Fine WoodWorking

BEST TIPS

■■■ *on* ■■■

Finishing, Sharpening, Gluing, Storage,

and more

From the **Editors,**
Readers, and Contributors of
Fine Woodworking

The Taunton Press

The Taunton Press
Inspiration for hands-on living®

The Taunton Press, Inc.
63 South Main Street
PO Box 5506
Newtown, CT 06470-5506
e-mail: tp@taunton.com

Editor: Jessica DiDonato
Copy editor: Seth Reichgott
Indexer: Jay Kreider
Cover & interior design: Chika Azuma
Layout: Chika Azuma

Library of Congress Cataloging-in-Publication Data
Fine woodworking best tips on finishing, sharpening, gluing, storage, and more / editors, contributors
& readers of Fine woodworking magazine.
     p. cm.
  ISBN 978-1-60085-338-8
  1. Woodwork. I. Taunton Press. II. Fine woodworking.
  TT180.F5537 2011
  684'.08--dc22
                              2010040210

About Your Safety: Working wood is inherently dangerous. Using hand or power tools improperly or
ignoring safety practices can lead to permanent injury or even death. Don't try to perform operations
you learn about here (or elsewhere) unless you're certain they are safe for you. If something about
an operation doesn't feel right, don't do it. Look for another way. We want you to enjoy the craft, so
please keep safety foremost in your mind whenever you're in the shop.

ACKNOWLEDGMENTS

Thank you to the editors, contributors, and readers of *Fine Woodworking* whose willingness to share their innovations and revelations will inspire others to do the same and provide practical shop solutions for years and years to come.

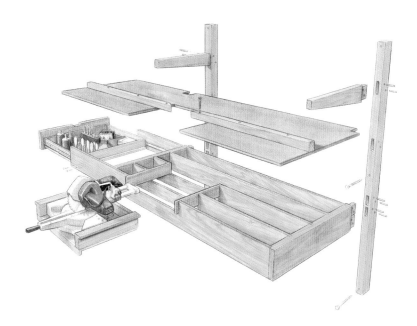

CONTENTS

INTRODUCTION

When the first issue of *Fine Woodworking* was published in 1975, I was a young computer-programmer-by-day, amateur-woodworker-by-night living in Houston, Texas, and was immediately smitten with the magazine. I signed up as a charter subscriber and even submitted a couple of articles which, to my surprise, were published. When the *Methods of Work* column was started in 1976, I sent in several tips accompanied by rough pencil drawings. John Kelsey was the editor in those days and saw something he liked in those drawings. Out of the blue, he called me and asked if I could help him out of a bind. He was short of staff and wondered if I could take over the selection of tips and illustration of the *Methods of Work* column from my home in Houston. This was to be a temporary job—just for a couple of issues until John could get his staff built back up.

After several cycles, the (at the time) unusual out-of-house arrangement became permanent. Today, more than thirty years later, the same arrangement continues. But the *Methods of Work* column has always been very much a collaborative exercise, and over the years I've had the pleasure to work with several talented in-house editors who help put together the column.

The *Methods of Work* column has evolved and changed noticeably over the years. Initially we mostly published simple jigs, many of which were in common usage around the woodworking community. As the years have passed, the tips have become more sophisticated and complex—sometimes requiring multiple drawings and a whole page of text—as the ever-evolving technology of woodworking continues to bring in a whole new wave of tips based on battery-powered tools, sliding chopsaws, dust collection systems, and much more. In April 1999 we began awarding a prize for the tip we deemed the most innovative and useful of the bunch we select to run in the column. Much of the material in this book is based on these unique and creative tips.

And why do woodworkers love tips so much? I believe that we enjoy the creativity that is the hallmark of a good tip—the "Aha! factor" that causes us to say, "I wish I thought of that." This book would not exist without those individual woodworkers who first had a spark of genius, then had the generosity to share it with the rest of us. I thank you.

—Jim Richey

SHOP HELPERS

SAWHORSES

Short horse gives a lift

My shortest sawhorse is really a larger version of a foot-stool or a small bench. It works well for sawing long planks to rough length. But most often I use one or a pair of these to bring a case piece up to a comfortable working height.

For example, I'm over 6 ft. tall, so a 30-in.-tall cabinet that needs to be planed or sanded is in a much better working position for me with this horse placed underneath it. When edging wide panels or case backs, I set one end into my bench vise and support the other end on the short horse.

I also find it handy as a step stool. My ancient Skil belt sander weighs close to 15 lb., and I prefer to use it in the horizontal position. Consequently, when finish-sanding the top of a 5-ft.-tall cabinet, I stand on the short horse to make the job easier. When working on a nearly completed piece, I pad the top of the horse with carpet scraps to protect the piece from unwanted dings, dents, and scratches.

CHRISTIAN BECKSVOORT, New Gloucester, Maine

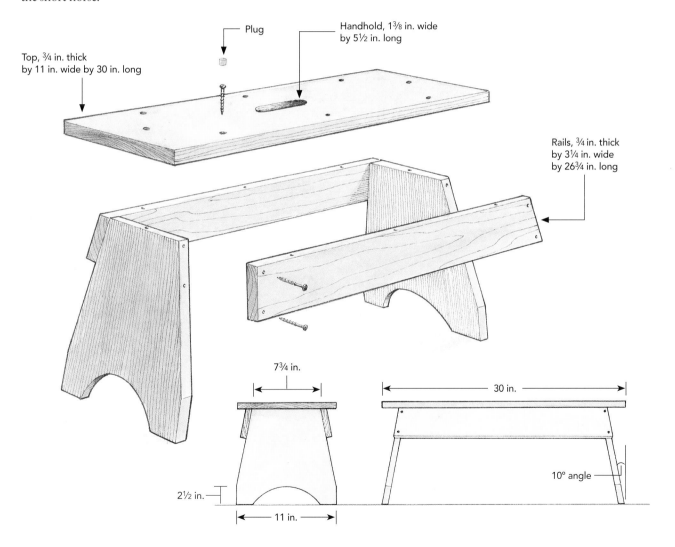

Plug

Handhold, 1⅜ in. wide by 5½ in. long

Top, ¾ in. thick by 11 in. wide by 30 in. long

Rails, ¾ in. thick by 3¼ in. wide by 26¾ in. long

7¾ in.

2½ in.

11 in.

30 in.

10° angle

Adjustable horse raises the bar

I use a pair of these horses mainly for sanding and finishing. Even though they're 36 in. tall, they can be raised to 55 in. for real close-up work, like carving or inlay. The design is also useful for supporting work at the bandsaw or drill press.

The tall horses are built almost like the two-footers on the facing page. The major difference is that I have enclosed the ends and added diagonal braces for strength.

The extenders are connected to a ¾-in.-thick crossbar and are drilled at ½-in. intervals for the adjustment dowels. The extenders fit into slots in the top and the lower shelf, much like a centerboard of a sailboat. I pad the crossbar with ¾-in.-dia. foam pipe insulation to protect workpieces. The foam also provides grip to prevent panels from sliding around when they're being sanded.

—**CHRISTIAN BECKSVOORT**, New Gloucester, Maine

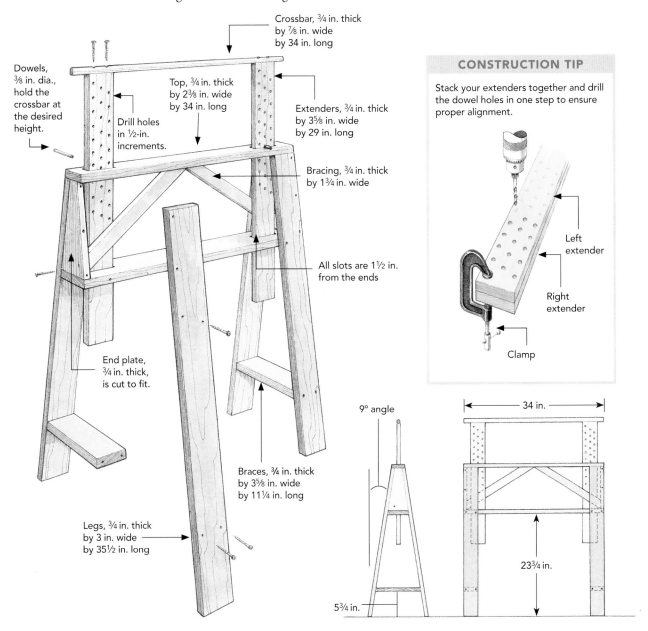

Crossbar, ¾ in. thick by ⅞ in. wide by 34 in. long

Dowels, ⅜ in. dia., hold the crossbar at the desired height.

Top, ¾ in. thick by 2⅜ in. wide by 34 in. long

Drill holes in ½-in. increments.

Extenders, ¾ in. thick by 3⅝ in. wide by 29 in. long

Bracing, ¾ in. thick by 1¾ in. wide

All slots are 1½ in. from the ends

End plate, ¾ in. thick, is cut to fit.

Braces, ¾ in. thick by 3⅝ in. wide by 11¼ in. long

Legs, ¾ in. thick by 3 in. wide by 35½ in. long

CONSTRUCTION TIP

Stack your extenders together and drill the dowel holes in one step to ensure proper alignment.

Left extender

Right extender

Clamp

9° angle

34 in.

23¾ in.

5¾ in.

Stackable horse saves space

This sawhorse is the workhorse in my shop. It is easy to make and easy to move around. I make them in pairs, and the design allows the horses to be stacked when not in use. I also stapled carpeting to the top to prevent pieces from being damaged while they are on the horses.

Their primary use is for holding case pieces at working height. When fitting face frames, backs, or doors, or when sanding or installing hinges, I find these midheight horses indispensable. And because the braces are inboard of the legs, I can clamp onto the ends as well as the middle of the top. This is a real handy feature when working alone.

A shelf on the lower braces not only adds strength to the horse, but it comes in handy for holding tools. For a while I had side strips installed along the shelf that kept tools from rolling off. But they collected all sorts of debris and were difficult to keep clean, so I took them off.

— **CHRISTIAN BECKSVOORT**, New Gloucester, Maine

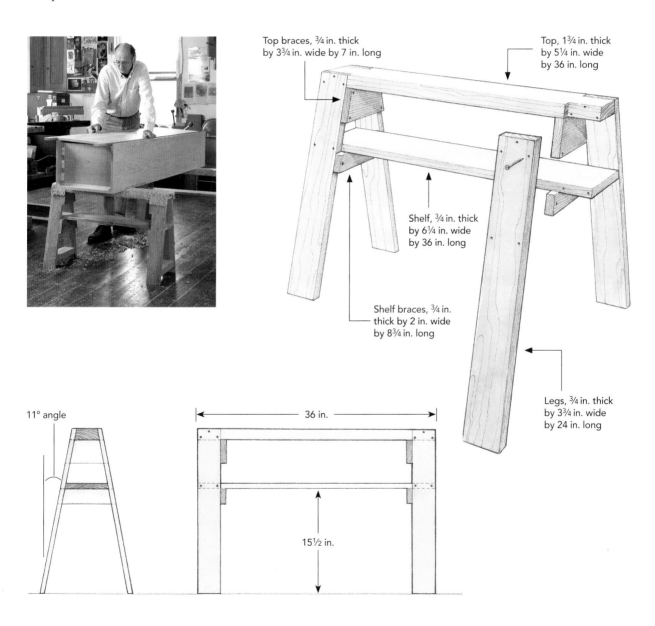

Top braces, ¾ in. thick by 3¾ in. wide by 7 in. long

Top, 1¾ in. thick by 5¼ in. wide by 36 in. long

Shelf, ¾ in. thick by 6¼ in. wide by 36 in. long

Shelf braces, ¾ in. thick by 2 in. wide by 8¾ in. long

Legs, ¾ in. thick by 3¾ in. wide by 24 in. long

11° angle

36 in.

15½ in.

Light, strong sawhorses stack neatly

I've used these sawhorses in the shop since about 1978. Even though they're light, the horses have never failed. It's easy to make a bunch of them, and the entire lot can be stored in one neat stack.

The legs are attached to the sawhorse with a scarf joint that is glued, clamped, and screwed. A spline added to the joint boosts shear strength and maintains the correct angle for the splay during assembly.

Cutting the scarf on the leg is tricky. You'll need a jig similar to the one shown in the drawing below. First,

miter both ends of the leg with a compound miter, 15° and 15°. Then clamp a pair of legs in the jig, which holds them splayed both 15° front to back and 15° side to side. With the tablesaw blade set vertically, cut the cheeks. To cut the spline slot in a leg, first set both the miter gauge and the tablesaw blade at 15°. Then, with the scarf joint facing down, use the miter gauge to support the leg as it's passed over the blade.

—LOUIS MACKALL, Guilford, Conn.

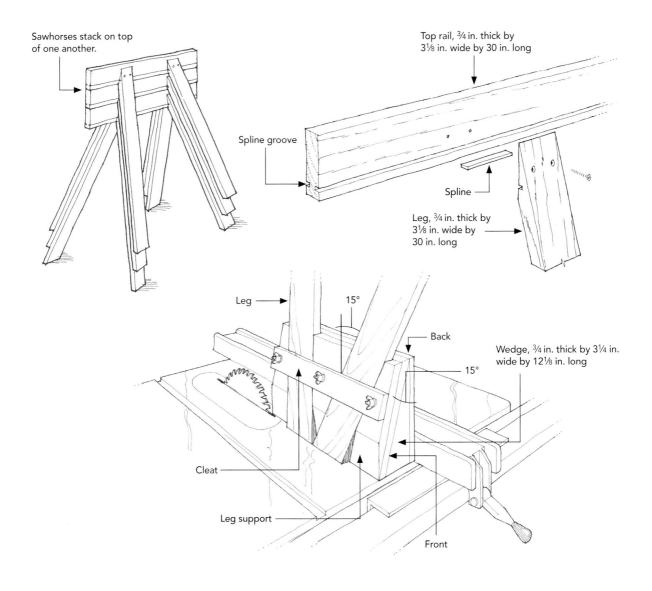

Sawhorses stack on top of one another.

Top rail, ¾ in. thick by 3⅛ in. wide by 30 in. long

Spline groove

Spline

Leg, ¾ in. thick by 3⅛ in. wide by 30 in. long

Leg

15°

Back

15°

Wedge, ¾ in. thick by 3¼ in. wide by 12⅛ in. long

Cleat

Leg support

Front

Sawhorse folds up when you lift it

This folding sawhorse is simplicity itself. Just pick it up and it folds. I make these out of milled 2×4s and nylon rope. The legs are canted 100° and their bottoms are beveled, so they sit flat on the floor to prevent cords from hanging up on them. Leave the top boards square to create a channel above the hinge. This may save your sawblade someday. I have been using a pair of these almost every day for 30 years.

—HUGH GRUBB, Hillsboro, Va.

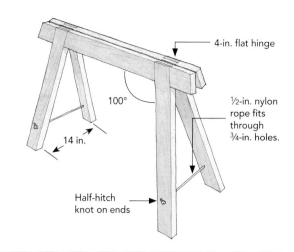

4-in. flat hinge

100°

14 in.

½-in. nylon rope fits through ¾-in. holes.

Half-hitch knot on ends

Improved sawhorse design

I've seen a lot of different designs for sawhorses, but none of them had all of the features I wanted. This one includes all of the improvements I was looking for: The horses are stackable, have a replaceable sawing insert, and feature a flip-up tool tray.

Make the main structure of the sawhorse from 2×4s with plywood brackets. The 1½-in. slot through the top of the sawhorse allows you to stand a sacrificial 2×4 insert in the slot. Use this when you're cutting plywood so that you won't destroy the body of the sawhorse. When the insert is full of sawcuts, throw it away and cut a new one to replace it.

The tray is simply a plywood piece edged with ¾-in.-thick stock. The tray pivots on dowel pins on one side and rests on a 2×4 stretcher on the other.

—KEVIN MCLAUGHLIN, Helena, Ala.

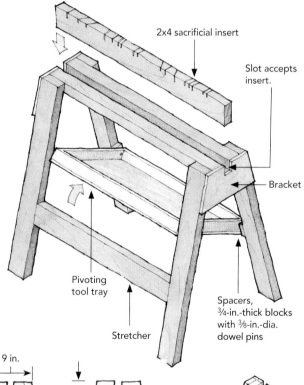

2x4 sacrificial insert

Slot accepts insert.

Bracket

Pivoting tool tray

Stretcher

Spacers, ¾-in.-thick blocks with ⅜-in.-dia. dowel pins

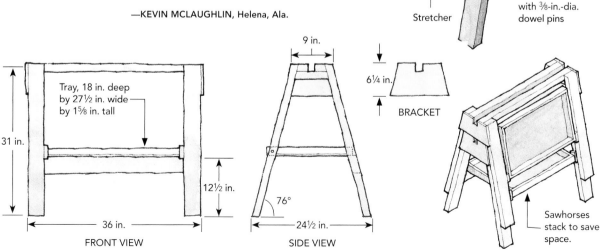

Tray, 18 in. deep by 27½ in. wide by 1⅝ in. tall

31 in.

12½ in.

36 in.

FRONT VIEW

9 in.

76°

24½ in.

SIDE VIEW

6¼ in.

BRACKET

Sawhorses stack to save space.

WORKBENCHES

Extension lengthens clamping capacity

A few years ago, one of my customers wanted a 12-ft.-long tapered flagpole. My plan was to make an octagonal blank and then use a handplane to shape it into a tapered cylinder. But the pole was 5 ft. longer than my bench, and that introduced a clamping problem.

My solution was this workbench extension that effectively lengthened clamping capacity by several feet. Now that I have the extension, I use it whenever I have a workpiece longer than my bench, such as bedposts, tabletops, and countertops.

—AURELIO BOLOGNESI, Hardwick, Mass.

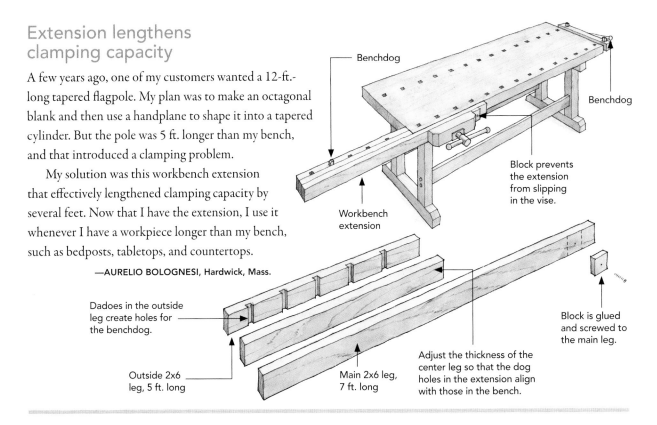

Benchdog

Benchdog

Block prevents the extension from slipping in the vise.

Workbench extension

Dadoes in the outside leg create holes for the benchdog.

Outside 2x6 leg, 5 ft. long

Main 2x6 leg, 7 ft. long

Adjust the thickness of the center leg so that the dog holes in the extension align with those in the bench.

Block is glued and screwed to the main leg.

Workbench support fixture for edge-planing long boards

When I edge-plane a long board on my workbench, the front vise usually won't support the entire board. To add extra support on the far end of the board without another "helper" that would be in the way as I worked, I came up with a removable support fixture.

When I need to plane a long board, I insert the top tenon up into any dog hole and pin the tenon with a locking dowel. To ensure that the front of the fixture would be flush with the front of the bench, I made the support by laminating several pieces. To accommodate various widths of lumber, a series of holes are bored in the front lamination. The holes, with centerpoints spaced 1-in. apart, accept a dowel that supports the board. When not in use, the fixture hangs on the wall.

—RICHARD J. GOTZ, Plymouth, Minn.

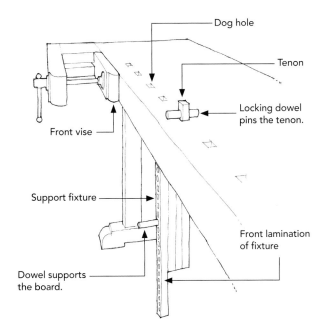

Dog hole

Tenon

Locking dowel pins the tenon.

Front vise

Support fixture

Front lamination of fixture

Dowel supports the board.

Sliding bench jack holds boards on edge at any height

To plane a long board on edge, woodworkers often clamp one end in a front vise and support the other end on a device known as a bench jack.

A traditional bench jack is clamped into the tail vise (either L-shaped or full width) and uses a dowel to support the workpiece. The jack often has holes from top to bottom that allow the dowel to be adjusted for different board widths and working heights. This adjustment method is relatively crude and doesn't restrict the board from wobbling from side to side as you plane it. So I came up with this design, which features a sliding shuttle equipped with a toggle clamp (DeStaCo® No. 225-U; www.grainger.com) to hold the board against the bench.

In use, the bench jack rests on the floor and is clamped into the tail vise (for a bench without a tail vise, you might attach the jack permanently). I adjust the shuttle by loosening the knobs and simply sliding it up or down its T-track. Once the height is locked in and the material is resting on the shuttle, I flip the toggle clamp. The toggle clamp can be adjusted to accept materials as thin as the shuttle (¾ in. in this case) or up to almost an inch thicker. If the workpiece is thinner than the shuttle, I add a spacer between the clamp head and the workpiece.

With the workpiece supported and clamped into the jack, it is ready for planing, shaping, or sanding. The material will be held firmly at the desired height with much less side-to-side movement.

—ABRAHAM TESSER, Athens, Ga.

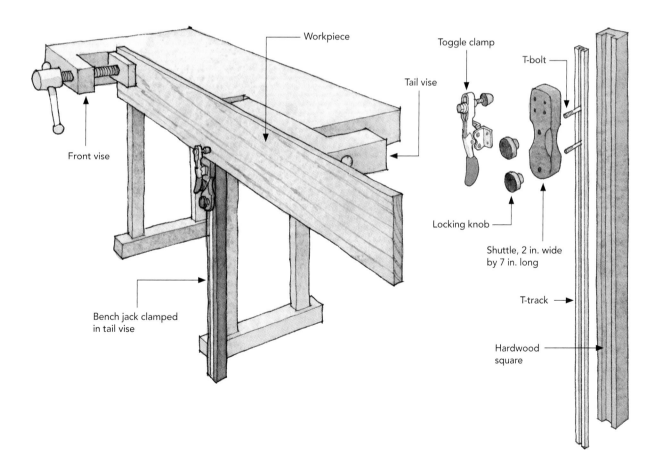

Long-board support

A while back when I was wrestling with a large board on my workbench, it occurred to me that the tail vise might come to my rescue. First, I cut a 1½-in.-wide board to a length equal to the height of the workbench. Then I drilled a ¾-in. hole in the edge of the board with the top of the hole the same distance above the floor as the top of the guide rods in the front vise. Next, I inserted a short piece of ¾-in. dowel into the hole and clamped the board in the tail vise.

I clamp the long workpiece in the front vise with the bottom edge resting on the guide rods and on the top of the peg.

—LEN URBAN, Rancho Mirage, Calif.

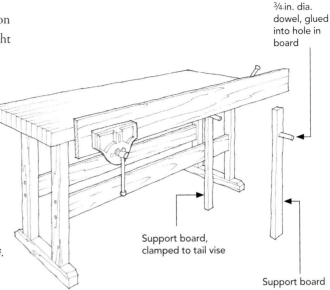

¾-in. dia. dowel, glued into hole in board

Support board, clamped to tail vise

Support board

Magnetic spring keeps benchdogs in place

Benchdogs are shop helpers that sit in holes in a workbench top. The dogs are raised above the benchtop so that a board can be secured against them for handplaning, for instance. When not in use, the dogs slide down below the benchtop.

Most dogs are held at the correct height with a metal or wood spring built into the sides. When I was making a bunch of dogs for a recently completed workbench, I realized that it takes a lot of fussing to fit each dog with a wooden spring. I wanted a quicker and easier way to hold the dog at the desired height.

My solution was to inset two rare-earth magnets into the side of each rectangular dog. I arranged the pair to repel each other, which causes the outer magnet to press against the side of the dog hole, holding the dog at the height you want.

Don't pull the dog out too far, though, or the magnets could pop out. It helps to locate the magnets as low as possible, so you can maximize the height of the dog.

—JIM SHAPIRO, San Francisco, Calif.

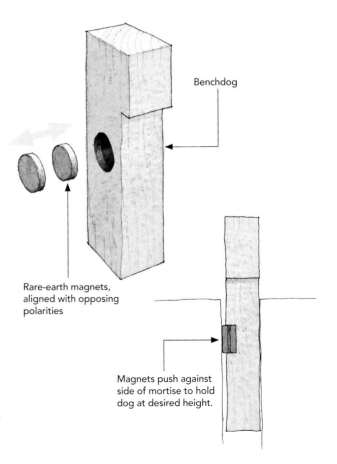

Benchdog

Rare-earth magnets, aligned with opposing polarities

Magnets push against side of mortise to hold dog at desired height.

Adjustable support for a workbench

I know how important it is to put work at the right height. This goes not only for the workbench itself but also for everything that you do on it. For example, when you want to plane the edge of a shelf, it is important to have it at just the right height—too low will wear out your back, and too high will wear out your arms.

To put work at the right height, we Dutch use an adjustable support called a *knecht*, which translates to "helping boy." To eliminate some inherent problems in the traditional *knecht* design, which is freestanding, I modified it so that the upright fits into the dog holes in a traditional European-style workbench. The device is so useful that I find myself using it every day for many purposes: gluing, routing, sanding, and planing.

To make the support, first cut the hardwood upright for a loose fit in your benchdog holes. Although the

upright looks fragile, it can handle several hundred pounds of weight easily. Next, drill a series of ¼-in.-dia. holes every 1½ in. or so near the back edge of the upright. With a bandsaw, open up each hole at an angle of 45°. Cut the work holder from stock that is the same thickness as the upright, and then make the catch mechanism from aluminum bar stock and a couple of bolts. Finally, glue a piece of carpeting to the top of the holder so that your workpiece won't be damaged.

To use the device, remove the work holder and slip the upright into a dog hole from the top. Slip the work holder back on the upright and, using the catch, set the height of the work holder for the job at hand. If you have a long workpiece to support, you may need two or even three of these fixtures.

—JOS MERTENS, Venray, The Netherlands

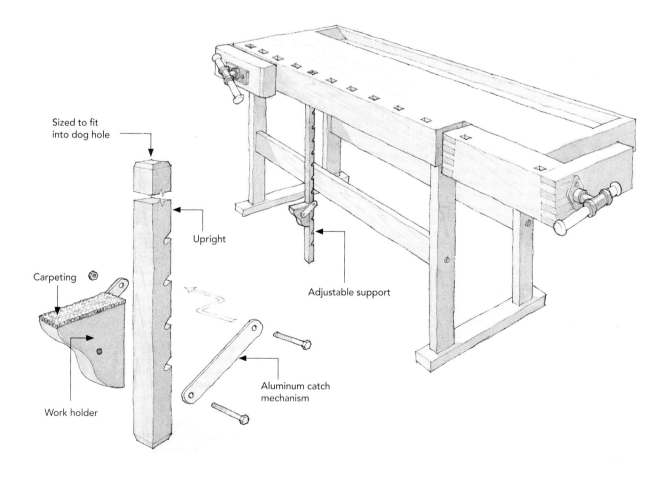

Sized to fit into dog hole

Upright

Carpeting

Work holder

Aluminum catch mechanism

Adjustable support

Miniature shaving horse

For those chair makers who like to work standing up or who don't have space for a full-size shaving horse, this little version—made to be held in a bench vise—is both compact and portable. To use it, simply clamp the keel in the bench vise, push back the lever arm to raise the upper jaw of the jig, and lower it onto the workpiece. The spring mechanism closes the jaw automatically and provides gripping force.

The key feature of the horse is a ⅝-in.-dia. steel shaft that goes through the wooden arms, the metal lever arms, the clamp head, and the springs. A second shaft through the body of the horse provides a fulcrum point for the lever arms. A third shaft provides an attachment point for the springs and can be moved to increase or decrease the clamping force. Clamping pressure can also be adjusted by using stronger or weaker springs. The clamp head has sandpaper on the business side to enhance the grip. You could also add a strip of sandpaper to the top edge of the body for an even better grip.

All of the wooden parts of the jig were made from ¾-in.-thick Baltic-birch plywood. The lever arms were welded up from 1-in.-wide, ⅛-in.-thick steel.

—LOUIS MENGOLI, La Mesa, Calif.

Push metal lever arm to raise the clamp head and tension the spring.

Clamp head

Plywood arm

Sandpaper on bottom of clamp head

Workpiece

Clamp the keel in a vise.

Steel rods, ⅝ in. dia.

Spring-tension adjustment holes

Push back the lever arm to release the jaw.

Improve a benchdog with a bullet catch

A benchdog that's too skinny will fall into the dog hole. One that's too fat is hard to adjust. I solved the problem with a bullet catch, an inexpensive item available at hardware stores.

When using a bullet catch, you'll want the benchdog slightly undersize in thickness, so it slides easily in the hole. Then, drill a hole in the side of the dog and install the catch. The spring inside the catch holds the

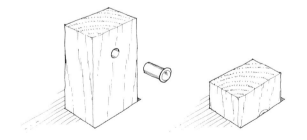

dog in position at any elevation. Use a pair of catches for especially long dogs.

—ROBERTO BIANCO, Napoli, Italy

Keeping vise jaws parallel

Uneven pressure caused by repeatedly clamping pieces on one side of a vise and not the other can eventually cause damage. I have a wooden vise, and nine times out of ten, I clamp my work on the right side of it. Therefore, the piece being held keeps the jaws apart on the right side only, while the screw is trying to pull the entire jaw in. Because there is no resistance on the left side of the vise, the evener bars (on either side of the screw) will eventually either bend (on a metal vise) or work loose from the wooden jaw (on a wooden vise).

Years ago, I made myself a set of five T-blocks to help keep the vise jaws parallel to each other. It took less than a board foot of scrap wood and about 30 minutes of work. First, I made five top blocks, about ¾ in. thick by 3 in. wide by 3 in. long. To the middle of the 3-in. by 3-in. faces, I glued five different-size spacer blocks: ⅞ in. by 1 in., ½ in. by 1⅛ in., ⅝ in. by 1½ in., ¾ in. by 1¾ in., 1¼ in. by 2 in. (all 2½ in. long). These blocks act as spacers for the left side of my vise, with the top blocks holding the spacer portion between the jaws. Note that I now have 10 different thicknesses of wood to use: ½ in., ⅝ in., ¾ in., ⅞ in., 1 in., 1⅛ in., 1¼ in., 1½ in., 1¾ in., and 2 in.—all 2½ in. long. Other thicknesses can be made for whatever dimensions you need.

If I'm planing a 1-in.-thick board, I drop the appropriate block between the jaws on the opposite side of the vise. If I then choose to clamp a ⅞-in. board, I simply open the vise, turn the block 90° and retighten. The blocks can be stored in the tool trough of the bench or on a small shelf below, or they can hang below using small screw eyes and string.

—CHRISTIAN BECKSVOORT, New Gloucester, Maine

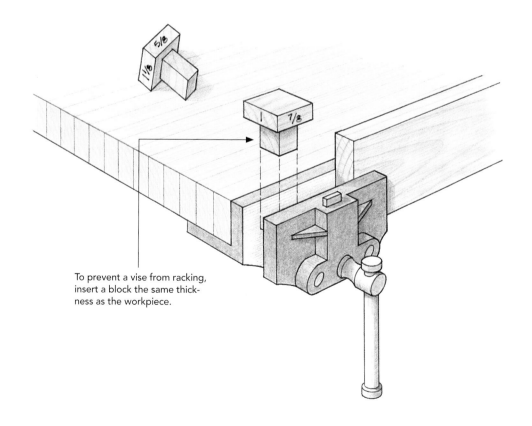

To prevent a vise from racking, insert a block the same thickness as the workpiece.

Idler holds tapered workpiece in vise

It's often a challenge to clamp tapered workpieces in a bench vise. Although shims and wedges work fine, they can be fussy to cut and fit. A patternmaker's vise eliminates the fuss, but at a steep price. This simple device, made from scrapwood, is easy to use and works great. I call it an idler.

Start with a chunk of hardwood, 2 in. thick by 3 in. wide, the same length as the vise jaws. Drill a through-hole (the diameter isn't critical; ½ in. is fine) near one edge, then bevel the piece so that only half the hole remains. Glue a 3-in.-long dowel in that half hole.

Long ago, I added a wood face to each vise jaw to help protect workpieces from denting when squeezed by the vise. I found that by cutting a V-groove in each of the wood faces, positioning the idler in the vise got a little easier.

To use the idler, place it in the vise with the dowel in one of the V-grooves. Then place the tapered piece in the vise and close the jaws. As the jaws close, the idler automatically pivots to match the angle of the taper, and the workpiece is held securely.

—PHILIP A. HOUCK, Boston, Mass.

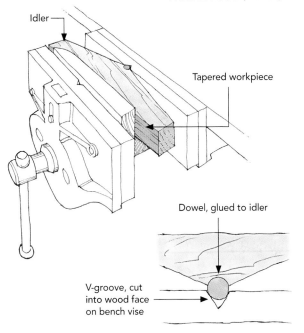

Idler

Tapered workpiece

Dowel, glued to idler

V-groove, cut into wood face on bench vise

Insert prevents vise from racking

This simple little shopmade gadget prevents my vise from racking when the pressure gets cranked up on one end of the jaw. To make it, cut a couple of dozen ⅛-in.- to ¼-in.-thick plywood scraps, each one 2 in. wide by 4 in. long. Then drill a ⅜-in.-dia. hole near one end of each piece. Fasten the pieces together with a ¼-in. bolt, washers, and a wing nut. After snugging up the vise to the workpiece, pivot the plywood spacers down into position as needed at the opposite side of the vise. With the insert in place, the vise won't rack, even if you tighten it down hard.

—SCOTT CULLEN, Edina, Minn.

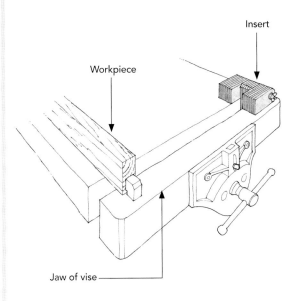

Insert

Workpiece

Jaw of vise

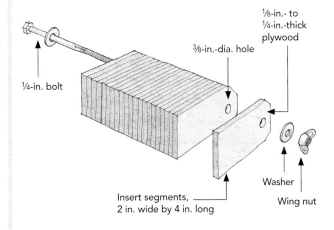

¼-in. bolt

⅜-in.-dia. hole

⅛-in.- to ¼-in.-thick plywood

Insert segments, 2 in. wide by 4 in. long

Washer

Wing nut

Clamping odd shapes in a vise

To hold odd-shaped workpieces in your bench vise, cut a section of heavy plastic or iron pipe in half and place the half-round against the workpiece. The pipe will distribute the pressure and hold the workpiece securely.

—ALBERT T. PIPPI, Baltimore, Md.

Workpiece

Half-section of heavy plastic pipe distributes pressure on irregular stock.

Clamping keel for a machinist's vise

When I needed to change the clamping orientation of some panels I was sanding, I attached a 2×4 keel to my machinist's vise, clamped it in my bench vise and reoriented the workpiece as shown in the sketch. This dual-vise arrangement worked so well that I've used it for other jobs. It provides an endless variety of holding angles, is quick to set up, costs nothing, and makes good use of my machinist's vise, which needed a good dusting anyway.

—JAMES J. RANKIN, Easton, Pa.

Auxiliary work rest for large panels

I attached metal shelf standards and brackets to the legs of my workbench. With the aid of a small shelf resting on the brackets, I can support large awkward workpieces, such as doors, at the right height for planing or installing hardware. I clamp one corner of the workpiece in my bench vise to hold the work steady and upright and add a pipe clamp to the other corner if needed.

—ROY H. HOFFMAN, Oriental, N.C.

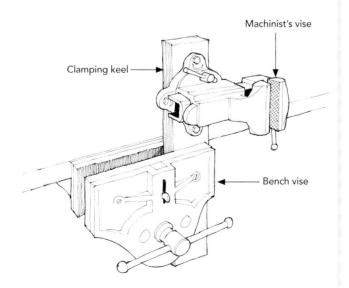

Machinist's vise

Clamping keel

Bench vise

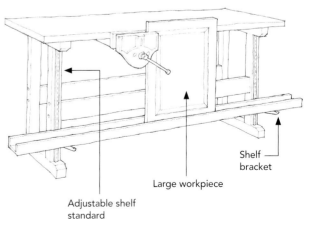

Adjustable shelf standard

Large workpiece

Shelf bracket

Pipe-clamp parts make workbench more versatile

While drilling dog holes in my new maple benchtop, I realized that ¾ in. is the tap drill size for a ½-in. pipe thread. After drilling the dog holes to size, I tapped them with a ½-in. pipe tap, going deeper than the normal thread depth for a pipe to give the threads more holding strength in wood. This allowed me to screw a threaded section of ½-in.-dia. pipe into the tapped dog hole and, in turn, screw a pipe-clamp head to the pipe's other end. I've been using this setup for two years now, and the tapped wooden threads in the hard maple have held up just fine in their double duty as dog hole and threaded insert.

I use the threaded dog holes in three ways: First, I can install a clamp perpendicular to the benchtop in any dog hole to use as a hold-down. Second, after drilling and tapping holes in the apron of the bench, I can use a clamp as a side vise against a dog. Finally, utilizing drilled and tapped holes on the opposite side of the apron, I can attach the quick-release end of the pipe clamp. This lets me hold items that are wider than the benchtop.

The tapped holes on the side of my bench are really neat—it is like having an extra vise. You can screw a short or long pipe into the hole. The arrangement gives a lot of latitude for clamping. When locating the side holes, it is important to put them at the correct height below the top of the bench—too low and the clamp head will not be above the top of the bench.

—DANIEL THOMAS, Franklin Park, Ill.

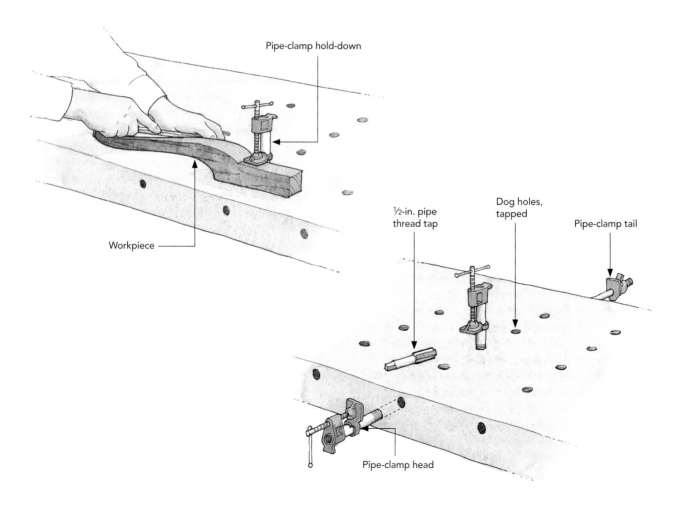

Pipe-clamp hold-down

Workpiece

½-in. pipe thread tap

Dog holes, tapped

Pipe-clamp tail

Pipe-clamp head

Multipurpose workbench is a space saver

My entire shop must fit into half of my garage, so I have to make the most of the available space. Toward that end, I've built a workbench that also serves as an outfeed table for my tablesaw, and a power-tool workstation with interchangeable modules.

When in outfeed-table mode, I increase the support area for sheet goods by sliding out an extension. This dovetailed, U-shaped frame attaches to the apron of the bench. Slots in the front and back of the extension allow it to slide open 16 in.

At the far end of the bench, I've built a square opening that's designed to receive one of four tool modules:

a down-draft sanding platform, a chopsaw, a bench grinder, or a router table. Cleats inside the opening support the modules when they are dropped in. I built the chopsaw module so that the table of the chopsaw is even with the top of the workbench. My default is to keep the down-draft module in place because it does not interfere with the tablesaw or other operations on the workbench. When the modules are not in use, I store them in a rack on the back wall of my shop.

—PHILIP WILSON, Buda, Texas

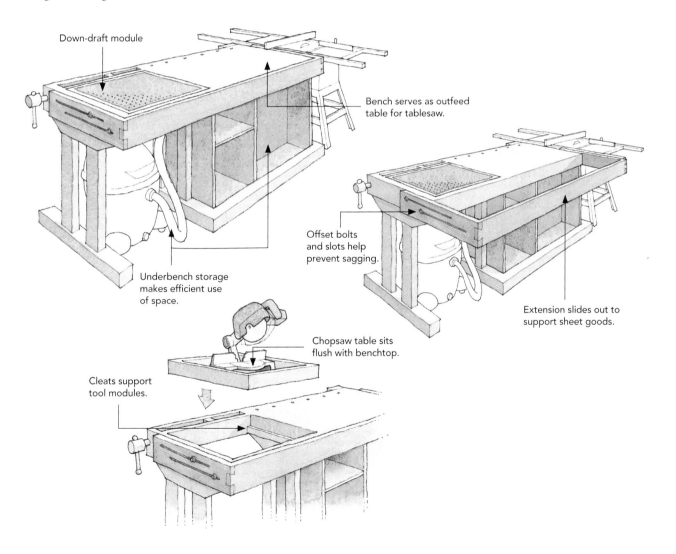

Down-draft module

Bench serves as outfeed table for tablesaw.

Underbench storage makes efficient use of space.

Offset bolts and slots help prevent sagging.

Extension slides out to support sheet goods.

Chopsaw table sits flush with benchtop.

Cleats support tool modules.

Steam out dents in benchtop

Small, shallow dents in a benchtop can be steamed out with the tip of an iron. Put some water in the dent, let it stand for a few minutes, and then place a wet cotton rag over the area. Apply the leading inch or two of a hot steam iron over the rag. Keep adding water to the rag as you go. Be persistent; hardwoods like maple and beech are slow to swell when steamed.

—RICHARD L. HUMPHREVILLE, New London, Conn.

Fill small holes in benchtop with epoxy and sawdust mixture

To fill shallow chipouts and holes in your benchtop, mix epoxy with very fine sawdust. A loose mix with a minimum amount of sawdust is best to enable the epoxy to sink thoroughly into the affected areas. Add a little dye powder to help match the color of the filler to the bench. To reduce mess, frame each hole with masking tape.

—RICHARD L. HUMPHREVILLE, New London, Conn.

A Dutchman repairs benchtop gouges

To patch deep gouges, use a "Dutchman," a piece of wood slightly deeper, wider, and longer than the gouge and of the same species and appearance as the benchtop. Lay the Dutchman over the gouge with the grain aligned, then use a marking knife to scribe a line around it. Next, use a router or chisel to remove the wood from the benchtop within the scribe lines. A pressure fit with no gaps around the edges is your goal. To make it easier to fit the Dutchman, chamfer its leading edges lightly. Then, glue it in place and use a plane to bring it flush with the benchtop.

—RICHARD L. HUMPHREVILLE, New London, Conn.

Movable bench lighting

Because my workshop has little natural light, I needed a versatile system for concentrating strong light where it was needed for executing very detailed wood carving. I cut a thick hardwood block with a benchdog-size pin protruding from the bottom. Holes in the block accept the mounting pins in my lamp. I can move the block anywhere along the row of benchdog holes on either side of my carver's bench to put the lamp and the light right where they are needed.

—FREDERICK WILBUR, Lovingston, Va.

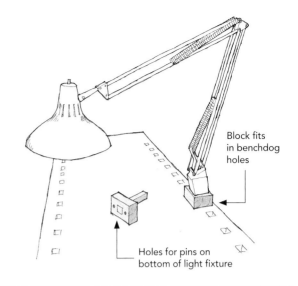

Block fits in benchdog holes

Holes for pins on bottom of light fixture

Wooden pegs patch large benchtop holes

Large holes in a benchtop are easy to fix. First, clean up the hole using a Forstner bit (bottom left). Then cut a square peg slightly larger than the hole, taper two opposite sides at the tip, and round over the corners using a block plane (right). Put some glue in the hole, align the untapered edges of the peg parallel to the direction of the bench grain to prevent the bench surface from splitting, and tap in the peg. When dry, saw off the protruding part of the peg, and chisel the surface flat (bottom right).

—RICHARD L. HUMPHREVILLE, New London, Conn.

AIR COMPRESSORS

Quieting an air compressor

To quiet an air compressor, enclose a small compressor in a plywood or medium-density fiberboard (MDF) box, provided that you make the cabinet large enough to allow good air circulation around the compressor and drill enough vent holes.

The number of vent holes and their locations will vary from one compressor to another, and it takes trial and error to get the ventilation right.

You can use a thermostat to monitor the temperature inside the cabinet. If it gets too hot—and especially if the compressor overheats—drill more vent holes.

—CHRIS ERMIDES, Beacon, N.Y.

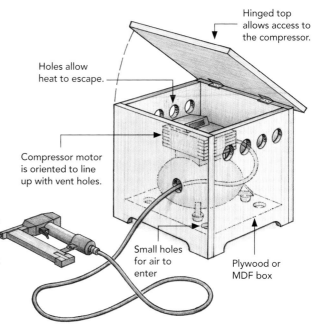

Hinged top allows access to the compressor.

Holes allow heat to escape.

Compressor motor is oriented to line up with vent holes.

Small holes for air to enter

Plywood or MDF box

Wrench for air-compressor drain valve

I know it is important to drain water from my compressor often to prevent rust in the tank. But the ditzy little drain valve, or petcock, mounted on the underside of the tank is difficult to use. So I solved the problem by making a new wrench. I routed a channel in a hardwood block to fit the valve and drilled a hole through the block to let air and water escape. I then shaped the outer edges to make the wood wrench easy to hold and glued it onto the valve with epoxy.

—JOHN WEIDNER, San Francisco, Calif.

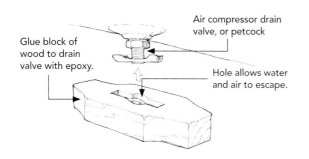

Air compressor drain valve, or petcock

Glue block of wood to drain valve with epoxy.

Hole allows water and air to escape.

Use your air compressor to blow sawdust away from your workspace

If you have a compressor, I strongly recommend using a jet of air to remove wood dust from your machines and projects as you're working to minimize distraction. I have my compressor hooked up to an adjustable nozzle with a magnetic base. The one I use is made by Woodtek® and sold by Woodworker's Supply Inc. (Part No. 826-182;

www.woodworker.com; 800-645-9292). The adjustable stream of air blows away the dust so that you can see the layout lines.

—WILL NEPTUNE, Acton, Mass.

DUST COLLECTION

Dust collection under the floor—three successful accounts

When I built my new shop, one major concern I had was how to run a dust-collection duct and power cord to my tablesaw. I wanted the tablesaw in the middle of my shop for convenience, but I didn't want electric lines or sheet-metal ducts hanging down from the ceiling or cluttering the floor. Also, I was uncomfortable about permanently embedding an air duct in the concrete floor.

After much thought, I came up with an idea that has worked out well. Before the floor slab was poured, I built a 5-in.-deep, 6-in.-wide plywood form to place in the floor where I wanted to run a channel (see the drawing below). I capped the form with a piece of plywood that would create a lip at the top of the concrete channel. I assembled the form with easily accessible screws, so that I could disassemble it from the top after the concrete cured. I then placed the form into the floor and poured the concrete around it.

After the concrete had cured, I removed the form and had a perfect channel in which to run a 4-in. vacuum duct and a couple of extension cords to the middle of the shop floor. I topped off the channel with steel plates that fit neatly into the lip left by the form.

—BOB CHANDLER, Rathdrum, Idaho

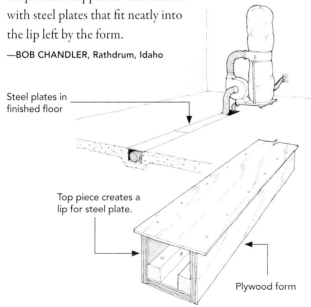

Steel plates in finished floor

Top piece creates a lip for steel plate.

Plywood form

When I built my shop several years ago, I too didn't want to stumble over air hoses, dust-collection ducts, or electrical cables on the floor. My solution was to have the contractor drop the cement floor 6 in. below the top of the footings (see the drawing below). I then put in 2×6 joists and ¾-in. flooring to bring up the floor to the top of the footings. This allowed me to put all of the hoses, wires, and ducts under the floor between the joists. In addition, this gave me a wood floor to work on, which is much easier on legs and dropped tools.

—HOWARD L. ALTHOUSE, St. George, Utah

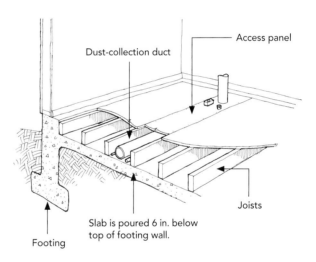

Dust-collection duct

Access panel

Joists

Slab is poured 6 in. below top of footing wall.

Footing

For our new shop we designed a dust-collection system that rests on top of the concrete pad and between the 2×6 floor joists that support a ¾-in. plywood floor. The floor joists are 12 in. o.c., creating a channel that is deep and wide enough to house a 4-in.-dia. PVC dust-collection pipe, a compressed-air hose, and electrical cables for floor outlets. The channel is topped off with an access panel. We also ran dust collection to the workbench, a very practical added feature.

—JULIE WHITTAKER, Charlevoix, Mich.

Closet muffles cyclone's roar, and backlight shows when bucket is full

A cyclone dust collector is great, but it can be noisy and it's hard to tell when the dust bin is filled without lifting the lid. But if you overfill the system and clog the ductwork, it takes an inordinate amount of time to disassemble, clean, and then reassemble the system. I solved both of those issues when I designed my new shop.

I built a special closet for the dust collector that deadens the sounds via noise-reducing insulation in the walls (www.soundprooffoam.com). I also added an incandescent light fixture behind the hose that connects the dust bucket to the cyclone unit. The light makes it easy to see when the dust bucket is getting filled. The light switch is right next to the dust-collector switch on the outside wall of the closet. This technique has worked very well, and I have not had an overfill problem in my new shop.

—BOB NASH, Newtown, Conn.

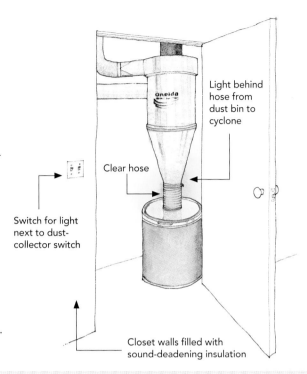

Light behind hose from dust bin to cyclone

Clear hose

Switch for light next to dust-collector switch

Closet walls filled with sound-deadening insulation

Running a 1.5-hp portable dust collector off of a duct

Portable dust collectors generally lack the power to be run off of a central duct system. They are designed to provide optimum air volume at the end of a 5-ft. length of flexible hose, not a 25-ft. duct run. Woodworkers who have tried to use a 1.5-hp collector in an overhead system have not been all that successful (too much duct).

However, they have been successful with running a 20-ft. main duct along a wall, about 3 ft. off the floor, with several gated tap locations on the duct. The collector stays in one place, and the stationary power tools are connected with short lengths of 4-in.-dia. flexible hose.

CURT CORUM, Woodbridge, Conn.

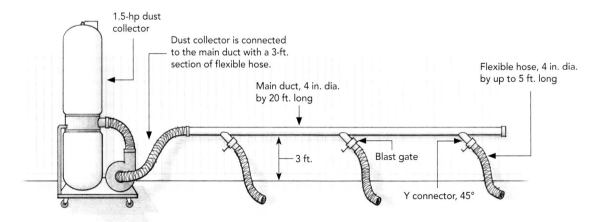

1.5-hp dust collector

Dust collector is connected to the main duct with a 3-ft. section of flexible hose.

Main duct, 4 in. dia. by 20 ft. long

Flexible hose, 4 in. dia. by up to 5 ft. long

3 ft.

Blast gate

Y connector, 45°

Proper dust collection
near a gas or oil furnace

It is essential that you use proper methods of dust collection if you have a gas or oil furnace in your shop; otherwise you are putting yourself in danger. If you create dense clouds of fine sawdust, almost any source of ignition could create an explosion—static electricity, smoking, open flames, even a spark from a faulty light switch. If you were to run a heavy-duty sander until the room was filled with fine sawdust, the furnace kicking on could be a source of ignition. This threat is a good reason to install reliable dust collection. In reality, however, the threat to a sensible hobbyist is slim. The cloud of dust necessary to cause a fire or explosion would be so thick that I can't imagine working in it.

On an industrial scale, if you were to blow a 1-qt. container of fine wood dust into the air in a 4,500-sq.-ft. shop with a 10-ft. ceiling, you would be in violation of the permissible exposure limit set by the Occupational Safety and Health Administration (OSHA).

All shops should at least have spot dust collection (right at the machine) by using portable or central dust-collection systems. To prevent dust clouds in the shop, the proper-size, self-contained dust collector, filter material, and hooding are very critical. A self-contained, ceiling-suspended air cleaner is also a good idea. The object is to keep dust out of the air so that there will be neither fire nor health risks. Hand-sanding operations should be done over a downdraft table with sufficient airflow.

Many commercial and non-commercial woodshops, especially in New England, heat with oil- or gas-fired furnaces that are located in the shop. One customer in Connecticut heats his woodshop every winter with two woodstoves. He operates a two-man shop with 11 woodworking machines. He has proper dust collection and good housekeeping. So as long as you're sensible about the amount of dust that gets into the air of your shop, there shouldn't be a problem.

—CURT CORUM, Woodbridge, Conn.

Mesh-bag vacuum filter keeps
small parts on the bench

Horizontal surfaces such as benchtops are great collecting areas, not only for wood dust but also for miscellaneous small parts and hardware, such as screws, that might be needed for a current project. Here's how I solved the problem of vacuuming that dust without devouring the small parts. I put a small mesh bag, the kind used to hold practice tennis balls or used for sweater or lingerie laundry bags (www.handylaundry.com), over the business end of my shop vacuum. The vacuum sucks up the unwanted dust while the mesh keeps out the small parts. It really works well.

—CHRISTOPHER AMAN, Webster, N.Y.

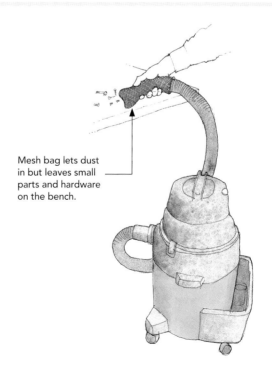

Mesh bag lets dust in but leaves small parts and hardware on the bench.

Improving dust collection on a bandsaw

When I use my bandsaw, a good deal of sawdust tends to migrate to the lower part of the saw. To improve the dust-collection efficiency, I cut a hole in the bottom of the door and added a vacuum port, connecting it to the bandsaw's regular vacuum fitting with 1½-in.-dia. PVC pipe and connectors.

—CARL N. PAULI, Mt. Tabor, N.J.

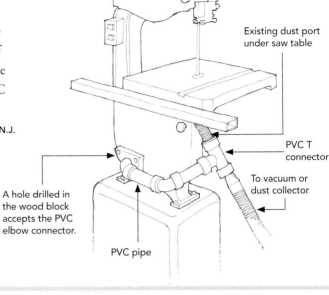

Existing dust port under saw table

PVC T connector

To vacuum or dust collector

A hole drilled in the wood block accepts the PVC elbow connector.

PVC pipe

Shop-built sanding filter

We do a lot of sanding in our prefinishing shop, and the fine dust often clogged the filter on the shop vacuum. Cleaning the vacuum filter was messy and time-consuming, so I looked for an alternative. After considering expensive commercial filters, I decided to build my own out of medium-density fiberboard and a 1-in.-thick fiberglass furnace filter.

Whatever size filter you choose (some are rectangular, some square) build the box around it for a tight fit. Holes in the top of the box receive the hoses from the sander and the vacuum, one on each side of the filter. The filter slides in from the front between wooden cleats. The door, attached with hinges, locks with screen-door hooks and eyes. I caulked all joints in the carcase and put a rubber gasket around the door to make it airtight.

I was surprised how well this simple and cheap device actually works. The vacuum filter still clogs, but now I clean it weekly instead of daily. A light tap on the furnace filter every few days helps keep it clear.

—DAN STANDLEY, Portland, Ore.

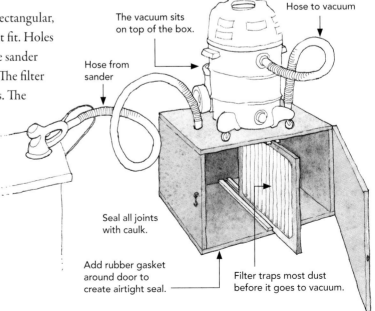

Hose to vacuum

The vacuum sits on top of the box.

Hose from sander

Seal all joints with caulk.

Add rubber gasket around door to create airtight seal.

Filter traps most dust before it goes to vacuum.

Adjustable overarm blade guard with dust collection

When I decided to build a blade guard for my tablesaw, I wanted one that not only would protect my fingers but also would provide excellent dust collection. I believe I achieved this in the design shown below and for a cost of less than $100. One important safety feature is that during use, the guard head is locked into position just $1/16$ in. above the workpiece. In my opinion, this feature provides more protection than a guard head that can be lifted by the workpiece during the cut. The dust-collection component works so well that there is virtually no dust generated when ripping a board and very little when making crosscuts.

The blade guard consists of three main parts: the head, the height-adjustment arm, and the suspension leg. For the guard head, I chose $3/8$-in.-thick Lexan® plastic because I wanted a clear material that would be almost bulletproof. I cut the Lexan pieces on my tablesaw and assembled them with screws, which allows me to replace one piece at a time if it gets damaged.

(continues on p. 28)

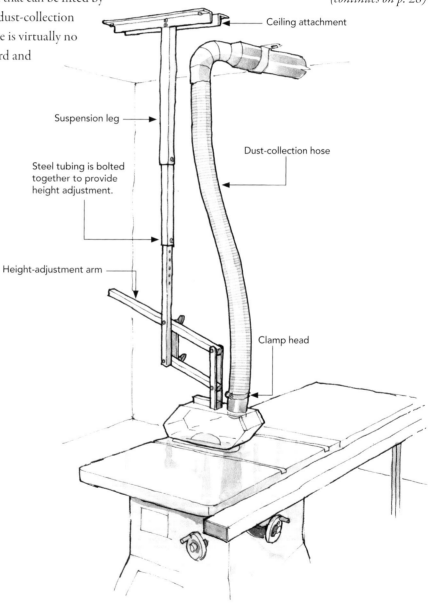

Ceiling attachment

Suspension leg

Steel tubing is bolted together to provide height adjustment.

Dust-collection hose

Height-adjustment arm

Clamp head

(continues from p. 27)

I made the height-adjustment arm with 1-in.-square aluminum tubing and 1-in.-wide aluminum bar stock. The arm locks in place with T-knobs to hold the head at the right height over the sawblade. The parallelogram-shaped mechanism keeps the head level with the table at any height, and it easily can be raised several inches when changing blades or cleaning the tabletop. To remove the head from the adjustment arm, I simply have to remove a couple of cotter pins.

I made the suspension leg from 1½-in.-, 1¼-in.-, and 1-in.-square steel tubing. These sizes fit inside each other, telescoping to allow gross height adjustments and quick removal of the entire unit, if necessary. I bolted the top of the suspension leg between two heavy angle irons that are in turn lag-bolted into the ceiling joists. A sturdy connection to the ceiling is important, so you may have to improvise, depending on the particulars of your shop. In my case, I also was able to bolt the suspension leg to a garage-door support for additional stability.

Once I had the unit supported and ready to use, I attached a 3-in. plastic splice to a length of 3-in.-dia. plastic dust-collection hose and inserted the splice into the hole in the top of the blade guard. Now my tablesaw is safer and dust-free (well, almost dust-free).

—GORDON J. SAMPSON, Pearland, Texas

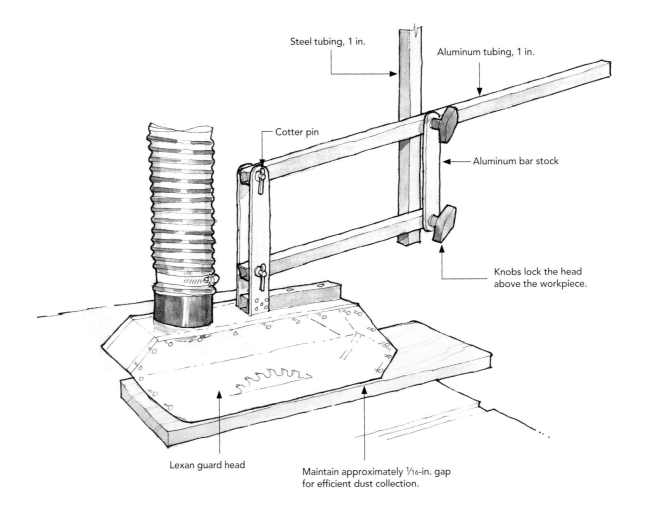

Steel tubing, 1 in.

Aluminum tubing, 1 in.

Cotter pin

Aluminum bar stock

Knobs lock the head above the workpiece.

Lexan guard head

Maintain approximately 1⁄16-in. gap for efficient dust collection.

ROUTER TABLES

Basic plywood table gets the job done

This uncomplicated router table is at the other end of the scale from those ultimate router tables replete with bells and whistles. It is just a router mounted upside down on a piece of plywood. The simplicity of the design makes it far more flexible than most router tables. You can build it in about 20 minutes and add a simple fence in another 10. Additional fences are made easily for special purposes.

To make the table, start with a piece of ¾-in.-thick plywood about 2 ft. by 3 ft. Cut a hole in the center of the table. Make and install a ¼-in.-thick plastic insert to fit around the bit. Make additional inserts as needed to provide a close fit around other bits in your collection. Also, to prevent the insert from lifting when the router runs, screw the insert to the table. Attach the router to the table by running machine screws through the recess for the insert.

The fence is simply a 1×4 that pivots on one end and is clamped on the other. A small movement at the clamp end provides very close and precise movement at the bit, allowing for adjustment in the thousandths of an inch. When the standard flat fence does not fit the application, I just make a new fence. For instance, I use a tall fence for making lock miters and raised panels.

To use the table, simply clamp it to your workbench with wooden hand screws. When you're done, just unclamp the whole fixture and store it out of the way to save space.

— DOUG STOWE, Eureka Springs, Ark.

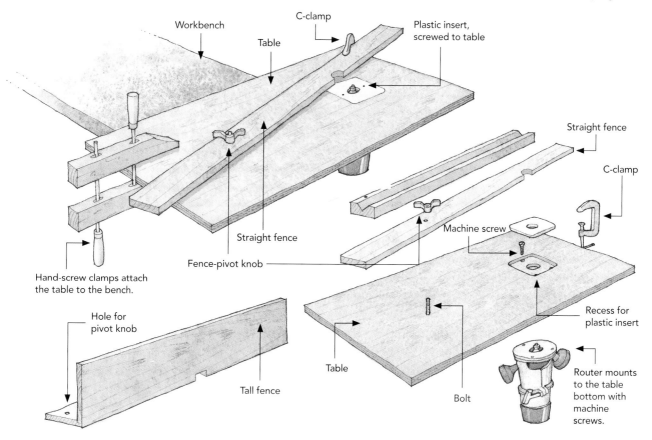

Workbench

C-clamp

Table

Plastic insert, screwed to table

Straight fence

C-clamp

Straight fence

Machine screw

Fence-pivot knob

Hand-screw clamps attach the table to the bench.

Hole for pivot knob

Tall fence

Table

Bolt

Recess for plastic insert

Router mounts to the table bottom with machine screws.

Zero-clearance router-table fence

This zero-clearance fence is an easy project that improves the performance of almost any router bit. The fence is made of ½-in.-thick medium-density fiberboard (MDF). Construction details are shown in the drawing below. To use this setup with a new router bit, screw a new replaceable insert into the rabbeted recess in the fence. Place the pivoting end of the fence over a dowel in the router-table top, turn on the router, and swing the fence slowly through the bit to cut a reverse opening in the insert. The final placement of the fence is secured with two C-clamps. When you change the bit, you will need to install a new insert and repeat the operation.

—ERNIE CONOVER, Parkman, Ohio

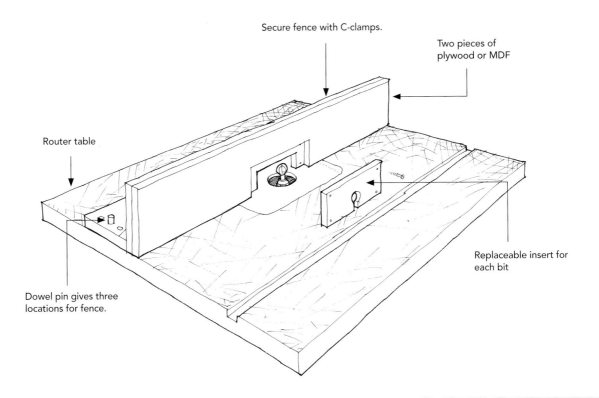

Secure fence with C-clamps.

Two pieces of plywood or MDF

Router table

Dowel pin gives three locations for fence.

Replaceable insert for each bit

An inexpensive alternative to phenolic and acrylic inserts

When I wanted to build a router table, I checked out the phenolic and acrylic inserts in the mail-order catalogs and decided they were too expensive. Then I came up with the idea to use a plastic cutting board, the kind found at any store that sells cooking utensils. The board machined well and cost less than $5.

—RICK GRINSTEAD, Charlotte, N.C.

Remove small router burn marks

To remove small router burn marks on shaped profiles, take the router bit out of the chuck, hold the bit in a gloved hand and delicately scrape off the burn mark. This avoids dulling the crisp features of the routed edge, as you would using sandpaper.

—MATTHEW C. JACKSON, Rapid City, S.D.

Two-part hold-down makes routing safer

This versatile two-part fixture uses sections of PVC pipe to hold the workpiece against the router table and the fence to reduce the chance of kickback and to make a cleaner, more consistent cut.

To make the fixture, cut two pieces of ¾-in.-thick plywood 4½ in. wide and as long as your router table. On the vertical hold-down piece, rout two ⅜-in. adjustment slots. Now, use a drill press and Forstner bit to make four 1⅞-in.-dia. through-holes, aligning the bit so that it will overlap the edge by about ⁷⁄₁₆ in. Drill three holes in the horizontal hold-in piece, centering them between the holes in the vertical hold-down.

Cut the ⅝-in.-wide rings on the tablesaw from a 1½-in.-dia. schedule 40 PVC pipe. The rings should be slightly thinner than the plywood; otherwise, their freedom of action will be impaired when the hold-down is clamped in place. Next, use a bandsaw to remove a 1¼-in. section from each ring.

Insert the rings with all the openings facing the same direction. Holding a Phillips-head screwdriver in the opening at about 45° to the bottom edge, rotate the PVC ring to pinch the screwdriver shaft (see the bottom drawing at right) and mark the inside where the tip touches the PVC. Drill a ⁵⁄₃₂-in.-dia. hole through the PVC only and then attach it to the plywood with a 1-in. self-piercing lath screw.

To use the fixture, place the stock flat on the router table under the rings of the hold-down. Push the hold-down onto the workpiece so that the rings deflect slightly, roughly ¹⁄₃₂ in. Do the same for the hold-in.

The pressure the rings exert on the workpiece helps keep it against the table and the fence, and will prevent the stock from kicking back. Use moderate feed pressure, and be sure to use a push stick at the end of the cut.

—RICHARD BABBITT, Friday Harbor, Wash.

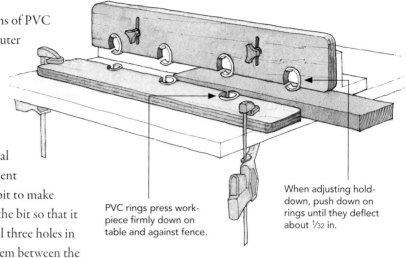

PVC rings press workpiece firmly down on table and against fence.

When adjusting hold-down, push down on rings until they deflect about ¹⁄₃₂ in.

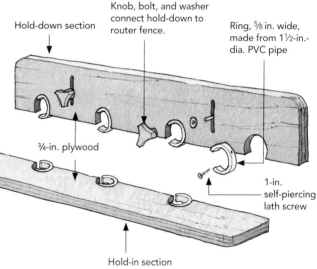

Hold-down section

Knob, bolt, and washer connect hold-down to router fence.

Ring, ⅝ in. wide, made from 1½-in.-dia. PVC pipe

¾-in. plywood

1-in. self-piercing lath screw

Hold-in section

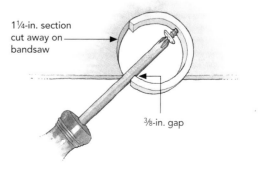

1¼-in. section cut away on bandsaw

⅜-in. gap

Backer block handles all cross-grain routing

This router-table push block, or backer block as I like to call it, stabilizes the workpiece and reduces tearout. It is handy for backing up the cut across the grain, such as when profiling a panel, but it's especially useful for milling the ends of narrow stock, such as when cutting stub tenons in a frame or using cope-and-stick bits.

Made of medium-density fiberboard, it features a skewed handle that keeps fingers away from the cutting action and automatically applies pressure against the fence as you push the workpiece through the cutter. The two finger holes make holding long, thin workpieces much easier.

To use, simply hold the workpiece against the block and push through, keeping the block firmly against the fence. The block can be reversed to make a new zero-clearance backer, and it's easy to replace when it gets worn out.

—SERGE DUCLOS, Delson, Que., Canada

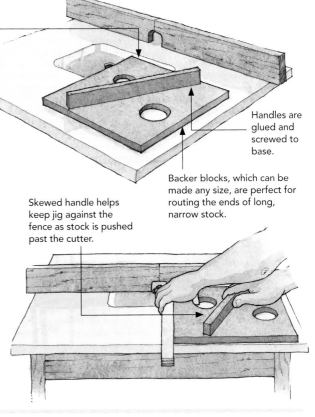

Corners must be exactly 90°.

Handles are glued and screwed to base.

Backer blocks, which can be made any size, are perfect for routing the ends of long, narrow stock.

Skewed handle helps keep jig against the fence as stock is pushed past the cutter.

Push stick for routing vertical workpieces

While using a router table to cut the key, or pin, for a sliding dovetail joint, it's a challenge to keep the vertical workpiece against the fence and on the router table while keeping your fingers away from the spinning bit. I've devised a surefire, safe method that also ensures a good, clean cut. It utilizes a tall fence and a vertical push stick.

The push stick also serves as the handle, helping you to keep the board tight and plumb against the router-table fence. The adjustable (and replaceable) backer block hooks the board to help keep it from rocking and also helps to prevent tearout at the end of the cut.

—SERGE DUCLOS,
Delson, Que., Canada

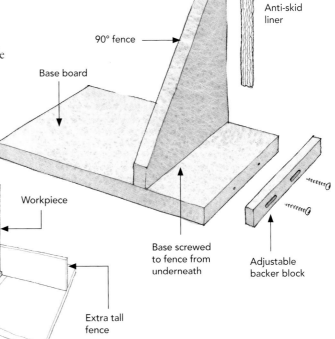

Anti-skid liner

90° fence

Base board

Base screwed to fence from underneath

Adjustable backer block

Workpiece

Router table

Extra tall fence

Making a segmented column on the router table

I recently needed to make a large coopered oak column that was 12 in. dia. by 4 ft. long. Because these dimensions exceeded the capacity of my lathe, I devised a method for making the cylinder on my router table.

First, I glued up the coopered cylinder and removed most of the waste from the corners with a power plane. Then I screwed a plywood disc to each end and drilled centered holes in the discs through which I placed a 1¼-in.-dia. iron pipe to serve as an axle. To hold the coopered column in place, I built a carriage with uprights on each end that kept the rough cylinder suspended so that it just cleared the top of my router table. I also clamped a guide board to the router table to keep the cylinder centered directly over the router bit.

By rotating the cylinder over the router bit as I gradually advanced the carriage across the table, I was able to turn a perfect cylinder that required only moderate sanding.

—CALEB CARLSON, Sandpoint, Idaho

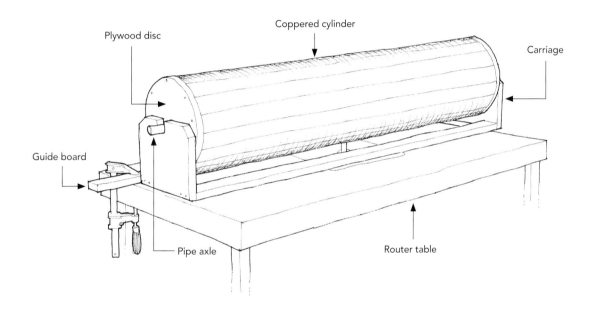

Plywood disc

Coppered cylinder

Carriage

Guide board

Pipe axle

Router table

Improved router-chuck wrench

That cheap chuck wrench that comes with your router is an awkward knuckle-banger to use. A low-cost, low-tech remedy to this problem is to clamp the jaw end of the wrench in your vise and bend the handle about 15°. This should angle the wrench just about right to reach in through the opening in the router base.

—FRED TABSHEY, Omaha, Neb.

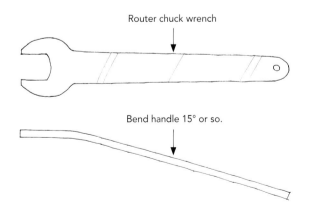

Router chuck wrench

Bend handle 15° or so.

Movable toggle clamps

With a slight modification in the mounting holes, you can move your DeStaCo toggle clamps instantly from one jig to another. Make the front holes into slots by opening them up with a hacksaw and file. Then extend the rear holes by boring a second hole in front of the existing hole and filing out the waste between the two holes. The size of the second hole should be larger so that a screw head will pass through it.

—VINCENT A. LAVARENNE, Bruney, France

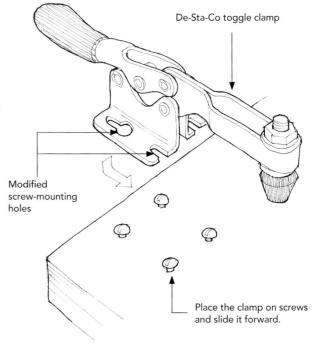

De-Sta-Co toggle clamp

Modified screw-mounting holes

Place the clamp on screws and slide it forward.

Deep socket fits router collet

Until I made this discovery, every time I needed to change bits in my table-mounted router I had to lift it out of the table to get at the collet nut. Over the duration of a project, the time spent removing and replacing the router adds up. But I just discovered that a deep socket (in my case a 7⁄8-in. spark-plug socket) will fit my router's collet nut and has plenty of room to fit over many of my router bits. Use of the socket greatly reduces the effort required to change a bit. This method should work with any router that has a shaft lock feature, although the size of the socket may vary.

Make sure your router is unplugged before you try this, because a socket-driver handle spinning at 20,000 rpm could really put a crimp in your workday.

—ROBERT F. REYNOLDS, Columbia, Md.

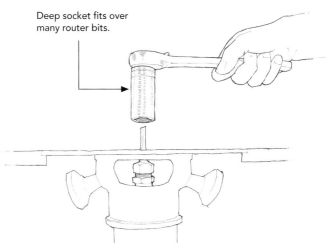

Deep socket fits over many router bits.

Router table borrows tablesaw's fixtures

One of the unique advantages of the high-end European combination machines is that you can use the sliding table and the crosscut fence with both the shaper and the tablesaw. I decided to do something similar on my tablesaw by mounting a router in the extension table and installing two miter-gauge slots in the extension table that matched the spacing of those on the saw table. This allows me to use not only the rip fence and the miter gauge but also any sliding fixtures I've made for the saw.

To make this setup, you need to purchase aluminum miter-track inserts (sold by Rockler® and other mail-order woodworking suppliers). These inserts are necessary because most extension tables are made from sheet goods that will not hold up to extended wear.

Installation is easy. Simply use your saw's rip fence to guide a router fitted with a straight bit. Rout two parallel dadoes in the top of the extension table, matching the spacing of the slots in the saw table. Screw the aluminum miter-track inserts in place, and you are ready to go.

One word of caution: Be sure to grind or file away the lip of the angle iron at the front and back of the extension table, as needed, to provide enough clearance before routing the groove.

—JUDD FANCHER, Glendale, Ariz.

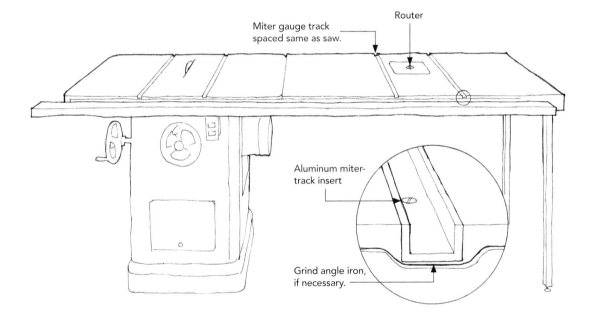

Miter gauge track spaced same as saw.

Router

Aluminum miter-track insert

Grind angle iron, if necessary.

Fence transforms tablesaw into a real router table

Installing a router table in my tablesaw's extension table saved a huge amount of shop space, but I needed to turn the rip fence into a router-table fence and figure out how to collect dust. I solved the problem with an auxiliary fence that is simple to build, fast to put on and take off, and gives a neat way to collect dust at the source.

The fence is basically a hollow box made from ¾-in.-thick plywood that attaches to the tablesaw fence with two universal fence clamps (www.rockler.com; No. 31373). I used slippery high-density polyethylene (HDPE) for the fence faces and bottom, but melamine or plywood would work, too.

The faces are mounted on T-tracks so they can be slid back and forth to create an opening for different-size bits. They can also slide together to create a zero-clearance effect, if desired. The T-track above the fence faces is for hold-downs and stops.

I drilled a hole in one end of the fence to match my shop-vacuum hose, which draws air through the opening in the fence and almost eliminates dust. The entire setup works great.

—DAVID DIAMAN, Abingdon, Md.

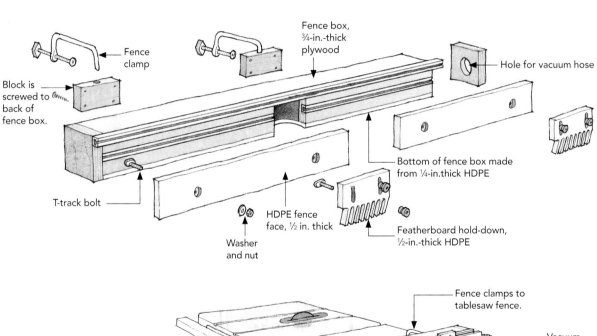

Fence clamp

Block is screwed to back of fence box.

Fence box, ¾-in.-thick plywood

Hole for vacuum hose

T-track bolt

Washer and nut

HDPE fence face, ½ in. thick

Bottom of fence box made from ¼-in.-thick HDPE

Featherboard hold-down, ½-in.-thick HDPE

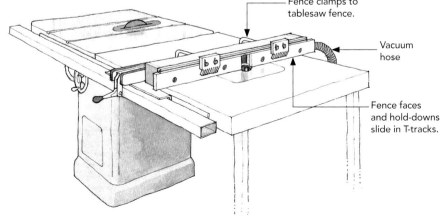

Fence clamps to tablesaw fence.

Vacuum hose

Fence faces and hold-downs slide in T-tracks.

TABLESAWS

Tablesaw outfeed with PVC rollers

In a one-man shop, ripping sheet goods and long lumber is difficult. I decided to solve this problem by building a roller extension on the back of my tablesaw. When I discovered that the commercially available rollers were a bit pricey, I went shopping. For a few bucks I bought a 10-ft. length of 1½-in.-dia. PVC plumbing pipe, a short length of nylon bar stock, several lengths of ½-in.-dia. steel bar stock, and some angle iron.

I made up four rollers by cutting lengths of the PVC and fitting each end of the pipe with bearings made from the nylon bar stock. I made axles from the ½-in.-dia. steel bar stock and drilled and tapped holes in each end to attach the axles to the frame. I then made a cantilevered framework with angle iron and bolted the framework to the back of the saw as shown, so that the rollers are level with the top of the tablesaw. This extension has made the handling of large stock much easier, quicker and safer.

—DON GILLIEM, Milford, Mich.

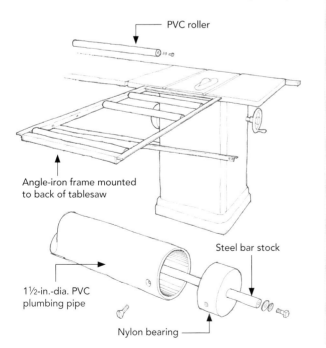

PVC roller

Angle-iron frame mounted to back of tablesaw

Steel bar stock

1½-in.-dia. PVC plumbing pipe

Nylon bearing

Improved tablesaw splitter

Many woodworkers never attached the splitter that came with their new tablesaw because it is cumbersome and inconvenient to use and has to be removed for some operations, such as cutting dadoes. After experiencing kickback on a friend's saw that had no splitter, I was determined to work out a convenient solution for the splitter on my own saw (General). With the design shown below, the splitter can be left in place even when using a crosscut sled. And because it uses the same arbor mount as the factory-supplied splitter, it tilts for a miter cut. Not all splitters work that way.

To make the splitter, cut the basic shape shown from ³⁄₃₂-in.-thick aluminum stock. This thickness will leave ¹⁄₆₄ in. of clearance on each side of a standard sawblade kerf. You can modify the shape as you wish, but mine sits 2½ in. above the table.

The best part of this design is the way the splitter attaches to the mount. Replace the old splitter attachment bolt with an adjustable ratchet-type of handle that has the same size threads. These ratchet handles are available from Reid Supply Company (www.reidsupply.com) and other sources. The handle will clear the blade and will make it easier to remove and install the splitter.

—BUD RUBY, Oakland, Calif.

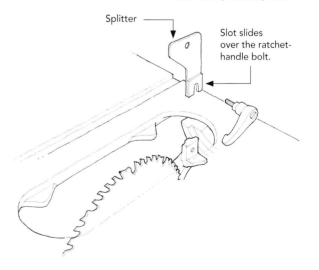

Splitter

Slot slides over the ratchet-handle bolt.

A safer crosscut sled

I once saw a beginner in our shop using a cutoff sled to crosscut a heavy workpiece. As he neared the end of the cut, with the far edge of the sled hanging over the back of the saw table, the sled reared up on him. Luckily, someone else was nearby and kept him from flopping the sled back onto the table and into a spinning blade. After that, the first thing we did was to build an outfeed table for that saw. I also decided to make a new, safer crosscut sled.

I made the sled of ¾-in.-thick medium-density fiberboard because it's inexpensive, it's about as hard as soft maple, and it's very stable. I milled some scraps of hardwood for the runners and cut a 24-in. by 32-in. piece of MDF for the base. I laminated two pieces of MDF for the front and back fences and three pieces for the middle fence.

I secured the runners with glue and screws because I didn't want to risk any possibility of them coming loose during a cutting operation. After installing the runners, I sealed and lubricated them with several coats of paste wax.

Before attaching the fences, I cut a kerf into the base of the sled to give me a reference edge to which I could square them. Last, I added a block of MDF (three pieces thick) to fit between the middle and back fences. That block of MDF makes it virtually impossible to cut your fingers at the end of a crosscut operation because the blade is completely buried within the MDF.

—JOE SANTAPAU, Yardley, Pa.

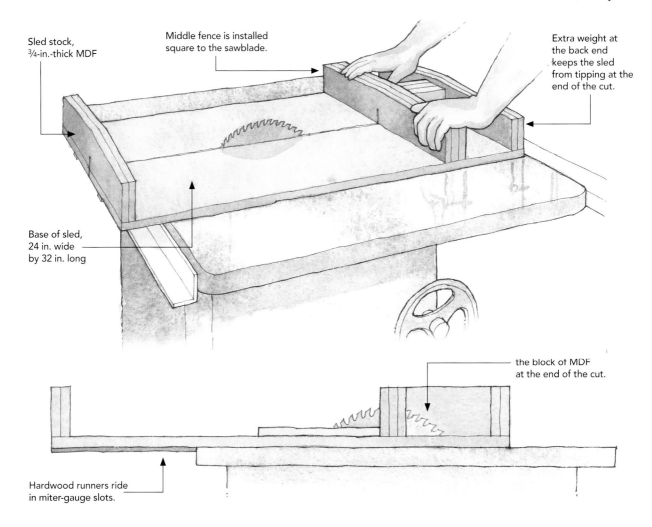

Sled stock, ¾-in.-thick MDF

Middle fence is installed square to the sawblade.

Extra weight at the back end keeps the sled from tipping at the end of the cut.

Base of sled, 24 in. wide by 32 in. long

the block ot MDF at the end of the cut.

Hardwood runners ride in miter-gauge slots.

Shopmade fence for a miter gauge

A long, straight sacrificial fence attached to the table-saw's miter gauge provides better support for workpieces, which yields more precise cuts. It also provides a mounting surface for stop blocks or a stop extension stick, and it prevents chipout on the back edge.

To construct a flat, stable fence, start with two ½-in.-thick pieces of hardwood or plywood. Make them about 20 in. long by 2½ in. tall and face-glue them against a flat reference surface. Before securing the fence to the miter gauge, cut a small rabbet along the bottom front edge to give sawdust a place to go.

Mount the fence so that one side can act as a sweep for moving cutoffs past the blade. That means having a few inches of fence extending past the blade. To make a nonslip surface, you can glue fine sandpaper to the fence.

—TIM ALBERS, Ventura, Calif.

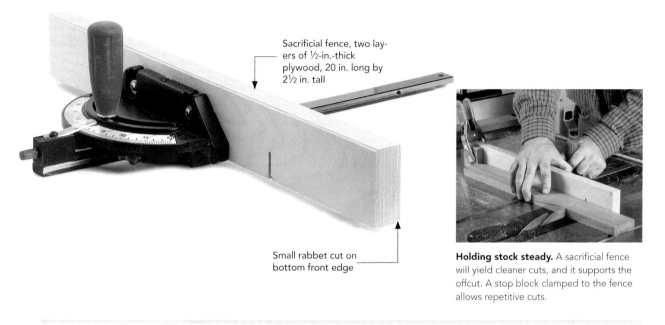

Sacrificial fence, two layers of ½-in.-thick plywood, 20 in. long by 2½ in. tall

Small rabbet cut on bottom front edge

Holding stock steady. A sacrificial fence will yield cleaner cuts, and it supports the offcut. A stop block clamped to the fence allows repetitive cuts.

Nonslip push stick for the tablesaw

When I used my ordinary push stick on a tablesaw, I had good control in the north/south direction but less in the east/west direction, especially when trying to keep small workpieces tight against the rip fence. So I added a nonslip shelf-liner strip to the sole of the push stick. The shelf liner grabs the workpiece, giving me more control in all directions.

To attach the liner, first sand the sole of the push stick to help ensure a good bond, then attach the strip with double-faced tape.

—SERGE DUCLOS, Delson, Que., Canada

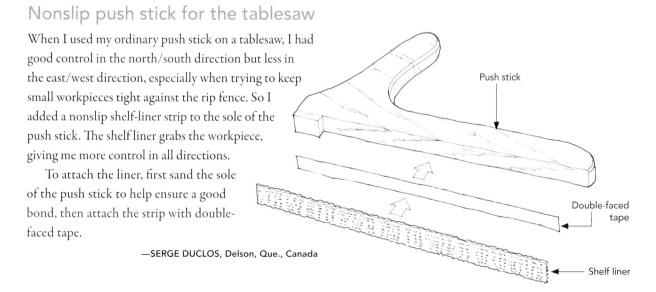

Push stick

Double-faced tape

Shelf liner

Tablesaw extension supports large workpieces

When crosscutting wide materials on the tablesaw, you need extra support at the front and side of the saw. My support extension slides right into the end of the fence tubing and can be used or stored in seconds. It is simply a length of aluminum angle lag-bolted to a length of hardwood that's cut to fit snugly against the top and bottom of the tube. When the extension is in position, the aluminum angle should be the same height as the top of the table. When it's not in use, I pull out the extension, rotate it 180°, and reinsert it. It is easily accessible yet out of the way at the same time.

—BOB HARTIG, Sheboygan, Wis.

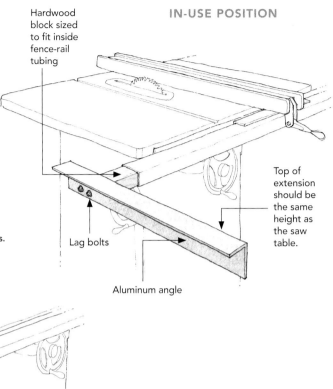

Hardwood block sized to fit inside fence-rail tubing

IN-USE POSITION

Top of extension should be the same height as the saw table.

Lag bolts

Aluminum angle

STORED POSITION

Low-dust lubricants for a tablesaw

If the gears of your tablesaw often become clogged with sawdust, making them hard to turn, there are two choices of lubricants that can be applied to the gears to prevent dust buildup. I use a white grease stick by Panef® that has the consistency of soft soap. You can find it in the automotive aisle of most hardware stores. A toothbrush will let you apply a thin coat to the gears that won't attract much dust.

If you can't find the stick grease, use a furniture wax like Johnson's® paste wax. It works nearly as well.

To help clean the gears before applying the grease, use a spray penetrating oil such as WD-40® and a stiff brush.

—JOHN WHITE, Rochester, Vt.

Lubricant keeps dust from sticking. A thin coat of Panef's white stick lubricant is easy to apply with a toothbrush and isn't a dust magnet. After scraping some grease onto a toothbrush, press the bristles into the gears as you rotate them with the handle.

Tablesaw-blade tightening technique

It can be difficult to get sufficient leverage on the blade of a cabinet saw when tightening it to the arbor. The goal is to attach the nut to the arbor bracket firmly without inadvertently warping the blade by doing so. Jamming a block of wood against the blade's rim or clamping the blade can permanently distort it. I've developed a method that doesn't put any stress on the blade. After you get the nut finger-tight against the blade, place the wrench on the nut, hold the blade with one hand, and strike the wrench with a block of hardwood, taking two or three moderate blows. This method simulates the action of an impact wrench, using the inertia of the saw's drive system to keep the arbor still while the nut is tightened with a series of blows.

Because of the way a saw is designed, you don't have to worry about the nut coming loose and the blade flying off. The direction of the threads on the arbor run in the opposite direction of the arbor's rotation; so even if the nut were loose, it wouldn't spin off the shaft while the saw was running.

To remove the nut, reverse the procedure. Place a shop rag on the edge of the table-insert opening to prevent the wrench handle from dinging the edge of the opening when the nut comes loose.

—JOHN WHITE, Rochester, Vt.

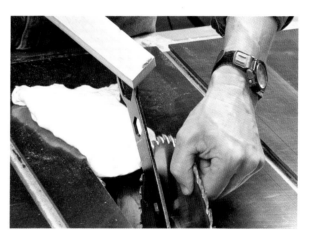

Steady the blade with slight hand pressure. Then rap on the free end of the wrench a few times with a piece of hardwood to tighten the nut (left). Loosen the blade the same way (right), but protect the tabletop from the loosened wrench.

Sacrificial rip-fence cover

Make a box to fit over your tablesaw's rip fence. It must be a snug slip fit in both width and length. Use melamine pieces on the outside, and you'll have an almost friction-free fence you can saw or dado into without damaging your regular rip fence. The cover is very easy to take on and off, and mine has lasted longer than I thought it would.

—BLAISE GASTON, Earlysville, Va.

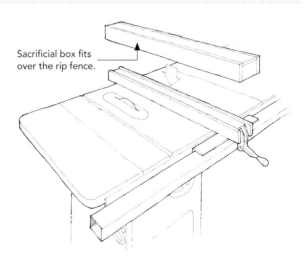

Sacrificial box fits over the rip fence.

Rolling lift for the tablesaw

I often have to move my tablesaw around, so I made a rolling lift that raises the saw onto casters.

My design has a couple of advantages over the typical commercially made rolling platforms. Unlike those, it does not raise the height of the saw by 3 in. to 4 in. Also, when lowered, the base of the saw rests on the shop floor, so there's no intermediate platform to compromise sturdiness.

To build the lift, you need four swivel casters, four butt hinges, a screen-door latch, some scrap hardwood, and a few assorted nuts, bolts, and washers. Also, you need a small piece of metal (I used ⅛-in.-thick aluminum) for a striker plate.

The lift has two main parts: a pedal beam and a catch beam. Attached to each beam are pairs of casters and butt hinges. The hinges mount to the base of the saw.

With the lift installed, you raise the saw simply by pushing down on the pedal-beam arm until the striker plate engages the screen-door latch. Once engaged, the two beams lock together to hold the saw up on the casters. The beams pivot up when the screen-door latch is released, lowering the saw base to the floor.

—TIM JANSSEN, Toronto, Ont., Canada

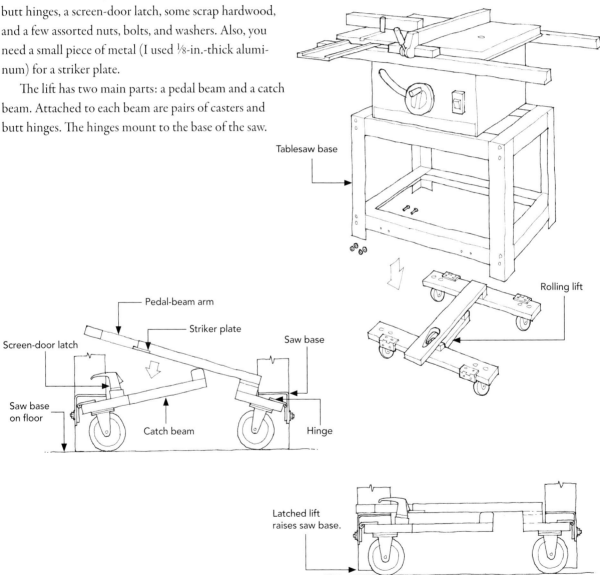

Tablesaw base

Rolling lift

Pedal-beam arm

Striker plate

Screen-door latch

Saw base

Saw base on floor

Catch beam

Hinge

Latched lift raises saw base.

Multiuse joinery jig for the tablesaw

Instead of making multiple jigs for cutting different joints on the tablesaw, I saved time, materials, and space by making one that can do multiple jobs. It consists of a carriage that rides my Biesemeyer-style fence and interchangeable fixtures designed to cut various joints. I have three fixtures: one for cutting tenons, one for keyed miters, and one for cutting spline slots.

The carriage is made from ¾-in. Baltic-birch plywood, but MDF would work as well. To ensure that the mounting holes in all fixtures align with those in the carriage, make a ¼-in.-thick plywood template the same size as the carriage side. Drill the five ¼-in.-dia. holes in the template and use it to drill the mounting holes in the carriage and in the fixture base. Install any fences, hold-downs, or clamps you need with glue and/or screws from behind.

I finished the carriage and fixtures with two coats of shellac and applied paste wax on the interior of the carriage so it slides freely on the rip fence.

—DOUGLAS BLACKE, Olivenhain, Calif.

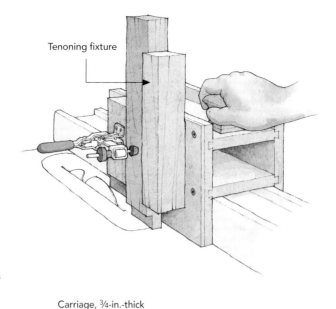

Tenoning fixture

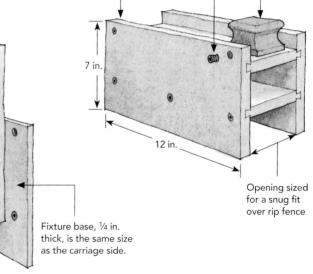

Carriage, ¾-in.-thick MDF or plywood

¼-20 threaded insert

Handle

7 in.

12 in.

Opening sized for a snug fit over rip fence

TENONING FIXTURE

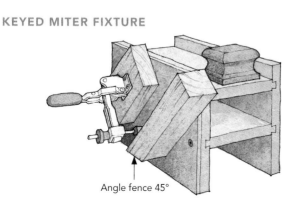

Machine screws secure each fixture to the carriage.

Fixture base, ¼ in. thick, is the same size as the carriage side.

KEYED MITER FIXTURE

Angle fence 45°

SPLINE SLOT FIXTURE

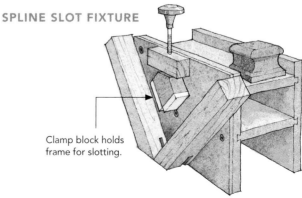

Clamp block holds frame for slotting.

Blocks improve clamping area under cast-iron machine tops

From time to time, I need to clamp featherboards and other devices to the top of my tablesaw and shaper. Both tools have cast-iron tabletops with ribs on the underside, which makes it difficult to find the right place for a large clamp. The solution for both machines is to glue blocks of wood to the underside of the tops to provide a level clamping surface. I used construction adhesive as the glue.

—LARY SHAFFER, Scarborough, Maine

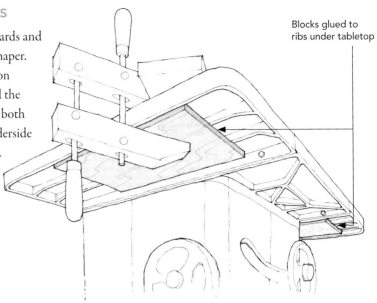

Blocks glued to ribs under tabletop

Smoother cuts on the tablesaw

Tablesaws need accurate alignment to perform well. The miter-gauge slots must be adjusted parallel with the blade, and the rip fence should be adjusted slightly out of parallel, which can be done by referencing off the miter slot. Otherwise the rear of the blade will re-cut wood that has already passed through the front of the blade.

To keep the rear of the blade from re-cutting the stock when ripping, the rip fence needs to be out of parallel by $\frac{1}{64}$ in. to $\frac{1}{32}$ in. over its length. In this way, only the first three or four teeth will be engaged in the actual cutting, and then the good wood will feed freely past the rear of the blade—no burning and no sawmarks.

In addition, use a splitter in the table insert or attach one to the arbor assembly to prevent the work from coming off the fence and into the blade (causing dangerous kickback) should it decide to bow on you during a cut.

—GARY ROGOWSKI, Portland, Ore.

Offset the fence and add a splitter. For cuts free of burns and sawmarks, adjust the rip fence so that it is slightly out of parallel with the miter-gauge slot. A splitter attached to the arbor assembly, or integrated into the insert, keeps stock from drifting into the blade and catching.

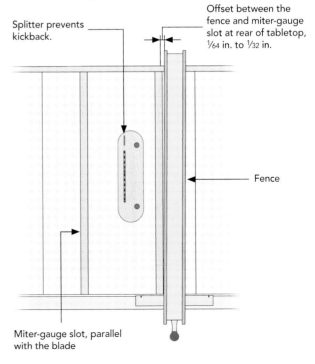

Splitter prevents kickback.

Offset between the fence and miter-gauge slot at rear of tabletop, $\frac{1}{64}$ in. to $\frac{1}{32}$ in.

Fence

Miter-gauge slot, parallel with the blade

Firm anchor for a tablesaw featherboard

A featherboard is designed to hold stock against a table-saw's fence and tabletop so you can keep your fingers away from the blade while ripping. Typically made of ¾-in.-thick hardwood with fingers cut into the end, a featherboard is clamped just ahead of the blade. To help anchor the featherboard, clamp a second board behind and at a right angle to it to act as a brace. This keeps the featherboard from pivoting on its clamp point and thereby releasing pressure on the workpiece being held in place.

—RICHARD BRENING, Bellevue, Wash.

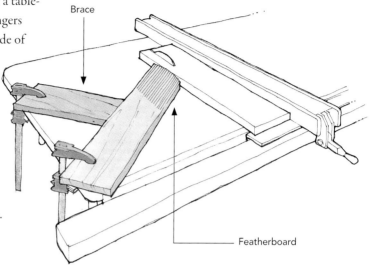

Brace

Featherboard

Tablesaw insert from a kitchen cutting board

When I discovered the cost of aftermarket zero-clearance throat inserts for my tablesaw, I decided to make my own. I bought an ordinary white, high-density-plastic kitchen cutting board, ½ in. thick. I marked and cut out several inserts, using the existing metal one as a template. I then drilled and tapped four holes in each insert to install leveling set screws. I also drilled a finger hole to make it easy to remove the insert from the saw table. The cutting-board material is ideal because it is inexpensive, friction-free, dense, and stable. I was able to make several inserts for less than the price of one commercially available piece.

—SCOTT SPIERLING, Sunnyvale, Calif.

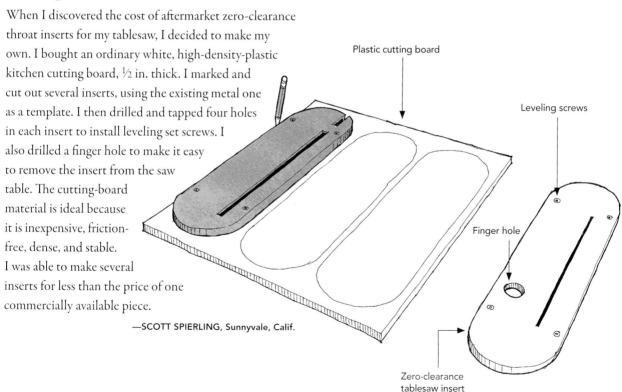

Plastic cutting board

Leveling screws

Finger hole

Zero-clearance tablesaw insert

A splitter you will actually use

Adding a splitter to a new tablesaw throat insert is an excellent safety practice. Once installed, neglecting it requires a conscious effort, so the odds are that it will see everyday, real-life use.

However, the procedure that's usually recommended —extending the kerf behind the blade and gluing in a wooden tongue—is hard to pull off without introducing minuscule errors. And the slightest error will result in a device that snags the workpiece. This method solves those problems.

Raise the sawblade through the new insert. Then place the insert against a fence on a drill-press table. Align things by lowering a drill bit of a diameter equal to the blade thickness (usually ⅛ in.) into the kerf. When the bit is centered in the kerf, lock the fence, change to a drill bit ½₂ in. smaller, switch on the drill press, and bore a hole near the outfeed end of the kerf. Now push that same drill bit into the hole, shank up, along with a dab of cyanoacrylate glue. The drill bit will now serve as the splitter pin. It will be aligned perfectly with the sawkerf and should have about ½₄ in. of clearance on each side.

MICHAEL STANDISH, Roxbury, Mass.

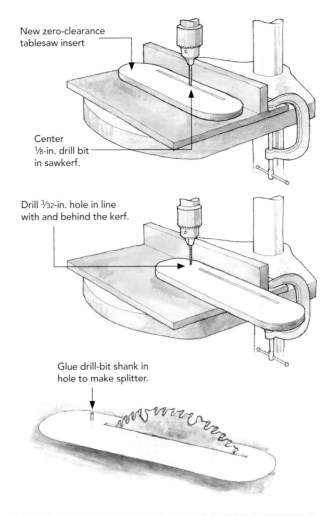

New zero-clearance tablesaw insert

Center ⅛-in. drill bit in sawkerf.

Drill ³⁄₃₂-in. hole in line with and behind the kerf.

Glue drill-bit shank in hole to make splitter.

Mark a roller stand for faster setups

I use my roller stand with several different tools with different table or outfeed heights. This requires me to adjust the stand frequently, with all the bending over, sighting, and readjusting that involves.

To speed up the process and save my back, I marked the extension shaft of the roller stand to indicate the correct height for different machines. Now all I have to do is adjust the extension to the right line, tighten the handle, and go to work.

—JOEL HARRELL, Raleigh, N.C.

Use permanent marker to highlight correct heights for individual tools.

Use easy-to-remember abbreviations for the tools (TS means tablesaw, for example).

Smart way to cut a new tablesaw insert to size

A zero-clearance throat plate insert makes a tablesaw safer and helps you make cleaner cuts. Sizing it right can be tricky, so here's an easy way to cut and trim a blank to size.

Because many saws are designed for a ½-in.-thick throat plate, make the insert from strong, ½-in.-thick birch plywood. On the tablesaw, cut it ⅛ in. wider and 1 in. longer than the saw's throat plate. Center the throat plate on the blank and attach it with double-faced tape.

Next, using the throat plate as a guide, round the ends of the blank with a bandsaw or jigsaw, leaving ¹⁄₁₆ in. of waste. Rout off the waste with a bottom-bearing, flush-trimming bit. The bearing runs against the throat plate as the bit removes the waste and trims the insert to size.

Keep the new insert attached to the old insert while you cut the blade and blade guard openings.

—TOM BEGNAL, Kent, Conn.

1. MAKE THE BLANK

Throat plate becomes template. Attach the throat plate to the blank with double-faced tape.

Round the ends. A bandsaw does this best, but a jigsaw also works. Leave about ¹⁄₁₆ in. of extra material.

Trim the blank. Rout the insert flush to the throat plate with a bottom-bearing, flush-trimming bit.

2. CUT THE OPENINGS

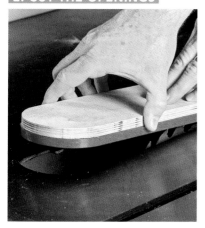

Don't remove the blank. Even at its lowest height, a 10-in. blade stops a blank from dropping into the throat. Cut the blade opening with the blank taped to the insert.

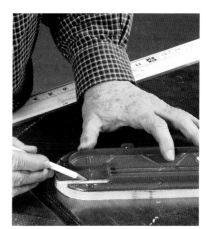

Two openings to cut. Hold down the blank with a push stick (left), staying away from the blade (you also can place a board across the insert, clamping it at the front and back of the saw table). Raise the blade slowly. Afterward, mark the opening for the blade-guard assembly (right) and cut it with a bandsaw or jigsaw.

Tablesaw cart keeps blades and accessories close by

When I first bought my tablesaw, I had one blade, an arbor wrench, and a rip fence. But after a few years, my collection of blades was hanging on the wall and my accessories were stored randomly all over the shop. I put an end to the tablesaw clutter by building a rolling storage cart that sits under the extension table of my saw.

The cart holds all the tablesaw's fixtures, including blades, miter gauge, setup squares, wrenches, and throat plates. Blades slip on and off the carriers easily. The carriers slide into an angled rack, which keeps the blades in place. All the materials and hardware can be purchased at your local home center.

The sides and drawer boxes are made of ½-in. plywood; the rest is ¾-in. Joinery is simple (screws). The cart should fit under the extension table of your saw (don't forget to allow for the casters). Its length should not exceed the front-to-back dimension of your saw's extension table. I use 10-in. blades, so I made the interior width 13 in. I left 1½ in. of clearance between the cart and the extension table. The extra space allows me to leave the carrier for the blade I'm using right on top of the other carriers. That way, when I change blades, I don't have to go looking for it.

—DAVID GROSZ, Stamford, Conn.

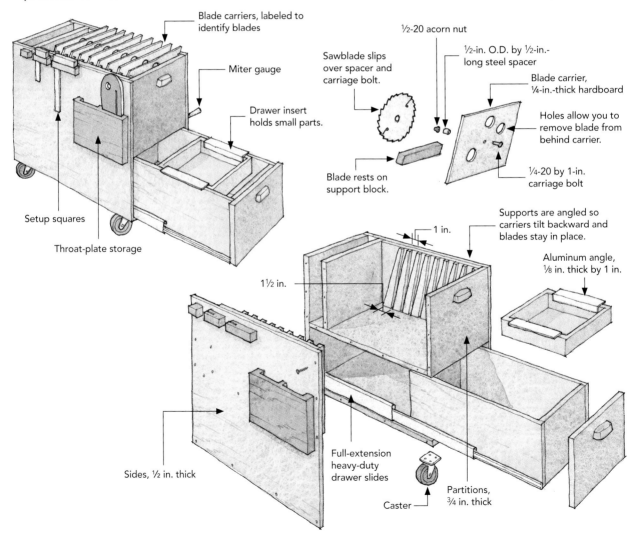

Blade carriers, labeled to identify blades

Miter gauge

Drawer insert holds small parts.

Setup squares

Throat-plate storage

½-20 acorn nut

½-in. O.D. by ½-in.-long steel spacer

Sawblade slips over spacer and carriage bolt.

Blade carrier, ¼-in.-thick hardboard

Holes allow you to remove blade from behind carrier.

¼-20 by 1-in. carriage bolt

Blade rests on support block.

1 in.

1½ in.

Supports are angled so carriers tilt backward and blades stay in place.

Aluminum angle, ⅛ in. thick by 1 in.

Full-extension heavy-duty drawer slides

Sides, ½ in. thick

Caster

Partitions, ¾ in. thick

BANDSAWS

Simple circle-cutting jig

Because the only piece of power equipment I have in my shop is a bandsaw, I try to make the most of it with jigs. When I set out to make a circle-cutting jig, most designs I found were too complicated, too limited, or too expensive. So I came up with a simple, effective jig that can be put together in about 10 minutes. It works as a sled in the miter-gauge slot to make a starting cut in the workpiece tangential to the circle. When the jig stops against the front edge of the saw table, rotate the workpiece to complete the cut.

The sled is a piece of plywood that's ⅜ in. or ½ in. thick and a couple of inches bigger than the bandsaw table. Attach a runner to the bottom that fits into the miter-gauge slot, and attach a stop that will engage the front edge of the saw table. Cut a kerf into the sled by running the jig into the blade until it stops. Mark a pencil line 90° from the point where the kerf ends.

To use this jig, drill a small hole on the 90° line at a distance from the sawkerf equal to the radius of the circle you want to cut. Tap a finish nail into the bottom center point of the workpiece and drop the nail into the hole.

Turn on the saw and run the whole jig into the blade until it stops. Rotate the workpiece to cut a perfect circle every time.

—BENJAMIN JOHNSTON, Chicago, Ill.

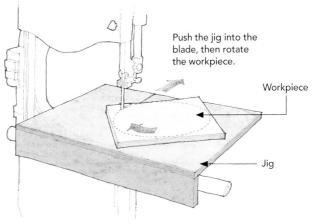

Push the jig into the blade, then rotate the workpiece.

Workpiece

Jig

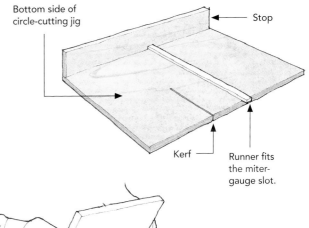

Bottom side of circle-cutting jig

Stop

Kerf

Runner fits the miter-gauge slot.

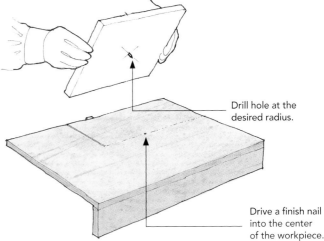

Drill hole at the desired radius.

Drive a finish nail into the center of the workpiece.

Safety bumpers from tennis balls

In smaller shops like mine, where space is at a premium, there's the constant danger of bumping into protruding fence rails, like those on my bandsaw. A used tennis ball slipped over the end of a fence rail serves as a bold visual reminder of possible danger and as a cushion against the inevitable bump. Simply cut an X-shaped incision with a hobby knife, and press-fit a ball over the fence rail or similar protruding object.

—ROBERT R. LLEWELLYN, Memphis, Tenn.

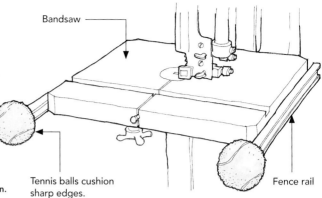

Bandsaw

Tennis balls cushion sharp edges.

Fence rail

Keep bandsaw tires clean

Here's a simple way to clean embedded sawdust off bandsaw tires and minimize the problem of dust building up on the tires.

With the saw turned off and unplugged, scrub off embedded sawdust with a brass brush. Spin the wheel by hand and hold the brush in place against the wheel. Avoid using oil-based solvents such as paint thinner because they may damage the rubber of the tire.

To avoid the buildup in the first place, you can make three simple modifications. First, install a deflector to channel the dust toward the pickup chute. A piece of stiff rubber or flexible plastic can be attached with self-tapping screws or double-faced tape.

Second, install an additional dust pickup in the bottom left-hand corner of the lower housing, where a pile of dust tends to collect. You can use a metal-cutting hole saw to drill the hole. A sawdust pickup chute available from tool suppliers can be attached with screws over the hole.

Finally and most important, keep any remaining dust off the wheels by installing a stiff brush that cleans the lower wheel as it rotates. I use a wooden scrub brush with stiff natural bristles that I cut to size and attach with wood screws, inserted through holes in the metal casting. You also can buy brushes for certain bandsaw models.

With these modifications, I haven't had to replace the tires that came with my bandsaw 30 years ago.

—MICHAEL FORTUNE, Lakefield, Ont., Canada

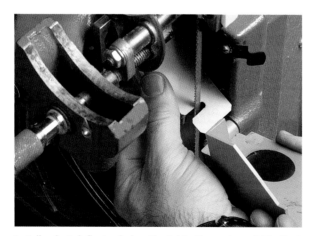

Install a dust deflector below the table. Use a piece of thin, flexible cutting board and align it with the existing dust-collection port.

Install a brush in the lower housing, against the wheel. Iturra Design carries a brush that fits the Delta® 14-in. bandsaw.

Miter gauge can act
as rip fence, too

Ripping and resawing on the bandsaw is always a problem because of the natural tendency of each blade to lead the cut in a slightly different direction, called drift. The traditional method of compensation is to find the drift angle, mark a line on the table, and then clamp a makeshift fence parallel to this line. This auxiliary table improves on that solution by borrowing your tablesaw's miter gauge for ripping as well as crosscutting on your bandsaw.

I made my auxiliary table from a discarded laminated kitchen countertop, but a good grade of plywood would work just as well. Size it a little larger than the original table, then drill through both tables and fasten them together with four countersunk carriage bolts. Cut a slot for blade entry. Now cut two ¾-in. dadoes to fit the miter gauge. Cut one parallel to the blade for standard crosscutting operations and then a second dado 90° to the first for ripping and resawing.

To find a blade's drift angle, mark a centerline on a piece of 1×2 scrap stock. Carefully rip freehand along this line until the stock reaches the rear of the table. Leave the 1×2 in this position and insert the miter gauge in the second slot as shown. Loosen the protractor adjustment knob and slide the miter gauge up to the workpiece. Adjust the fence angle to the drift angle you just found, then tighten the protractor knob. Remove the 1×2, position the miter gauge for the desired cut width, measuring from the front of the blade, and clamp the gauge in place. You're now set up for accurate, repeatable ripping and resawing.

—ANTHONY P. MATLOSZ, Howell, N.J.

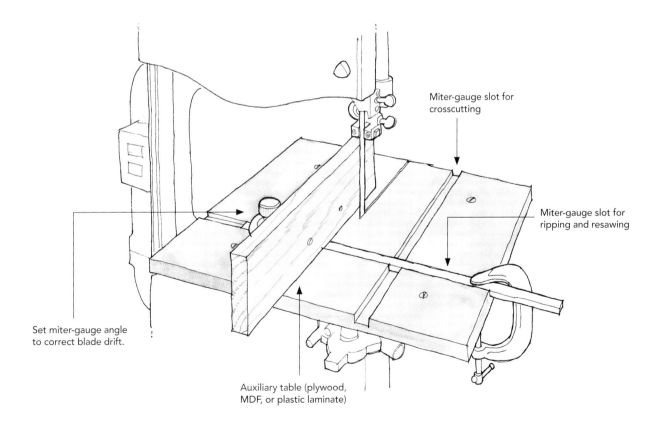

Miter-gauge slot for crosscutting

Miter-gauge slot for ripping and resawing

Set miter-gauge angle to correct blade drift.

Auxiliary table (plywood, MDF, or plastic laminate)

Shimming Taiwanese bandsaw wheels for blade alignment

Typically, on Taiwanese saws, the nut holding on the upper wheel stops on a shoulder machined in the axle, and there is no spacer tube in the upper wheel's hub to separate the inside races of the two wheel bearings. If this is the case with your saw, the position of the upper wheel can't be adjusted with shim washers; only the bottom wheel can be adjusted. Without a spacer tube, adding shim washers behind the upper wheel and tightening the nut against the shoulder on the axle will apply excess pressure on the wheel bearings.

On Taiwanese bandsaws, such as Grizzly® saws, wheel alignment can be adjusted by adding or removing shim washers behind the lower wheel. Usually, the wheel will be held in place by a bolt with a 13mm head and washer. It is quite likely that the bolt is a left-hand thread, so you will need to turn the bolt clockwise to remove it. If the wheel won't come off the axle after the nut has been removed, do not pry against the wheel's rim, because it can be bent easily. The only safe way to remove a solidly stuck wheel is with a gear puller, available at auto-supply stores.

Once the wheel is off, you can add shim washers behind it to move it outward. If the wheel has factory-installed washers behind it, you can remove them to move the wheel inward. If there aren't any washers behind the lower wheel, and you need to move it backward to line up the wheels, you are stuck: The machine was built out of line, and you will need to contact the manufacturer to see if there's a fix for the problem.

Iturra Designs in Florida sells an inexpensive set of shim washers for the lower wheel on Jet® bandsaws; I suspect that these also will fit the Grizzly saw because all of the Taiwanese saws are of similar design. Iturra's phone number is 904-642-2802.

—JOHN WHITE, Rochester, Vt.

Remove the lower wheel and shim it flush to the top wheel. A gear puller (left) makes quick work of removing a wheel that is seized in place. Once the wheel has been removed, simply shim it out (right) until it is aligned with the upper wheel.

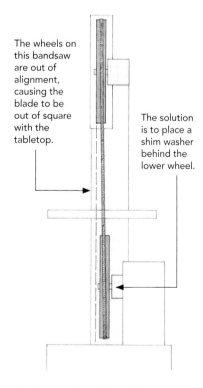

The wheels on this bandsaw are out of alignment, causing the blade to be out of square with the tabletop.

The solution is to place a shim washer behind the lower wheel.

Aligning bandsaw wheels. On many bandsaws manufactured in Taiwan, only the lower wheel may be adjusted.

Outfeed table for the bandsaw

When cutting long boards on a bandsaw, an outfeed table is a big help. This one folds up to hang on the wall when it's not in use.

To make this table, cut a ¾-in.-thick pine or ply-wood platform as wide as your saw table and about 6 ft. long. Bolt a notched 1-in. by 1-in. length of angle iron to the front of the outfeed table. Cut slots in the angle iron so that it fits over hex-head machine screws installed in the fence-attachment holes on the back of your saw table. When cutting the slots, start shallow and then slowly file the slots deeper to bring the top of the outfeed table flush with the bandsaw table. Finally, attach a hinged fold-down leg underneath. The weight of the outfeed table will be enough to hold the fold-down leg in place.

—WILLIE LOCHHEAD, E. Falmouth, Mass.

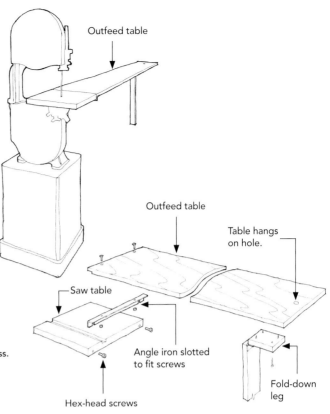

Outfeed table

Outfeed table

Table hangs on hole.

Saw table

Angle iron slotted to fit screws

Hex-head screws

Fold-down leg

DRILLING

Cure for puny knobs

If you find the puny knobs on your benchtop drill press (or any other tool) difficult to grasp, here's an easy solution. Buy some 1½-in.-dia. hardwood balls from a craft store, drill a hole in the balls the same size as the handle shafts and force-thread them onto the shafts. Secure the balls with some epoxy. Wipe on a couple of coats of finish, and you're set.

For variation, craft stores also carry egg-shaped and "doll's-head" wooden balls. A complete set is very inexpensive.

—R.B. HIMES, Vienna, Ohio

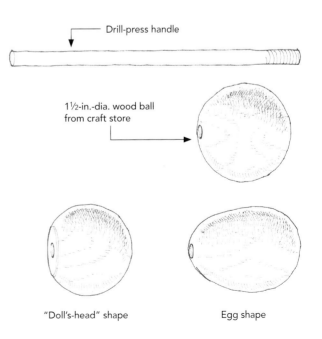

Drill-press handle

1½-in.-dia. wood ball from craft store

"Doll's-head" shape

Egg shape

Durable jig for shelf-support pins

Most jigs for drilling shelf-pin holes are awkward to use and bulky to store. In contrast, this simple homemade jig is small, accurate, easy to use, and built to last.

Start with a scrap block of ¾-in.-thick medium-density fiberboard and screw a hardwood fence to one edge. Measure in from the fence and install a registration dowel sized to fit the shelf-pin hole. Both the fence and the registration dowel should extend past the surface on both sides of the block: This allows the jig to be flipped over and used along both edges of the workpiece. Now drill the guide hole. The distance from the registration pin to the guide hole will set the spacing of the shelf-pin holes. I prefer a spacing of 2 in. If you plan to use the jig just once, you can use the guide hole as is. However, if you want a jig you can use over and over, install a steel bushing for the guide hole.

To use the jig, install a depth stop on the drill bit. For this, use a ¾-in.-dia. dowel drilled along its axis and then cut to length so that only the correct amount of drill bit protrudes. Measure down from the top of the workpiece and drill two starting holes, one on each edge. Place the jig's registration pin in the first hole and, while holding or clamping the fence against the edge of the workpiece, drill the second hole. Repeat this sequence while walking the jig down the workpiece until you have drilled all of the shelf-pin holes along one edge. Flip over the jig and repeat the process along the other edge.

—ANDREW FAIRBANK, Hammondville, NSW, Australia

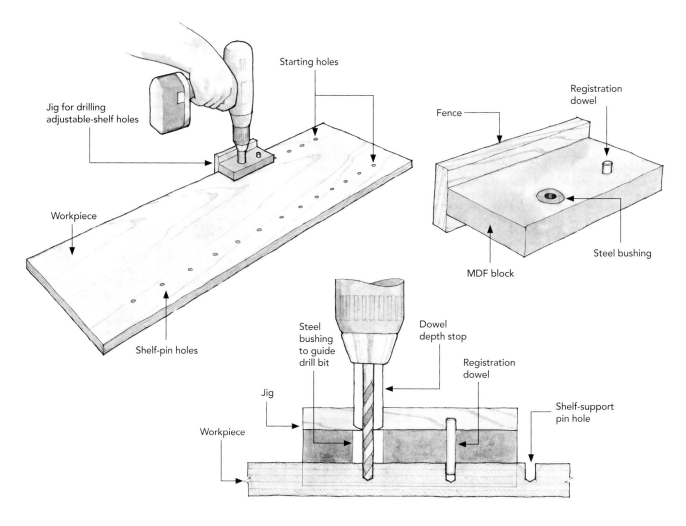

Easy drill-press fence

This quick-to-make drill-press fence is a big improvement over the clumsy strip of wood and two clamps that most of us use. The fixture consists of a ¾-in.-thick plywood auxiliary table and a movable fence. Attach the auxiliary table to the regular drill-press table—arrangements will vary from drill press to drill press. Make the fence from a length of 1½-in. by 1½-in. aluminum angle faced with plywood. The fence adjusts via two slots in the plywood table and locks in place by tightening vertical black handles that engage industrial T-nuts below. You can get both items at www.grainger.com: item No. 2YJL1 (T-nuts) and No. 4X501 (handle).

—DAVID M. GROSZ, Stamford, Conn.

Tapered handle with threaded insert

⁹⁄₁₆-in. slot in auxiliary table

T-nut, base size 1⅛ in.

Loosen handles to slide fence.

1½-in. by 1½-in. aluminum angle

¾-in. plywood face

Auxiliary drill-press table, ¾-in.-thick plywood

Keep chuck key close at hand

When I finally tired of having to search for my drill-press chuck key every time I needed to change a bit, I made a little nest for it right on the drill-press column using a ballpoint pen cap and a hose clamp.

I placed the keeper high enough so that it doesn't disturb the travel of the table and low enough to clear the head assembly when I pull out the key from the cap.

—SERGE DUCLOS, Delson, Que., Canada

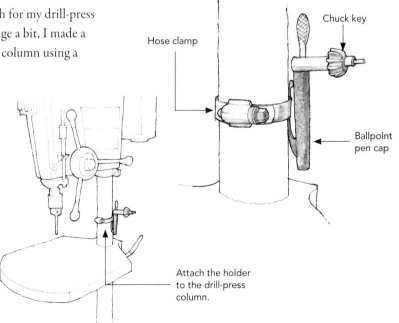

Hose clamp

Chuck key

Ballpoint pen cap

Attach the holder to the drill-press column.

Magnetic drill-press fence

This magnetic drill-press fence is easy to build, simple to adjust, and locks down tight. As an added bonus it has a handy magnetic cup for holding loose drill bits.

In the first version I made, the strong pull of the magnets made it difficult to fine-tune the fence's location on the drill-press table. To solve this problem, I installed a handle with a lever that raises the fence enough to break the magnetic pull. This improvement made it easier to adjust the fence. Once the fence is located where I want it, I lower the handle and the strong magnetic pull takes over, securing the jig to the iron drill-press table. It works great, but you need to take care not to bang your workpiece too hard against the fence, which may cause it to move slightly.

—LYLE MOSHER, San Jose, Calif.

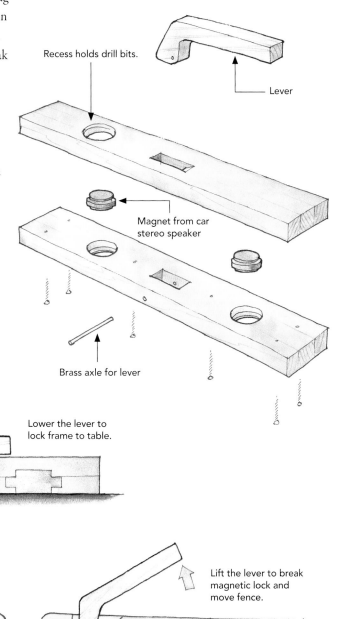

Recess holds drill bits.

Lever

Magnet from car stereo speaker

Brass axle for lever

Lower the lever to lock frame to table.

Lift the lever to break magnetic lock and move fence.

Drill-press table with a sacrificial insert

When drilling through wood, it always helps to have a backup to prevent tearout. Glue two pieces of beveled ½-in.-thick medium-density fiberboard onto a base of ¾-in.-thick MDF, creating a dovetailed channel into which a beveled sacrificial board can slide. Offset the slot with respect to the drill chuck (instead of centering it) so that when one strip of the sliding board is used up, reverse it and have a fresh area to drill into. The sacrificial board locks into the channel with a wedge. Fasten the auxiliary table to the drill-press table with screws from underneath.

Besides solving the problem of backing up holes, the auxiliary table is larger than the table that came with the drill press. This helps when drilling bigger pieces. The overhang also makes it easier to clamp fences and jigs, or the work itself, without fighting the ribs and unevenness of the cast table. It has been a great addition to my shop.

—DEAN MALMSTROM, Cedar Hills, Utah

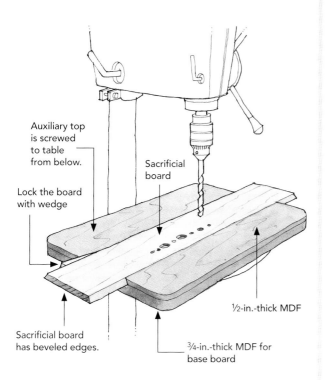

Auxiliary top is screwed to table from below.

Sacrificial board

Lock the board with wedge

Sacrificial board has beveled edges.

½-in.-thick MDF

¾-in.-thick MDF for base board

Center finders—two variations

To make a handy homemade guide for center-drilling holes in the edges of boards to be doweled and edge-glued, screw five sticks of hardwood together in the configuration shown in the drawing below.

The sticks pivot so the device collapses like a parallelogram. For the drill guide, fit the center strip with a hex-head bolt ⅛ in. larger than the bit size. Then, using a drill press for accuracy, drill a pilot hole through the bolt using a bit one number larger than the bit you'll use for doweling. To use, align the edges of the boards and mark the dowel locations with a square. To center the dowels, straddle the device on each board's edge and squeeze the guide shut. Then slide the device to each mark and drill.

—JOHN HUENING, Seffner, Fla.

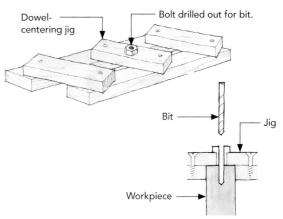

Dowel-centering jig

Bolt drilled out for bit.

Bit

Jig

Workpiece

A self-centering jig for boring drawer-pull holes (below) should have pivoting sticks long enough to span your deepest drawer. Fit the center plate with drill-bit guide bushings or small holes for marking with an awl.

—J.B. SMALL, Newville, Pa.

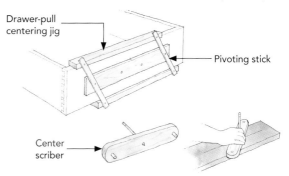

Drawer-pull centering jig

Pivoting stick

Center scriber

Two depth-stops for your drill bits

A great depth-stop for a portable electric drill is a masking-tape flag around the bit stem, as shown in the drawing. Masking tape works on all kinds of bits, is easy to set to the right depth, and never mars the workpiece. The advantage of the flag is that you don't have to strain your eyes to tell when the tape reaches the surface: You simply stop drilling when the flag sweeps the chips away.

—RICHARD R. KRUEGER, Seattle, Wash., and
NORMAN CROWFOOT, Pinetop, Ariz.

An alternative to wrapping masking tape around a drill bit to make a depth gauge is to wrap the bit with a length of brass wire instead. It is just as simple to use, and it makes a more accurate, longer-lasting depth gauge.

Starting with thin brass wire (about 1/64 in. thick), cut a length about 30 times the bit diameter (7½ in. or so for a ¼-in.-dia. bit). Hold the bit in one hand and coil the wire around the bit with your other hand, as shown below. Wind the wire in a clockwise direction as you face the tip end of the bit. That way the wire won't uncoil as you drill a hole. Don't use iron wire because it's too brittle, and it has some springback.

—VINCENT LAVARENNE, Brunoy, France

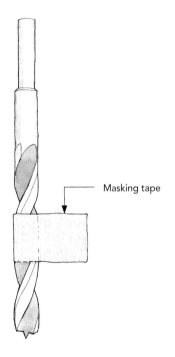

Masking tape

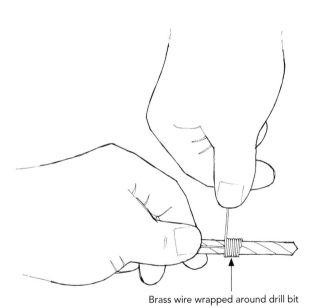

Brass wire wrapped around drill bit

Improving the performance of spade bits

Woodworkers often overlook the lowly spade bit, but it does have some advantages. It certainly is the cheapest bit and the easiest to sharpen. And if you need a nonstandard size or a tapered hole, you can easily grind a bit off the sides.

To drill a clean hole, just file a notch on each edge of the blade, as shown in the sketch. Essentially you are making spurs to sever the wood fibers cleanly on the wall of the hole. As you drill, go slowly when the flat of the bit first contacts the work. You will find that the wall of the hole will be crisp and clean—maybe even cleaner than with those other fancier bits.

—TIM HANSON, Indianapolis, Ind.

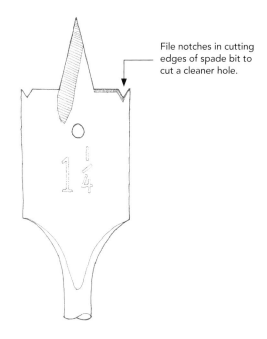

File notches in cutting edges of spade bit to cut a cleaner hole.

HANDPLANING

Block of wax makes setting a plane blade easier

I find it difficult to set the depth and tilt of a plane blade by sighting down the sole of the plane or by rubbing my finger across the blade. The alternative method I use is quick, simple, and accurate.

I take a block of ordinary paraffin wax and run it edgewise along the sole of the plane, engaging the blade and producing small shavings on each side of it. The blade depth and tilt are adjusted easily to produce balanced, thin shavings. As a bonus, the paraffin lubricates the sole of the plane so that it glides easily over the wood.

—LOUIS MENGOLI, La Mesa, Calif.

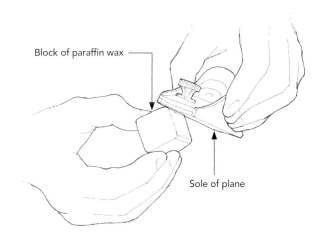

Block of paraffin wax

Sole of plane

Reducing handplane chatter

Chatter shows up as ripples in the surface where the plane stuttered and didn't cut smoothly (see left photo below). It can often be easily felt, heard, or even seen. Typically, chatter will occur at the start of a cut, before the plane is firmly supported on the surface. The uneven cutting is caused by the buildup of pressure against the iron to the point that it starts to vibrate. As the iron springs forward and back, the cutting depth is raised or lowered slightly, enough to leave distinct parallel cuts in the surface.

You can reduce chatter by applying less pressure on the iron or by giving it more support. The simplest solution is to use a thicker, more stable iron. Alternatively, you can skew the cut (see right photo below) to reduce pressure on the iron, or take a lighter cut. To make sure the iron is getting

adequate support, check some of the tuning to be sure the bed is flat and even; the cap iron is fitted to the iron; the frog is adjusted too far forward, leaving the iron with little support near the cutting edge.

—GARRETT HACK, Thetford Center, Vt.

Troubleshooting clogging

Clogging can occur even with the best-tuned planes. Shavings bind up so tightly in the throat that the plane no longer cuts. The most obvious cause is that the throat is too tight. The solution is to open the throat or back off the cap iron $\frac{1}{16}$ in. or so. Clogging often can be eliminated simply by clearing the throat of large shavings at the end of each stroke.

Also, nothing clogs up a plane faster than a dull iron. Be sure to keep your iron sharp.

Clogging can also be caused by a poor fit on the cap iron and iron, which allows some shavings to build up under the cap iron. The cap iron should be smooth and waxed. The cap iron might be somehow blocking the shavings from escape. Bevel the front edge of the throat forward slightly to give the shavings extra room. A light cut always helps, but sometimes, no matter what you do, clogging is going to be a problem.

—GARRETT HACK, Thetford Center, Vt.

A flat iron is key to controlling chatter in a shoulder plane

If you're experiencing blade chatter while using a shoulder plane, you might need to flatten the back of the iron, level the bed it rests on, reposition the screw cap that holds the iron snug against the bed, or all three. Try moving the screw cap first. Push it as far forward as possible so that it applies pressure close to the bevel of the cutting edge. To level the bed, disassemble the plane and, with a fine jeweler's or needle file, flatten any high spots or roughness. Take off as little as necessary and check the flatness often with a small straightedge. Last, make sure that the back of the iron is not convex but flat for at least the last ½ in.

—GARRETT HACK, Thetford Center, Vt.

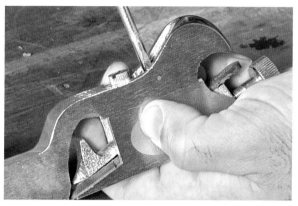

Move the screw cap forward to eliminate blade chatter. The screw cap on this Stanley No. 92 (top) is positioned too far back from the cutting edge. Adjust it forward (bottom) so that the pressure is concentrated near the blade's bevel.

Make clean cuts by making lateral adjustments

Lateral misalignment of the iron can be an annoyance. If the iron isn't parallel with the sole, one side cuts more deeply than the other. This is fine when rough surfacing a board, but for final smoothing, I want the iron parallel to the sole. I usually feel the depth of the iron projecting from the sole before starting and, if need be, make slight adjustments. By watching the thickness and width of the shavings while planing, I can make further adjustments by moving the lateral-adjustment lever toward the edge where shavings appear (bottom left and center). Ideally, I want to see a shaving of consistent thickness curling nearly the width of the throat (bottom right).

—GARRETT HACK, Thetford Center, Vt.

Two methods of repairing worn mouths on wooden planes

A highly used wooden-bodied plane may get worn to the point that its mouth becomes enlarged and causes tearout. One way to repair the mouth is to glue on an entirely new sole, made out of a hardwood such as rosewood or ebony. The new sole will glide smoothly when waxed and be long-wearing. Flat soles are easiest to repair—although reshaping a molding plane can be done—the only tricky part is opening the mouth just enough, but not too much. To avoid problems with setting the iron deep enough, keep the new sole less than ¼ in. thick. To attach the sole, flatten the bottom of the plane body, and glue it on with yellow glue or epoxy.

Inlaying a throat plate is an effective alternative that's not only faster to execute but also preserves the integrity of the original plane body. Choose a wood that is as hard as, or harder than, the wood of the plane body. Size the throat plate carefully for the right size mouth.

—GARRETT HACK, Thetford Center, Vt.

A worn wooden plane. An enlarged mouth will create coarse shavings and result in tearout. A narrower mouth will put pressure near the cutting action, minimizing tearout.

GLUE ON A NEW SOLE

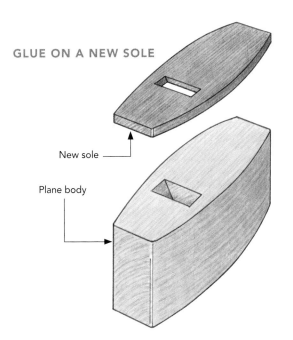

New sole

Plane body

INSERT A THROAT PLATE

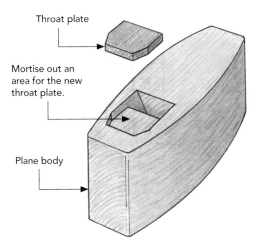

Throat plate

Mortise out an area for the new throat plate.

Plane body

Fifteen-minute vise

Here is a handy little device that is beyond simple to make. I originally made it to hold a door upright so that I could plane the edges. Since then I've used it in practically any way you might use a vise. The device is portable, and it's a great tool to have on installations. If you lose it, you can make another with scrap in only 15 minutes.

To make the vise, rip two 2×4s to make four 2×2 battens about 12 in. long. Choose the best of the four battens and cut it into a 3° or 4° wedge shape with a notch in the top of the thick end as shown. Choose two of the other battens as the jaws of the vise. Affix one of the jaws to a ¾-in.-thick plywood base with glue and screws. Use the fourth piece as a temporary spacer and set the wedge next to it. Place the second jaw against the wedge, and glue and screw it to the base as you did the first one.

To use the jig, place the workpiece between the jaws and tap the wedge into place. To release, tap the notch on the thick end of the wedge. If you need to hold a thin workpiece, just add another spacer, sized as needed.

—ALBERT KAUSLICK, Burlington, N.C.

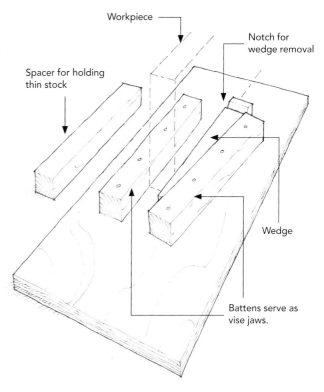

Workpiece

Notch for wedge removal

Spacer for holding thin stock

Wedge

Battens serve as vise jaws.

ACCESSORIES

File handle from a champagne cork

I find the best file handle is the cork from a champagne bottle. The method is simplicity itself. Starting from the bottom, drill a small hole (perhaps ⅛ in. dia.) halfway through the cork. Push the cork over the tang of the file. In use, the bulbous end of the cork fits comfortably into the palm of your hand.

—JERRY LEHNUS, Sandia Park, N.M.

File

Champagne cork

Wooden mallet

At least one wooden carpenter's mallet belongs in every woodworker's tool chest. The advantages of wood over steel are obvious—less damage to tools, work, thumbs, and eyes. For the price of one steel hammer, you can make a dozen mallets, each tailored to a particular job.

The traditional mallet has a solid-wood head mortised through for the wedge-shaped handle. My laminated head design is just as strong and much easier to make. Begin by cutting the handle and two center laminations for the head from the same 1-in.-thick board (this saves a lot of fitting later). Copy the handle's wedge angle (no more than ½ in. of taper) onto one of the side laminations. Then glue up the head, aligning the center laminations with the wedge-angle pencil lines. When the glue has cured, bandsaw the head to shape. Chamfer all the edges to reduce the chances of splitting and then insert the handle.

—DANIEL ARNOLD, Viroqua, Wis.

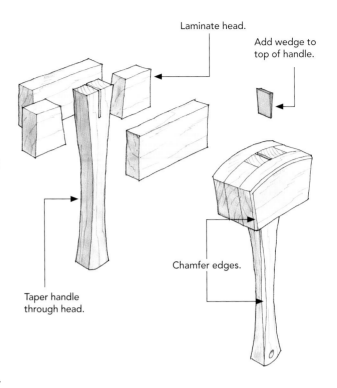

Laminate head.

Add wedge to top of handle.

Chamfer edges.

Taper handle through head.

Make a scraper from a metal spatula

The blade from a metal hamburger spatula is extremely flexible, so it makes a great scraper. Just file out the rivets that hold it to the handle, then file and burnish the edges.

—JEFF VAN DINE, Gold Bar, Wash.

Magnetic screw holder

I sometimes put a rare-earth magnet in my shirt pocket when I have to drive a bunch of screws. It allows me to keep a small handful of screws clinging to the outside of the pocket, and that makes it easy to grab one screw at a time.

—MARK A. FETTER, Fort Collins, Colo.

Printable magnets make cool tool note tags

Printable magnet sheets are commonly available at office-supply stores, like Staples. Cut the sheets into rectangles and attach them to your scrapers or other tools. Then make notes (like "needs sharpening") on the blank labels. Move the tags around as needed and keep the extras on your metal toolbox.

—BRUCE BARNETT, Troy, N.Y.

Handy notepad for tool setups

If you sometimes have trouble remembering the setup details on a tool from session to session, attach a small scrap of dry-erase board to the machine and write your setup notes there. You can jot down such things as the grit installed on a belt sander, the width/depth of the tablesaw dado head, or the rpm of the drill press.

—BARRY BURKE JR., Middletown, Conn.

Easy-to-move shop lights

If, like me, you are sentenced to work in a dim basement shop, you know there's always a need for more light. I solved this problem with a few steel electrical-box covers and a light with a magnetic base. I screwed the metal plates to ceiling joists in convenient places (the screw holes are already in the corners of the plate). Now I simply move the light where I need it and stick it to the metal plate. If I need light in a new place, I attach a plate at that location. To keep the extension cord out of the way, I drape it over two or three hooks I have screwed here and there into the ceiling joists.

—REGIS MCNICHOLAS, Kennebunkport, Maine1

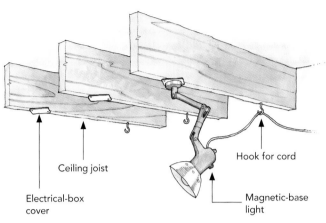

Ceiling joist

Hook for cord

Electrical-box cover

Magnetic-base light

Quick way to find the end of the tape

If, like me, you have fought with a roll of clear packing tape trying to find the end, here is a simple solution. Stick a plastic bag tab, the kind used to close the bag on a loaf of bread, under the end of the tape.

Now when you need some tape, just grab the tab and pull off what you need from the roll. Cut the tape to length, then stick the tab back on the end of the roll. Press down firmly on the tape to lock the bag tab in place. Everything is set for the next time.

—DAVID J. VALOVICH, Fairfield, Conn.

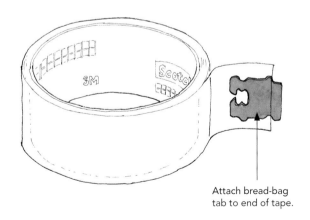

Attach bread-bag tab to end of tape.

Dry-erase panels for cabinet doors

When I built new cabinets for my workshop, I used white dry-erase boards for the panels in the cabinet doors. Now I can jot down notes and measurements right on the doors. And if I need to see the notes from the other side of the shop, I just open a door so it points in the proper direction.

The dry-erase panels have a slick, white surface applied to a 1/8-in.-thick Masonite® backing. To make the door panels, I added a piece of 1/4-in. plywood to the back of the dry-erase board so the inside of the door looks decent. I purchased the dry-erase panels from www.dryerase.com, a mail-order supplier that stocks several sizes.

—DAVE ZADROZNY, Morris Township, N.J.

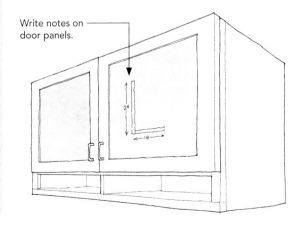

Write notes on door panels.

SHOP STORAGE

CLAMP STORAGE

A simpler pipe-clamp wall rack

Here's a pipe-clamp wall rack that is simple, compact, and elegant. It's just four boards glued together along their lengths and then screwed into wall studs.

What makes the system unique is how quickly clamps can be stored and removed. To store a clamp, you just slide the handle in at an angle, which allows the pipe to hang vertically. Angling the pipe away from the wall frees the head in one easy motion.

—JEFF SALES, Tucson, Ariz.

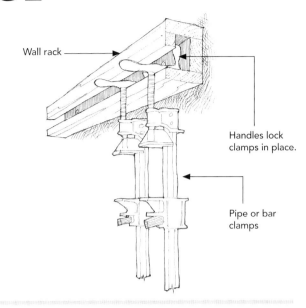

Wall rack

Handles lock clamps in place.

Pipe or bar clamps

Pipe-clamp rack

This simple rack not only stores clamps securely, but it also allows you to remove them quickly with just one hand. Simply grab a clamp and pull it toward you. Gravity helps the clamps stay put.

—ROY H. HOFFMAN, Oriental, N.C.

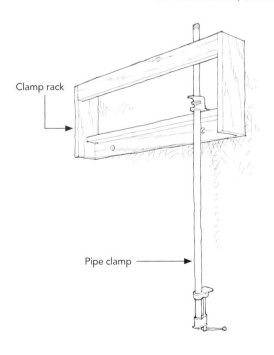

Clamp rack

Pipe clamp

Long clamps? Hang 'em high

I work in a basement shop, where wall and floor space are at a premium. I found the best place to store my long pipe clamps was to hang them from the floor joists with heavy-duty hooks. Problem solved!

—SERGE DUCLOS, Delson, Que., Canada

Space-saving rack for bar clamps

As my bar-clamp collection grew, I found that clamp racks were taking up precious wall real estate. To solve the problem, I built this space-saving rack.

The design is simple—just three wood frames of varying heights attached to each other with hinges. The hinges let the frames open like a book. Now I can store 30 clamps in a space that used to be limited to 10.

To make the racks, cut all the pieces and notch the top and bottom member of each rack. Size the notches wide enough for the thickest bar clamp and space them to allow the clamps to fit side by side.

Assemble the three frames with biscuits, glue, and screws. Use heavy-duty hinges to join the frames so that they won't sag from the weight of the clamps.

Reinforce the notches with support blocks. Also, add small pieces of foam weatherstripping between the notches on the top of each rack. The foam pieces serve as protective cushions and keep the clamps from moving around when you open the frames. Two magnetic cabinet-door latches keep the frames closed.

—SUWAT PHRUKSAWAN, Pleasant Hill, Calif.

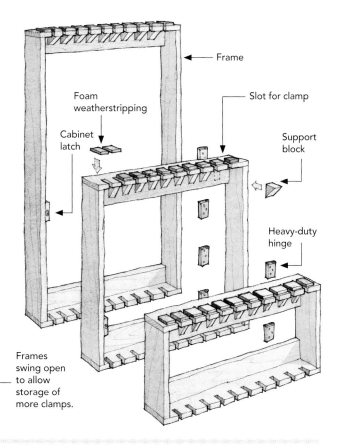

Frame

Foam weatherstripping

Slot for clamp

Cabinet latch

Support block

Heavy-duty hinge

Frames swing open to allow storage of more clamps.

Clever bar-clamp rack

I store my bar-clamp collection on a simple rack, consisting of two 24-in.-long, 1-in.-dia. oak dowels supported by two oak brackets that are mounted, in turn, to two oak backs. The dowels are positioned in the brackets so that the clamp handles slide down behind the top dowel and the clamp bars are supported vertically by the lower dowel. To fix the position of the large dowels, I use smaller dowels to pin them in the right-hand bracket.

—ANDREW BELOOUSSOV, Bolton, Ont., Canada

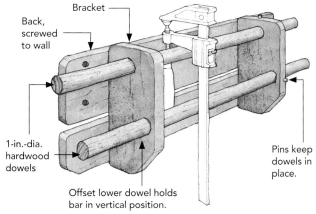

Bracket

Back, screwed to wall

1-in.-dia. hardwood dowels

Offset lower dowel holds bar in vertical position.

Pins keep dowels in place.

Wall rack for bar clamps

When I moved to a smaller shop, I had to find somewhere to store my fairly large collection of bar clamps and hand clamps. I decided against a fancy rack that rolls around the shop on casters because the floor space it would require is too dear. I wanted my clamps near the area where large glue-up projects will be done, but I also wanted to keep them out of the way when they're not needed. The solution was to hang them on the wall.

The racks I designed are quite simple, and they can store a variety of different-size clamps. I fastened a ¾-in.-thick hanger strip to the wall, using two screws at every stud location. Along the bottom of the hanger strip I screwed a ¾-in. plywood cleat with a 45° cut along the top edge. Then I made a matching plywood cleat with a 45° cut along the bottom edge to mate with the bottom cleat (the system is called a french cleat). I screwed blocks of wood into the front face from behind; clamps will hang between these blocks. After hanging the top cleat, I screwed it to the hanger strip for additional strength.

Depending on the type of clamps, they will hang better facing in or out, because of how the weight is balanced. You can arrange the racks on the wall to accommodate clamps of different sizes.

—JOHN WEST, Ridgefield, Conn.

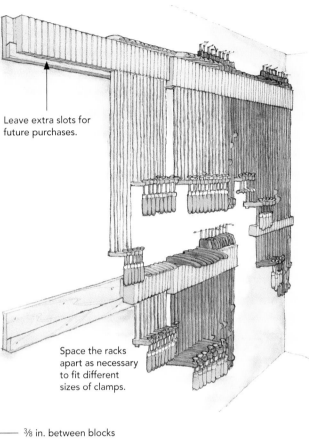

Leave extra slots for future purchases.

Space the racks apart as necessary to fit different sizes of clamps.

CLEAT DETAIL

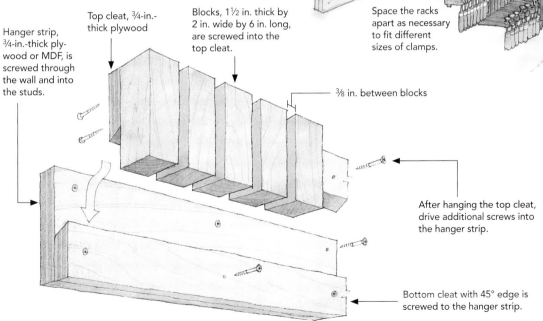

Hanger strip, ¾-in.-thick plywood or MDF, is screwed through the wall and into the studs.

Top cleat, ¾-in.-thick plywood

Blocks, 1½ in. thick by 2 in. wide by 6 in. long, are screwed into the top cleat.

⅜ in. between blocks

After hanging the top cleat, drive additional screws into the hanger strip.

Bottom cleat with 45° edge is screwed to the hanger strip.

Bar-clamp storage rack

When I built my workshop, I came up with this easily made rack to store bar clamps. It fits neatly between the wall studs and works well. The clamps are stored efficiently, yet each is readily available for use. I made the rack by ripping off the front edge from a piece of framing lumber at an angle of 15°. Then I cut slots at different depths, widths and spacing to accommodate my selection of clamps, with some extra slots for future purchases, of course (one can never have enough clamps). After that, I glued back on the front, mounted the rack between the studs and installed a shelf below the rack to complete the job.

—NICK ROWE, Greenlane, New Zealand

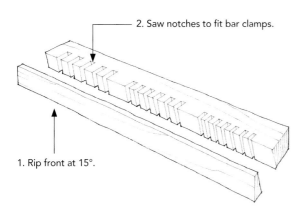

2. Saw notches to fit bar clamps.

1. Rip front at 15°.

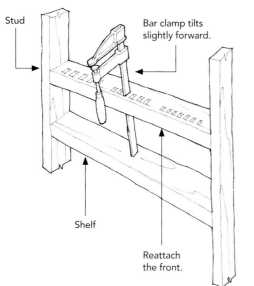

Stud

Bar clamp tilts slightly forward.

Shelf

Reattach the front.

Easy way to carry and store spring clamps

I use this caddy to organize my spring clamps. To make it, cut a 1-ft.-long handle, thin the lower edge with opposing rabbets, and pop the clamps onto the caddy. You can carry the clamps from place to place, where they stay neatly out of the way until you need them.

—JACK HEGARTY, Tottenham, Ont., Canada

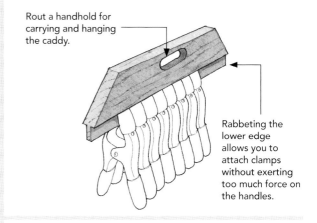

Rout a handhold for carrying and hanging the caddy.

Rabbeting the lower edge allows you to attach clamps without exerting too much force on the handles.

C-clamp rack

I store C-clamps on a narrow shelf. A rubber strip, cut from a black rubber stretch tie-down, prevents the clamps from falling off the front, while brackets prevent the clamps from falling off the ends. This storage shelf has several advantages. The clamps will stay put without having to screw them closed, and it is easy to pick out a particular clamp because they are all visible. If you have several sizes of C-clamps, build a shelf for each size.

—JOHN BEAL, Excelsior, Minn.

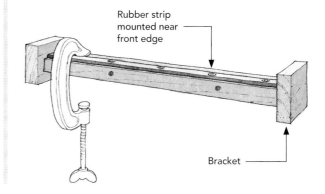

Rubber strip mounted near front edge

Bracket

Rack for Quick-Grip clamps

Everyone I have talked with loves Quick-Grip® clamps. Here's a simple hanger bracket that efficiently stores the awkward-to-hang clamps. Using a couple of side-by-side sawcuts, cut a groove just over ¼ in. wide and as deep, about ¾ in. from the edge of a board. Then cut slots, again just wider than ¼ in., into the board every couple of inches or so. Mount the board to a cleat on the wall or on the end of your workbench. Hang the clamps in the slots by the little compression pins in the ends of the bars.

—LLOYD W. WOOD, Virginia Beach, Va.

Mount clamp bracket to wall or bench.

¾ in.

Slots, 9/32 in., capture pins on clamp bars

Groove, 9/32 in.

Storing spring clamps

I have several dozen spring clamps, and I've struggled for years to find a simple, organized way to store and transport them between jobs. Recalling how my climbing buddies keep large amounts of gear organized and available on slings, I made a simple sling with a 2-ft. length of 1-in.-wide nylon webbing (available at most camping and climbing stores). This sling easily holds 10 of my 2-in.-capacity clamps. Keeping the same number of clamps on each sling is an easy way to quickly grab the number you need without counting. Use a narrower width of webbing for smaller clamps.

The sling makes it easy to carry a large number of clamps and to hang them over a nail or peg in my workshop or at a job site. You can tie the sling with a loose knot or use a quick-release buckle (also sold at camping stores). You can open the sling easily to dump the clamps onto a work surface, or thread them back onto the sling without having to squeeze them all.

—PHILIP JACOBS, Saint Paul, Minn.

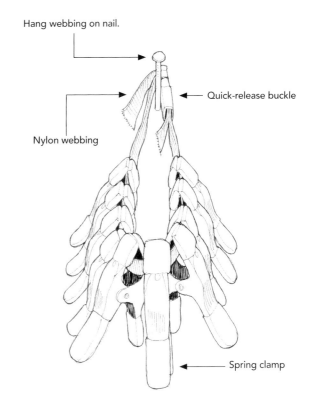

Hang webbing on nail.

Quick-release buckle

Nylon webbing

Spring clamp

LUMBER RACKS

Sturdy, simple rack

When I began thinking about a lumber-storage rack for my commercial shop, I was poised to purchase some of those huge, free-standing, cantilevered I-beam racks that would cost a small fortune. For the cost of materials and a few hours of labor, I built my own rack, and it's equally suitable for the home shop.

Each 24-in.-wide frame is made from 2×6 lumber and consists of two posts and a top and bottom plate. The frames are nailed together and connected with 2×4s at the top and bottom corners. Sixteen pieces of iron pipe make the four shelves that support the lumber. To stabilize the rack, you will need to attach it to joists overhead or add diagonal bracing on the sides.

Before assembling the frames, I measured and drilled holes through the 2×6s for the 1½-in. I.D. (slightly under 2 in. O.D.) cast-iron pipe. I drilled holes slightly larger with a 2-in.-dia. hole saw. The loose fit made it easy to insert the pipes, after which I wrapped the pipes with duct tape to make the fit more snug.

The shelf width is just right for stacking typical lumber. Dollar for dollar and square foot for square foot of storage, this is a great wood rack.

—TONY O'MALLEY, Emmaus, Pa.

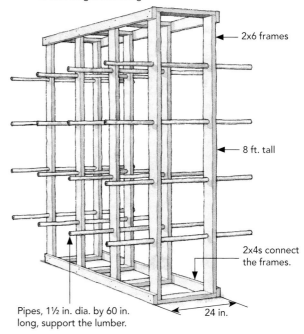

For stability, tie the frames into the ceiling joists or add diagonal bracing.

2x6 frames

8 ft. tall

2x4s connect the frames.

Pipes, 1½ in. dia. by 60 in. long, support the lumber.

24 in.

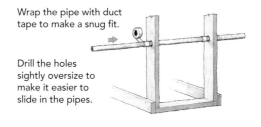

Wrap the pipe with duct tape to make a snug fit.

Drill the holes sightly oversize to make it easier to slide in the pipes.

Efficient plywood storage

Store plywood vertically if you are short on space. An added benefit is that you can access every piece. Build several dividers into the rack to separate the different kinds of plywood. Put pillow blocks with a 1-in.-dia. steel bar in front of the rack, and the sheets will roll in and out easily. Write the name of the face veneer on the front edge of each piece with a marker to make it easy to know what you have.

—BLAISE GASTON, Earlysville, Va.

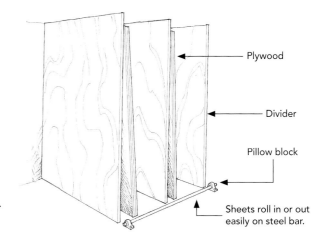

Plywood

Divider

Pillow block

Sheets roll in or out easily on steel bar.

Sturdy platform for rolling carts

A torsion-box base creates a rock-solid foundation for mobile carts. This design works well for lumber racks, but it also can be adapted to make assembly dollies and tables and tool carts. For stability, use 4-in.- to 6-in.-dia. casters and install them as close to the corners as possible. This size can be adapted for larger platforms.

—JOHN WHITE, Rochester, Vt.

Attach corner blocks to support casters. Corner blocks on this basic torsion box provide a structure where the casters are attached. Attach the blocks with countersunk 2-in. drywall screws (left). The top is applied using a bead of construction adhesive, then ribbed nails spaced 4 in. apart (right).

Attach the casters. Use 1½-in. lag screws to attach the casters securely to the base. Typically, the corner blocks will support lag screws for only three of each caster's mounting holes, but that's enough.

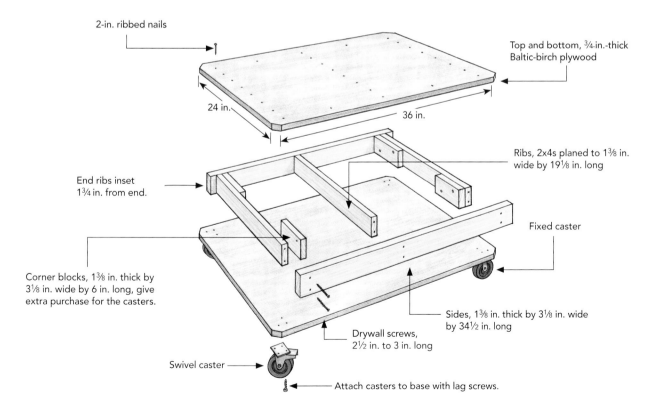

2-in. ribbed nails

Top and bottom, ¾-in.-thick Baltic-birch plywood

24 in.

36 in.

End ribs inset 1¾ in. from end.

Ribs, 2x4s planed to 1⅜ in. wide by 19⅛ in. long

Fixed caster

Corner blocks, 1⅜ in. thick by 3⅛ in. wide by 6 in. long, give extra purchase for the casters.

Sides, 1⅜ in. thick by 3⅛ in. wide by 34½ in. long

Drywall screws, 2½ in. to 3 in. long

Swivel caster

Attach casters to base with lag screws.

Stack and saw lumber
on the same rack

Storing lumber effectively is a challenge in any shop, but it's especially challenging in a small shop. When I designed my lumber rack, the efficient use of space was a priority. I wanted my lumber to be accessible and close to the chopsaw, where I cut it to rough length. Gradually, I developed the notion of a combination crosscutting table and lumber rack. While I was at it, I decided to make the chopsaw easily removable so that I could take it with me on jobs.

The rack's framework consists of two posts and a series of cantilevered arms that hold the lumber and support the crosscutting table. The hardwood posts are lag-bolted to the wall studs for maximum strength. The arms, also hardwood, are tenoned into the posts and secured with glue and draw-bored pegs. For ease of assembly, I glued the arms into the posts before bolting the posts to the wall.

The arms that support the crosscutting table are almost twice the width of the others. I modified the joinery for these arms, stacking two tenons for each arm rather than making a very wide one. This improves the joint because less material is removed from the post, which minimizes the risk of splitting. It also avoids wood-movement problems that can occur with wide tenons.

The arms for the chopsaw table have a series of dadoes cut on the inside faces to accept ¾-in.-thick plywood ribs that support the tabletop. I made the top of the table out of ¾-in.-thick medium-density fiberboard, because it is very flat and a good utility work surface. I also built a hardwood fence with stops for repetitive cutoff work. When I take the saw on the road, I remount the factory fence.

The chopsaw is mounted on a small tray that slides into place and is secured with two screws. With this setup, I can remove the two screws and take the saw with me.

My drill press is just a few feet away from the table, so I installed a drawer at one end to hold drill bits and drill-press accessories.

My rack is just inside the large door I use for bringing lumber into the shop. I simply back in my truck and unload lumber right onto the rack. Let the work begin.

—CHRIS GOCHNOUR, Murray, Utah

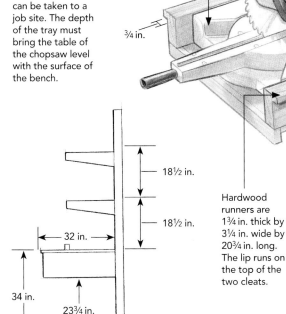

Chopsaw tray slides out so that the saw can be taken to a job site. The depth of the tray must bring the table of the chopsaw level with the surface of the bench.

¾ in.

18½ in.

18½ in.

Hardwood runners are 1¾ in. thick by 3¼ in. wide by 20¾ in. long. The lip runs on the top of the two cleats.

32 in.

34 in.

23¾ in.

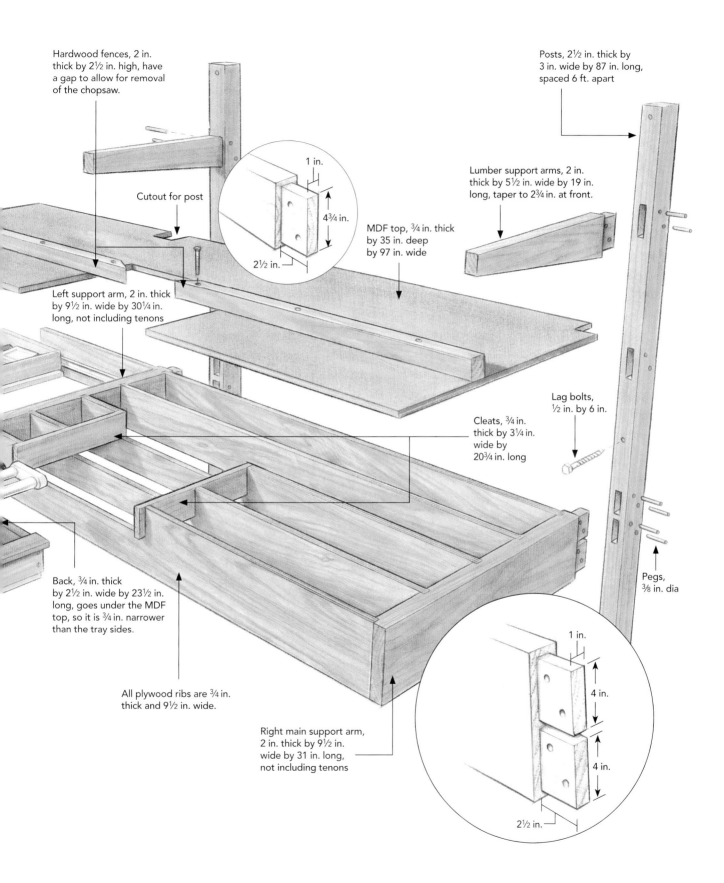

Hardwood fences, 2 in. thick by 2½ in. high, have a gap to allow for removal of the chopsaw.

Posts, 2½ in. thick by 3 in. wide by 87 in. long, spaced 6 ft. apart

Cutout for post

Lumber support arms, 2 in. thick by 5½ in. wide by 19 in. long, taper to 2¾ in. at front.

1 in.

4¾ in.

2½ in.

MDF top, ¾ in. thick by 35 in. deep by 97 in. wide

Left support arm, 2 in. thick by 9½ in. wide by 30¼ in. long, not including tenons

Cleats, ¾ in. thick by 3¼ in. wide by 20¾ in. long

Lag bolts, ½ in. by 6 in.

Back, ¾ in. thick by 2½ in. wide by 23½ in. long, goes under the MDF top, so it is ¾ in. narrower than the tray sides.

Pegs, ⅜ in. dia

All plywood ribs are ¾ in. thick and 9½ in. wide.

Right main support arm, 2 in. thick by 9½ in. wide by 31 in. long, not including tenons

1 in.

4 in.

4 in.

2½ in.

Bin for cutoffs allows quick access

A while back, as a means to store lumber scraps, I built a roll-around cart with bins about 2 ft. deep. I soon found, though, that short cutoffs—anything less than 10 in. or so—tended to get lost in the bottom of the cart. I spent way too much time pulling out the long pieces to see what was hiding in the bottom.

My solution was to rebuild the cart with sloped bins. The bins vary in height, allowing me to store short cutoffs at the front of the cart and longer ones at the back. Now it's a lot easier to spot a small, choice scrap of wood.

—WILL MOORE,
Georgetown, Tex.

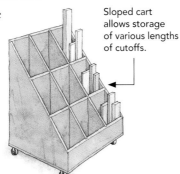

Sloped cart allows storage of various lengths of cutoffs.

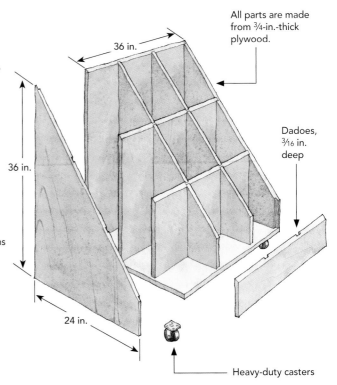

All parts are made from ¾-in.-thick plywood.

36 in.

36 in.

24 in.

Dadoes, ³⁄₁₆ in. deep

Heavy-duty casters

Rolling rack for sheet goods

This rolling rack is made to hold sheets of plywood and MDF. The keys to its design are a strong base and angled sides that prevent the sheets from flopping off as the rack is rolled around. The top 2× strip and the frame under the center shelf are beveled, as are the bottom blocks that help support the load. I covered one side of the blocks with an MDF strip so I could store smaller sheets easily. The blocks on the opposite side are left exposed, which leaves a gap so sheets are easy to grab at the bottom. I attached the stiffeners to the sides before attaching the sides to the top strip and the bottom frame. The triangular cubby between the sides can hold odd-size offcuts or lumber. All parts were assembled with drywall screws.

—JOHN WHITE, Rochester, Vt.

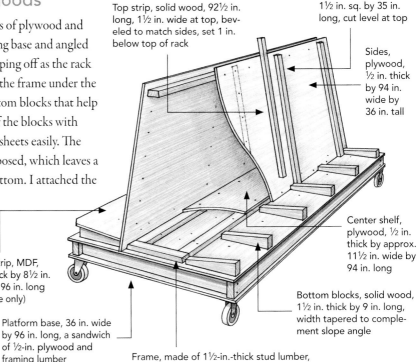

Top strip, solid wood, 92½ in. long, 1½ in. wide at top, beveled to match sides, set 1 in. below top of rack

Stiffeners, solid wood, 1½ in. sq. by 35 in. long, cut level at top

Sides, plywood, ½ in. thick by 94 in. wide by 36 in. tall

Center shelf, plywood, ½ in. thick by approx. 11½ in. wide by 94 in. long

Cover strip, MDF, ¾ in. thick by 8½ in. wide by 96 in. long (one side only)

Platform base, 36 in. wide by 96 in. long, a sandwich of ½-in. plywood and framing lumber

Frame, made of 1½-in.-thick stud lumber, is beveled on its sides and attached to base.

Bottom blocks, solid wood, 1½ in. thick by 9 in. long, width tapered to complement slope angle

TOOL STORAGE

Taming unruly power cords

Most portable power tools, such as drills, saws, and routers, have no provisions for holding the power cord in place. Try this.

Wrap a strip of hook-and-loop fastener (like Velcro®), with a self-adhesive backing, around the cord about 2 in. or 3 in. from the plug end. Then wrap the cord around the tool to determine where the strip will come in contact with the tool body and adhere the mating half of the strip at that location. Now you can wrap the cord around the tool and press the hook-and-loop strips together to fasten the cord. No knots, loops, or unraveling cords get in the way when you need to store or transport the tool.

—LEONARD FELDBERG, Chestnut Ridge, N.Y.

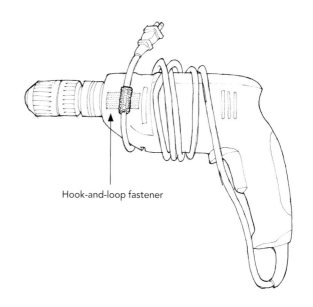

Hook-and-loop fastener

Holder keeps power cords tangle-free

I became tired of looking at and trying to work with the tangle of electric cords that I use both in my shop and outside for other projects. So I made a simple cord-winding rack that keeps both ends of the cord accessible and can be carried conveniently to and from the work locations. The rack is also easy to hang from its handhold.

It took about 30 minutes to make the ¾-in.-thick plywood rack shown here, which can hold up to 100 ft. of heavy-duty cable. Delighted with the results, I promptly made two more.

—JOE COLE, Escondido, Calif.

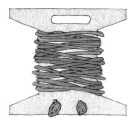

Milk-carton storage system

To make a simple and convenient storage system for nails and screws, simply cut an opening in the back of a 1-qt. or a ½-gal. milk container. Leave a ¼-in. strip of cardboard around the opening for strength and fasten a sample of the stored item to the top lip of the container to indicate the contents. The containers are sturdy, stackable, and very economical of shelf space, and the contents are readily accessible.

—DON ANDERSON, Sequim, Wash.

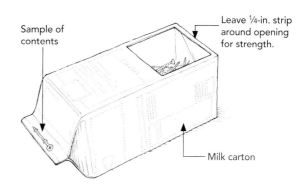

Sample of contents

Leave ¼-in. strip around opening for strength.

Milk carton

Carver's stand holds 30 gouges

I specialize in making reproduction 18th-century furniture, so it's not unusual for me to use 30 carving gouges on one piece. With that many tools in play, an efficient storage system is a must; otherwise, I'd spend more time looking for tools than using them. This double-decker stand lets me grab the right tool almost from memory.

The design is my impression of what an 18th-century furniture maker might have built. The stand has two sides, two tool trays, and a rack on top to display a sketch of the carving. All the parts are pine. Screws hold everything together.

The tool trays are the heart of the stand. They feature multiple coves, one for each tool. I plowed them with an antique round-bottom plane, but you could either drill 1-in. holes into 2-in.-thick stock and then rip it on the bandsaw or use a dado blade to cut recesses in 1-in. stock. I also cut a dado the length of the tray about where the tool handles meet the blades. This allows me to grab the neck of each tool easily with my fingers. Each tray also features a slat at the back to elevate each tool slightly. Finally I added blocks, hooks, and holders to the sides to accept a pencil, an awl, a mallet, and other tools I use when carving.

So that I can efficiently pull and replace gouges, I use a logical tool marking and placement system. First I mark each handle with the radius number and blade width in millimeters. Then I place them in ascending order by radius and width. After using this system for a time, I can locate the tool I need with just a glance.

—EUGENE LANDON, Montoursville, Pa.

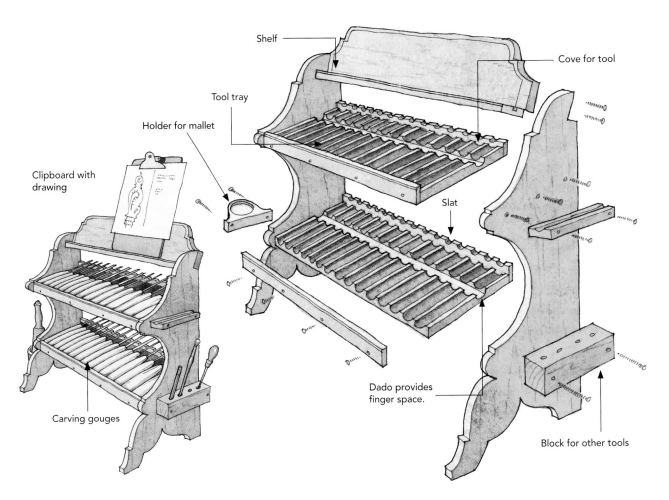

Shelf

Cove for tool

Tool tray

Holder for mallet

Clipboard with drawing

Slat

Carving gouges

Dado provides finger space.

Block for other tools

Prep woodworking machinery for long-term storage

If you're moving or building a new shop and must put your machines into storage indefinitely, they should be fine as long as you take some precautions. Built-up sawdust will soak up moisture like a sponge, so start with a thorough cleaning. Use a vacuum, brush, and air hose to blow out motors, and dig out every speck of sawdust you can. Don't forget to clean out electrical boxes.

Then use some synthetic steel wool lubricated with paint thinner, penetrating oil (such as WD-40), or kerosene to remove existing rust or tarnish on the bare steel or cast-iron surfaces, including gears and trunnion tracks on a tablesaw and the vertical support tube and quill on a drill press.

Next, apply a heavy coat of automotive or lithium grease to every unpainted steel or cast-iron surface, including all of the gears. Imbed a piece of heavy plastic sheeting into the grease, wrapping up the plastic using tape or string. Next, to help keep out critters, wrap motors tightly with plastic or cloth.

It's possible for a heavy cast-iron tabletop to warp if it isn't supported properly, so be sure your machines sit level and are supported on all four legs. If you'll be piling boxes atop your machines, cut a piece of heavy plywood to sit on top of the plastic sheeting.

Release the tension on all belts, remove bandsaw and tablesaw blades, and don't neglect such things as the chuck on a drill press. Squirt some motor oil in the chuck and wrap it with plastic and tape.

When you unwrap everything, remove the grease with solvent, and be sure to blow out motors and switch boxes again with compressed air. One more thing: Check to make sure mice or other varmints haven't made a meal of the insulation on any wires while your machines were in storage.

—LON SCHLEINING, Capistrano Beach, Calif.

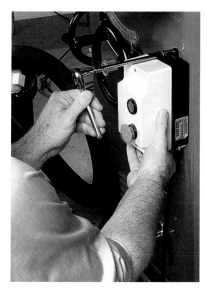

Remove the electrical box and clean out the dust. Also remove all arbor adjustments and knobs to eliminate the possibility of someone picking up the machine by one of these elements.

Brush out all dust. After vacuuming and blowing out the dust, take a brush to all stubborn dust spots, particularly gears and other areas that are lubricated.

Remove rust from unpainted surfaces. Then rub a generous portion of grease on the surface. Next, lay plastic sheeting on top and imbed it into the grease to form a good moisture barrier.

Rotating tower stores more hardware in less space

While rethinking the efficiency of my workshop, I came up with the idea of building a tower on top of a lazy Susan to manage 12 cases containing 252 small drawers full of screws, nuts, bolts, and other hardware. Before I built the tower, the cases ate up 15 sq. ft. of wall space. With this arrangement, the 12 cases take up less than 2 sq. ft. at the end of the countertop.

I simply stack the layers of cases on ¾-in.-thick MDF. Gravity keeps them in place, but if you have doubts, you could hold them with a nonskid material or double-faced tape. I chose 12-in.-dia. lazy-Susan hardware, the largest I could find to support all that weight. The tower spins easily, making every drawer instantly available.

—SERGE DUCLOS, Delson, Que., Canada

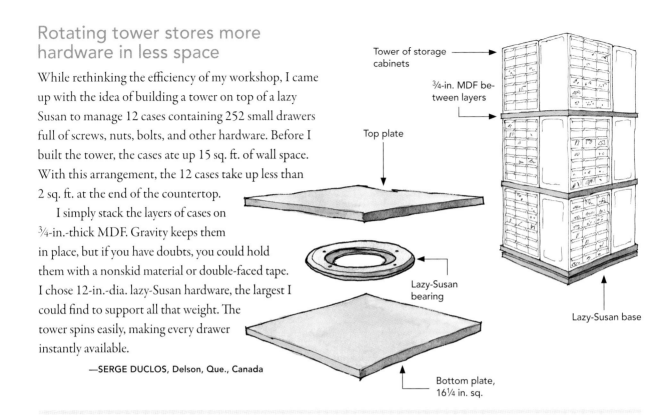

Tower of storage cabinets

¾-in. MDF between layers

Top plate

Lazy-Susan bearing

Lazy-Susan base

Bottom plate, 16¼ in. sq.

Hang tools where you need them

My workbench sits in the middle of my shop, which means I don't have any wall space nearby to store tools. So I suspended this hanging tool-storage unit above my bench to keep my most-used tools within easy reach. The unit is easy to move or raise, if necessary. I made it simply by screwing together two scraps of birch plywood into a T-shape and attaching end caps. To hang tools, I added wooden pegs and heavy-duty magnetic tool holders. To suspend the unit, I bolted two lengths of perforated angle iron (the stuff used to hang garage-door tracks) to the ceiling and attached the unit to the angle iron with three chains on each side. The three-chain configuration eliminates swinging.

—DICK ROCHESTER, Lafayette, Colo.

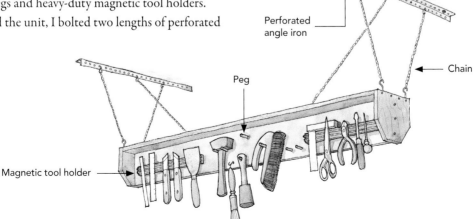

Perforated angle iron

Peg

Chain

Magnetic tool holder

Carousel holds lathe tools

Mounted on the wall near my lathe, this holder keeps my tools secure and within easy reach. To add a gouge, I just slip the cutting edge of the tool into a hole in the upper disk, then set the handle into the shallow hole in the lower disk. Holes drilled in the bracket provide a handy spot to store miscellaneous lathe tools.

It's important for the shaft hole to be vertical. To that end, it's best to drill the hole after the bracket is assembled.

Once all the rotating parts of the carousel have been cut and assembled, the steel shaft simply slips into the shaft hole.

—JAMES W. BOWLER, Lockport, N.Y.

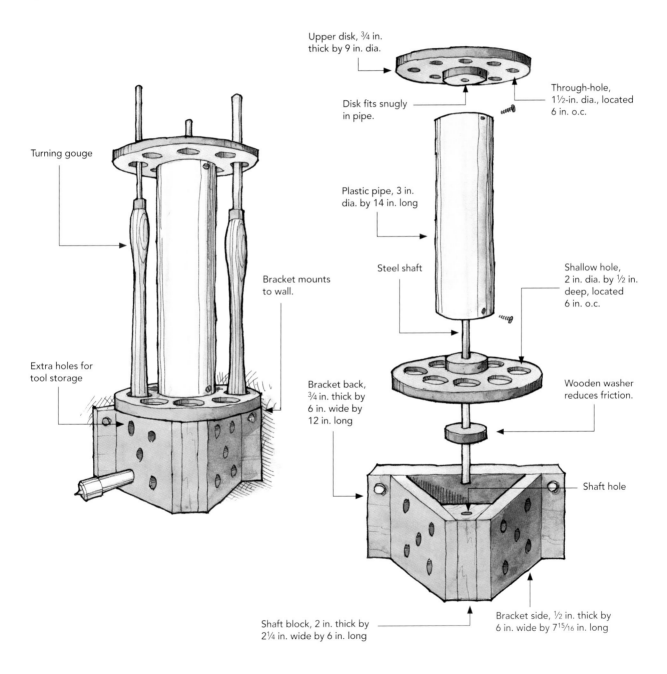

Turning gouge

Bracket mounts to wall.

Extra holes for tool storage

Upper disk, ¾ in. thick by 9 in. dia.

Disk fits snugly in pipe.

Through-hole, 1½-in. dia., located 6 in. o.c.

Plastic pipe, 3 in. dia. by 14 in. long

Steel shaft

Shallow hole, 2 in. dia. by ½ in. deep, located 6 in. o.c.

Wooden washer reduces friction.

Bracket back, ¾ in. thick by 6 in. wide by 12 in. long

Shaft hole

Shaft block, 2 in. thick by 2¼ in. wide by 6 in. long

Bracket side, ½ in. thick by 6 in. wide by 7¹⁵⁄₁₆ in. long

Rolling base for bench tools

This rolling cabinet is great for bench-mounted tools, such as thickness planers, drill presses, and miter saws. It allows you to move those tools around to make the most of your floor space and helps keep parts and accessories close by.

The cabinet is made entirely of Baltic-birch plywood. The 26-in. by 40-in. version shown here is sufficient for most benchtop tools. But you can alter the dimensions to any height (say, for an outfeed surface) or size you need, and you could even add drawers to increase storage versatility. The no-nonsense construction makes it easy to build in a day.

Simple butt joints suffice for putting the cabinet base together. Just make sure the edges are square, mark the screw locations carefully, predrill and countersink the holes, and attach with 2-in. deck screws for a better grip in the plywood end grain.

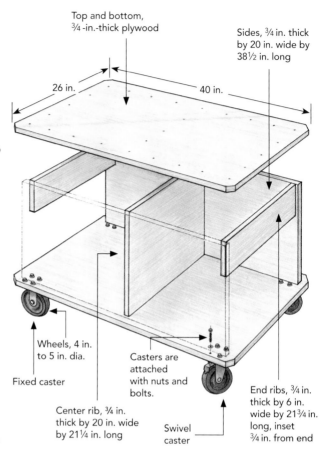

Top and bottom, ¾-in.-thick plywood

Sides, ¾ in. thick by 20 in. wide by 38½ in. long

26 in.

40 in.

Wheels, 4 in. to 5 in. dia.

Fixed caster

Casters are attached with nuts and bolts.

Center rib, ¾ in. thick by 20 in. wide by 21¼ in. long

Swivel caster

End ribs, ¾ in. thick by 6 in. wide by 21¾ in. long, inset ¾ in. from end

To prevent splitting, predrill the holes all the way into the plywood end grain. Use a tapered bit, or start with a bit narrower than the screw diameter, then widen the hole in the surface piece only.

—JOHN WHITE, Rochester, Vt.

Make a cabinet-style base. There's no need to put the cabinet base together with dadoes, rabbets, or even glue; a simple butt joint with screws is adequate.

Tips for installing casters. First attach casters with bolts, not lag screws. Then use a thread-locking compound (right) or nuts with nylon inserts to keep the bolts tight.

Stackable chisel chests

My first wooden chest to store my carving chisels held about 22 tools and hung vertically on a wall in my shop. As my collection of chisels grew, I ran out of room. I could have built a bigger chest, but wall space is scarce in my shop. So I built a second chest, stacked it on top of the first, and hung them both in the same space. When I need a particular chisel, I remove the chests from the wall and open them on my benchtop.

The drawings show the construction details. You need two identical finger-jointed chests with ¼-in.-thick plywood bottoms glued into a groove and ¼-in.-thick plywood tops that slide in a groove. To stack the chests, fasten the top of the lower chest to the bottom of the upper chest with appropriately sized spacers between them to provide a small gap that makes it easier to fit the chests together. Make the spacers from ½-in.-thick medium-density fiberboard or pine, milled to a thickness that can size the gap between the two chests. Glue the spacer strips to the top of the lid of the lower chest, and then with the two chests perfectly registered, screw through the bottom of the upper chest into the spacer strips to lock the combination bottom/lid together.

To make chisel keepers inside of the chest, use a dado blade or a router to crosscut ¼-in.-deep grooves in suitably wide stock about ⅝ in. thick. To minimize fore-and-aft movement of a chisel within its location, press-fit a small length of ¼-in. square stock crossways in the groove. You can pry them out if you need to fit another chisel in that location. To organize all of your tools more thoroughly, mark the sweep and width of each chisel on these stops for reference.

Hang the chests on a wall as you would a picture, but with more hangers and screws. Attach small rubber-bumper feet to the corners of the lower chest to prevent the hangers from marring the benchtop.

—GERALD C. LAUCHLE, State College, Pa.

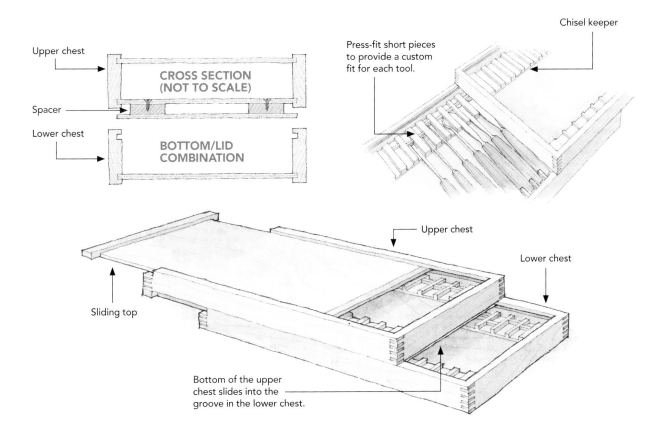

Upper chest

CROSS SECTION (NOT TO SCALE)

Spacer

Lower chest

BOTTOM/LID COMBINATION

Chisel keeper

Press-fit short pieces to provide a custom fit for each tool.

Sliding top

Bottom of the upper chest slides into the groove in the lower chest.

Upper chest

Lower chest

Lathe-tool holder

My turning gouges never seemed to be where I wanted them. I tried laying them across the bed of the lathe while I turned, but they sometimes fell off. I tried placing them on a table near the lathe, but I lost time looking for the tool I wanted to use next.

So I came up with this lathe-tool holder that has solved the problem. As you can see, the working ends of the tools are all visible when I place the stand to the side and slightly behind my work.

To make the stand, start with a heavy base (I used a recycled cast-iron stop-sign holder) and add casters to the base so that you can move it around easily. Turn a 2-in.-dia., 48-in.-long hardwood dowel (I used oak) and install it in the base. I secured the dowel with setscrews through a steel collar. Next, make three or four hard-wood tool racks with holes in the frame that allow each rack to rotate on the dowel. Install steel collars fastened with Allen-head screws to position the racks on the dowel. I think you will find this holder quite useful.

—GERALD Z. DUBINSKI SR., San Antonio, Tex.

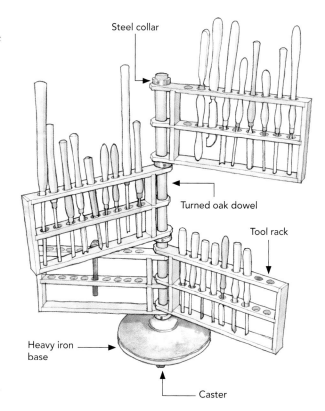

Steel collar

Turned oak dowel

Tool rack

Heavy iron base

Caster

Wall rack for open-end wrenches

I tried all sorts of holders for the tools I need in my shop, but none of them was completely satisfactory. I prefer a wall rack that positively indicates whether a tool has been returned after use. I built this rack to store open-end wrenches. The rack works well and could be adapted to other types of tools.

To make the rack, first cut a groove down the center of one edge of a piece of solid wood. The groove should be wide enough to hold the largest wrench in the set. Now, spread the wrenches along the workpiece, spacing them more or less equidistant from each other. With a pencil, mark the width of the shank of each wrench on the edge and cut a notch in the face of the workpiece for each wrench as indicated by the pencil marks. To complete the rack, drill a couple of mounting holes at both ends.

—LARY SHAFFER, Scarborough, Maine

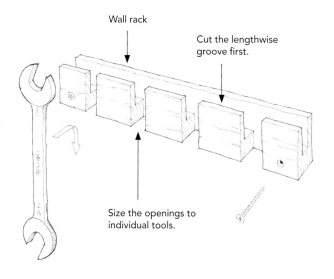

Wall rack

Cut the lengthwise groove first.

Size the openings to individual tools.

Sawblade storage box

Safely storing tablesaw blades was a problem until I constructed this box with drawers (below). The box minimizes the space required to store a bunch of blades, and it makes accessing them safe and easy. Each drawer is ¾ in. high and holds one blade. To retrieve a blade, I simply open a drawer, put my finger through the arbor hole in the blade, and lift it out. An added benefit is that one blade never contacts another, thus avoiding the problem of chipped or dulled teeth.

The box I built is about 13 in. wide by 12 in. deep by 12 in. high and holds eleven 10-in.-dia. blades. I made the carcase and drawer fronts from scraps of ¾-in.-thick lumber and the drawer bottoms from ¼-in.-thick plywood.

Begin by making the two sides of the box. Cut them larger than needed, and set up your saw to cut 5/16-in.-wide dadoes, ⅜ in. deep. Set the fence on your tablesaw 1 1/16 in. from the edge of the blade, which will provide 1/16-in. clearance between the bottom of the bottom drawer and the carcase, and cut the dadoes at the bottom edge of each side for the slides of the bottom drawer. Move the fence over 1 3/16 in. (the width of the drawer

plus 1/16 in. for clearance), and then cut the next dado in each side. Repeat until you've cut all the dadoes; trim the sides to height and width, and sand inside each dado so the drawers will slide freely.

Cut the top, back, and bottom of the box to size and assemble it using biscuit joinery. You can also chamfer the top, front, and side edges of the box with a router, or with a block plane or sandpaper, just to soften them a bit.

To make the drawers, mill ¾-in.-square strips of wood, and then cut a ¼-in.-wide groove down the middle of one side of each piece. Cut the strips to length for the drawer fronts, each as long as the box is wide. Next, cut the drawer bottoms from ¼-in.-thick birch plywood and use a hole saw to cut a 2-in.-dia. hole in the center of each drawer for lifting out the sawblade. Glue the plywood bottoms into the grooves in the drawer fronts. Then glue 3/16-in.-thick by ⅜-in.-wide strips to the sides and back of each drawer bottom to hold the blades in place, and keep the drawers from racking as they slide.

Finally, install a small pull knob on each drawer. Sand the outside corners of the carcase and the back corners of the drawer bottoms so that they won't catch on anything.

—DONALD F. COOLEY, Kansas City, Mo.

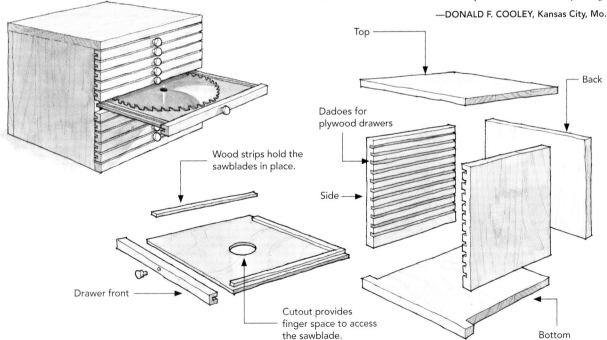

Wood strips hold the sawblades in place.

Top

Back

Dadoes for plywood drawers

Side

Drawer front

Cutout provides finger space to access the sawblade.

Bottom

Swinging rack adds wall space to garage

The double-car garage door severely limits wall space in my garage/woodworking shop. So I created a 4-ft. by 5-ft. swinging tool rack for hanging hand tools, clamps, and accessories. Mounted in the corner of the front of my garage, it can stay against the garage door until I have to get in or out that way. The rack does not interfere with storage on the adjoining wall.

I made the rack out of 2×4 and 2×2 lumber. Two heavy-duty fence hinges are bolted to two 10-in.-wide stand-offs to hold the rack away from the wall. The stand-offs, which can be any length, are lag-screwed into a stud in the garage wall. The outside vertical member of the rack is a leg that ends in a locking, swiveling caster, which provides needed stability.

I could have built the rack out of ¾-in.-thick plywood, but decided to use it as an exercise in making haunched and pegged mortise-and-tenon joints. The joints are quite strong, without a nail or screw in sight.

I also built two 4-ft.-long caddies, one for each side of the rack. I used ¾-in.-thick pine for the sides and ¼-in.-thick Masonite for the bottom. One caddy holds gluing supplies, and the other holds my small sanders.

—BILL PRATT, Helena, Mont.

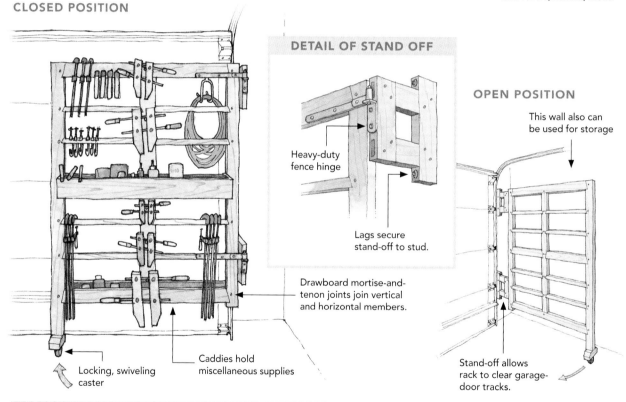

CLOSED POSITION

Locking, swiveling caster

Caddies hold miscellaneous supplies

DETAIL OF STAND OFF

Heavy-duty fence hinge

Lags secure stand-off to stud.

Drawboard mortise-and-tenon joints join vertical and horizontal members.

OPEN POSITION

This wall also can be used for storage

Stand-off allows rack to clear garage-door tracks.

Shoe organizer turned tool organizer

When setting up shop, I nailed three clear shoe organizers to the walls. The sturdy, see-through pockets are big enough to hold a hammer, Dremel tool, tape measure, or roll of duct tape—all those little items that clutter up your workspace or are misplaced easily. One quick glance and you can find what you're looking for.

—JOANNE INCLAN, Lone Tree, Colo.

Space-saving machine-storage stand

I recently purchased an oscillating spindle sander. Although I'm happy with the sander's performance, I discovered that the machine is too tall to use on my workbench and too low to set on the floor. I needed a stand on which to place the machine at the optimum working height, but I couldn't commit any of my valuable floor space to it. So I designed a pivoting stand that becomes a storage compartment when the sander is not in use.

Here's how it works: A platform screwed to the sander's base pivots in the stand, allowing the sander to rotate easily from working to stored position and back. Two barrel latches secure the sander in the working position. With the sander stored, the stand fits underneath my lathe, and I also can store assorted spindles and table inserts inside the stand.

Building the stand was pretty straightforward. One key to this design working smoothly is to install the pivots for the platform dead center, up and down and front to back, so that when the platform flips, it remains flush with the base and square in the opening.

—DWAYNE INTVELD, Hazel Green, Wis.

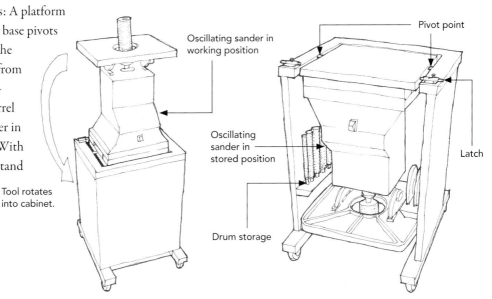

Oscillating sander in working position

Tool rotates into cabinet.

Pivot point

Oscillating sander in stored position

Latch

Drum storage

Caddy keeps sawblades protected, portable

Sawblades are expensive and easily damaged by poor storage and handling. So I came up with a sawblade caddy that protects the blades while minimizing storage space and permitting transport.

The caddy is simply a piece of ½-in.-thick Baltic-birch plywood with a ¼-in.-dia. carriage bolt protruding from the front. I place the blades over the bolt and separate them with ⅛-in.-thick hardboard disks, which I cut on the bandsaw using a circle-cutting jig. A threaded knob holds the stack of blades securely. I drilled a hole in the top of the caddy to hang it on the wall.

—BRUCE HARDING, Winnipeg, Man., Canada

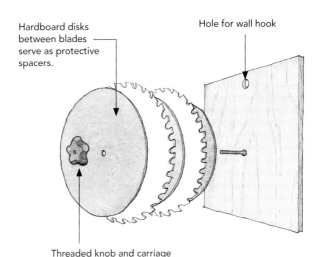

Hardboard disks between blades serve as protective spacers.

Hole for wall hook

Threaded knob and carriage bolt keep blades in place.

Hide-away planer table

I built a flip-up table for my portable thickness planer right into the auxiliary outfeed table of my tablesaw. I can swing the planer up into working position and then down out of the way when it's not in use. This arrangement not only saves space but it also gives me several feet of supporting table on the outfeed side.

Most of the parts are made from ¾-in.-thick plywood. When it is up, the platform is supported by a plywood leg that bolts to the front of the fixture. To install the leg, I prop up the table with a support that's slightly longer than the leg, giving the leg plenty of clearance to slide into place.

The planer's outfeed table must be aligned with the auxiliary table, so take that into consideration as you calculate the axle location and swing-arm length. Design the platform so that it sits below the auxiliary table. Then mill up two cleats to a thickness that will bring the planer's outfeed table level with the auxiliary table.

When I'm through using the planer I install the temporary prop, remove the support leg, remove the prop, and rotate the platform and planer down. I store the temporary prop between the auxiliary table legs and the planer to keep the planer from swinging out. Finally, I replace the removable table insert, and I'm ready to use the tablesaw.

—JOHN WANDLING, Sequim, Wash.

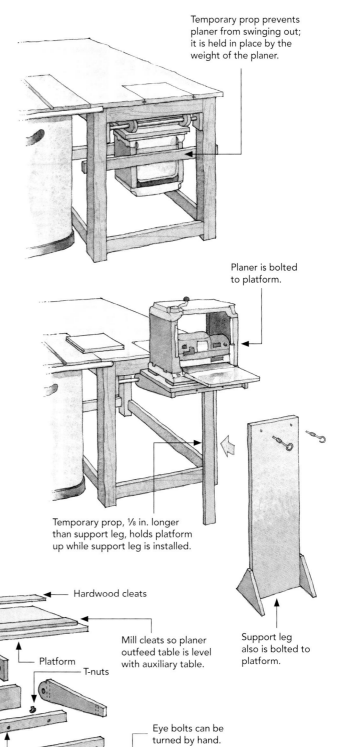

Temporary prop prevents planer from swinging out; it is held in place by the weight of the planer.

Planer is bolted to platform.

Temporary prop, ⅛ in. longer than support leg, holds platform up while support leg is installed.

Removable insert in table slides in and out on splines.

Hardwood cleats

Block between swing arms, screwed to apron, prevents lateral movement.

Mill cleats so planer outfeed table is level with auxiliary table.

Support leg also is bolted to platform.

Platform

T-nuts

Cleats for pipe are attached to legs with ⅜-in. carriage bolts.

Axle, 1-in.-dia. pipe

Eye bolts can be turned by hand.

Crossbeams stabilize platform.

Lock nuts

Planer cabinet doubles as outfeed table, stores out of the way

Because space is at a premium in my shop, I built a roll-around cabinet for my benchtop thickness planer. When in use, the planer sits atop the cabinet (right). When not in use, the planer is placed on a shelf under the cabinet, and the cabinet is rolled out of the way under the extension wing of my tablesaw (below). A pair of removable rollers on the top of the stand allow it to serve double duty as either an infeed or outfeed table for my tablesaw (right). The cabinet is made from ¾-in.-thick birch plywood, edged with solid birch.

The stand has a drawer on top, a pull-out shelf down below, and three storage bins along one side. Since the stand usually is parked under my tablesaw, I use the upper drawer and the bins to store tablesaw accessories—blades, miter gauge, dado set, inserts, and the like. The bins also serve as a place to store planer accessories.

To use the stand as an infeed or outfeed table, I add two rollers to the top of the stand. Each roller is mounted to a plywood base with dowels on the bottom that fit into holes drilled in the cabinet top.

—JURIS PUKINSKIS, Storrs, Conn.

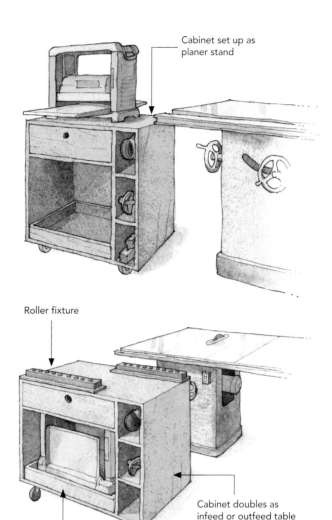

Cabinet set up as planer stand

Roller fixture

Pull-out shelf

Cabinet doubles as infeed or outfeed table for the tablesaw.

Tablesaw accessory storage

Miscellaneous storage

Planer storage

Sandpaper-storage cabinet with built-in cutter

I have a 12-in.-sq. by 36-in.-tall cabinet with about a dozen adjustable ¼-in. plywood shelves. The shelves ride in dadoes and pull out for access to the contents, making them the perfect place to store sheets of sandpaper. The sheets stay flatter and aren't as likely to curl on humid days.

To make the cabinet even more useful, I saved the serrated edge from a roll of plastic wrap and used duct tape to apply it to the outside edge of the cabinet door. The serrated edge makes it easy to tear full sheets of sandpaper into halves or quarters.

Also, I used two permanent markers (one black, one red) to draw lines on the front of the door. Using the lines as a guide, I can quickly position the sandpaper and tear it to the right size.

—BILL DUCKWORTH, Woodbury, Conn.

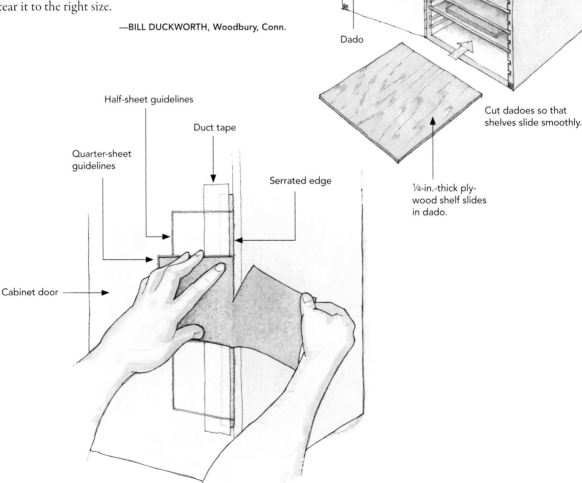

12-in.-sq. by 36-in.-tall cabinet

All parts (except shelves) are ¾-in.-thick plywood.

Dado

Cut dadoes so that shelves slide smoothly.

¼-in.-thick plywood shelf slides in dado.

Half-sheet guidelines

Duct tape

Quarter-sheet guidelines

Serrated edge

Cabinet door

Mouse pads for toolbox lining

Even worn-out computer-mouse pads have lots of useful life still in them. They're great for lining your toolbox or workbench drawers. The pads are durable, and planes and chisels can rest on them without being nicked or dulled.

—R.B. HIMES, Vienna, Ohio

Plastic tubing protects sharp tools

While looking for a way to protect my sharp chisels, turning gouges, and router bits, I remembered an old machinist's trick of sliding a piece of rubber hose onto an end-mill bit to protect it. At the hardware store, I bought several 1-ft. lengths of clear plastic tubing in different sizes. I then matched up each tool with the right-size tubing and clipped off a short length to protect the cutting end.

—JERRY HONEYCUTT, Winsted, Conn.

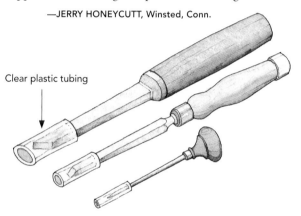

Clear plastic tubing

T-drawer for router bits

This little inverted-T drawer is handy for storing router bits or drill bits under the workbench. The drawer pulls out to full length to expose all the bits, and it tucks away in a jiffy. It uses only two pieces of wood: The vertical member is screwed to the lower horizontal member, which holds the bits. Mount the drawer to the underside of the benchtop with a full-extension ball-bearing drawer slide.

—BRIAN GEERTS, Brantford, Ont., Canada

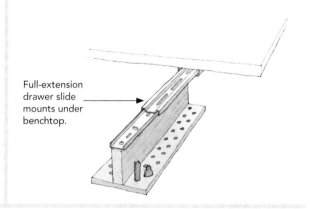

Full-extension drawer slide mounts under benchtop.

Compressor cart

Instead of lugging your portable air compressor around the shop, build this small wheeled cart that makes it easy to roll the compressor wherever it is needed. The cart, made mostly of ¾-in. material, also provides handy storage for air tools, nails, lubricant, and other supplies.

—JIM LEEDS, Flippin, Ark.

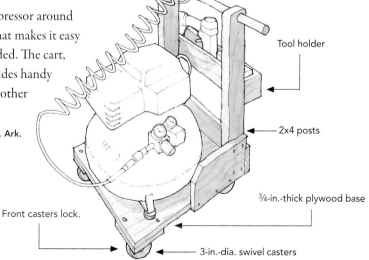

1½-in.-dia. closet pole

Tool holder

2x4 posts

¾-in.-thick plywood base

3-in.-dia. swivel casters

Front casters lock.

SHARPENING

SHARPENING TOOLS

Flattening waterstones

Because waterstones are designed to erode with use, they need to be flattened once in a while. I flatten stones using 180-grit or 240-grit wet-or-dry sandpaper stuck to a piece of ½-in.-thick plate glass, but you also could use a medium-grit diamond stone.

Mark a grid of pencil lines on the face of the stone and keep abrading it until all of the pencil lines have been removed. At that point, the surface is perfectly flat. After flattening the stone, ease the edges to prevent them from crumbling in use.

—DAVID CHARLESWORTH, Devon, England

1. Mark the stone.

2. Flatten the face.

3. Ease the edges.

Sharpening with a granite plate and sandpaper

My sharpening stones have been gathering dust ever since I discovered this sharpening technique. I use a granite surface plate, 2 in. thick by 9 in. wide by 12 in. long, and various grits of wet-or-dry sandpaper. The plate is available from Woodcraft Supply Corp. (www.woodcraft.com).

To use the system, I first pull a sheet of sandpaper through a bowl of water so that it is wet on both sides and spread it on the top of the granite plate. The sandpaper will stay in place because of the surface tension created by the water. The combination of stone and paper produces a large, heavy, water-lubricated, perfectly flat sharpening surface that can be changed from one grit size to another in no time. Going from 240-grit to 2,000-grit in stages, I can put a perfect edge on a new tool in less than five minutes.

—ROY FRAMPTON, Nashua, N.H.

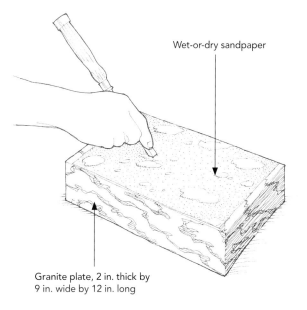

Wet-or-dry sandpaper

Granite plate, 2 in. thick by 9 in. wide by 12 in. long

Recovering sharpening stones

Woodworkers with ancient, oily, clogged natural Arkansas stones abandoned in shop drawers may be delighted to discover that the stones can be refurbished just like Japanese waterstones. The restoration process (which I confirmed with Woodcraft Supply Corp., www.woodcraft.com) is to lap the stones with water on 180-grit wet-or-dry sandpaper placed on a scrap of ¼-in.-thick plate glass. After 20 minutes of lapping and a few dollars worth of sandpaper, you can return the stone to service. Water, not oil, is the best lubricant to use on an Arkansas stone.

Also, I was able to resurface my vintage Norton Fine India stone using a coarse DMT-brand diamond sharpening stone.

—JOHN GREW SHERIDAN, San Francisco, Calif.

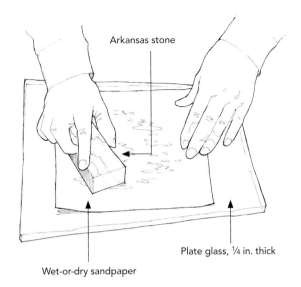

Arkansas stone

Plate glass, ¼ in. thick

Wet-or-dry sandpaper

Storing waterstones

I store coarser 800-grit and 1,200-grit waterstones on their sides in plastic trays of shallow water. A dash of household bleach can be added to the water to slow down the growth of mold. Don't store your stones in water if your workshop freezes at night, because the stones will shatter. Stones stored dry will be ready to use after a five-minute soak. Stones of 4,000-grit and finer always are stored dry and sprayed with water only prior to use.

—DAVID CHARLESWORTH, Devon, England

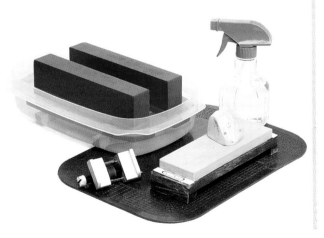

Stop collar makes it easier to dress a grinding wheel

I use a single-point diamond dresser to maintain the wheels on my bench grinder. To make the process easier, I slip a shaft collar on the dresser and use the collar as a depth stop. With the collar butted against the edge of the tool rest, and the business end of the tool just touching the wheel, I can slide the dresser from side to side and be sure that the cutting depth remains the same.

To make it easier to loosen or tighten the collar, I replaced the set screw in the shaft collar with a threaded knob.

—MIKE HOLZHAUER, Lorain, Ohio

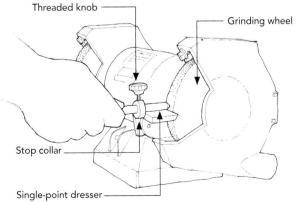

Threaded knob

Grinding wheel

Stop collar

Single-point dresser

BITS AND SAWBLADES

Sharpening a Forstner bit

To sharpen a Forstner bit, all you need is a small file and a slip stone. It takes only a few strokes to get a sharp edge, so there's no need to overdo it. It is also critical that you never hone or file the outside of the rim, which would lessen the bit's diameter, or the beveled side of the chippers, which could change their cutting angle.

Start by thoroughly cleaning the bit to remove any built-up pitch or other debris. Sharpen the inside of the rim, then the chippers, and the centering spur last.

—ROLAND JOHNSON, Sauk Rapids, Minn.

Some Forstner bits have a sawtooth rim.

Centering spur

Chipper

Rim

Hone the rim first. Use a slip stone with a rounded edge and sharpen the inside of the rim only.

File the back of the teeth. Some Forstner bits have sawlike teeth. A few strokes with a small triangular file will sharpen them.

Hone the front side of the chippers. Make sure the chipper and rim meet at a crisp 90° corner. A rounded corner won't shear the grain cleanly.

Right on point. Lightly file the centering spur to a sharp point, but keep the point centered. You can use an index card to protect the chippers from the file.

Clean lumber before milling to protect your cutting tools

Roughsawn lumber holds lots of dust and debris, which can act like sandpaper on cutting tools. A light brushing will not always get it out of the surface pores. The best way to clean the surface is to use compressed air and a wire brush. A quick blast will remove most of the debris, and a good brushing will dislodge the remaining grit.

—ROLAND JOHNSON, Sauk Rapids, Minn.

Blast and brush. Compressed air removes the bulk of surface dirt. Scrub the wood with a brush in the direction of the grain to remove debris.

Lubricating bits slows dulling and rust

Heat caused by friction is the enemy of a cutting edge. Dust buildup is a major cause of friction in blades. With drill bits and mortising bits, chip buildup can create a lot of heat. To help bits and blades repel dust and chips, I apply paraffin wax or a dry lubricant, such as Dri-Cote®.

—ROLAND JOHNSON, Sauk Rapids, Minn.

Apply a dry lubricant on chisel mortisers. The lubricant helps prevent chip buildup and keeps bits from dulling prematurely.

Wax bandsaw blades to reduce friction. With the blade running, hold a piece of paraffin wax on the table and against the blade.

Remove pitch and sawdust so blades won't dull

If the blades on bandsaws, tablesaws, and chopsaws are clogged with pitch or chips, they will heat up and dull quickly. I clean my round blades with OxiSolv Blade and Bit Cleaner or CMT® Formula 2050 Blade and Bit Cleaner.

To clear the narrow gullets of a bandsaw blade—especially important when resawing—I use a brass brush, which won't damage or dull the teeth.

—ROLAND JOHNSON, Sauk Rapids, Minn.

Clean bandsaw gullets. With the machine turned off, rotate the upper wheel by hand as you pass a brass brush over the blade.

Use a blade-and-bit cleaner on tablesaw blades. Spray it on the buildup and let it sit before scrubbing with a brass brush.

Save fingers when lapping small blades

When flattening and polishing the backs of plane blades and chisels, I use successively finer sheets of abrasive paper adhered to plate glass. When I began lapping the small blades for my Stanley® No. 45 combination plane, I realized that holding those little buggers in my hand was not the best way to get there.

A little old-fashioned Yankee ingenuity prevailed. I cut a shallow recess into a 2-in.-thick piece of scrap pine, deep enough that the back of the blade sits just proud of the heel of the jig. Then I mortised a rare-earth magnet into the hole to hold the blade. With the blade held in the jig, I can lap its back without grinding my fingers on the abrasive paper. I think a larger version of the jig could work for any size plane blades.

—BOB RAINVILLE, Colebrook, N.H.

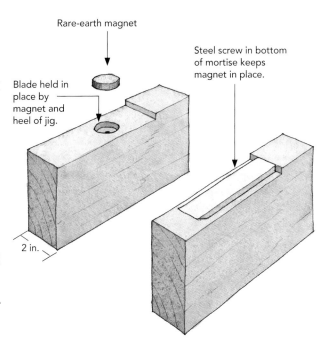

Rare-earth magnet

Steel screw in bottom of mortise keeps magnet in place.

Blade held in place by magnet and heel of jig.

2 in.

Protect blades and bits from harm

All cutting edges should be stored properly, to protect the edges as well as people working in the shop. These handy storage trays for bits and blades can be made in a day.

—ROLAND JOHNSON, Sauk Rapids, Minn.

Portable racks for your router bits. A small rack is portable and easy to make from scrap lumber.

Bit rack clamps directly to drill press. This two-tiered rack easily holds most commonly used bits.

Keep tablesaw blades separated. Cut dadoes into a case to accommodate ¼-in. plywood shelves, set 1 in. apart. Leave the shelves loose so they can slide out for easy blade access.

GET THE ANGLE RIGHT

Setup jig for a honing guide

I find it helpful to use a honing guide when sharpening plane blades. But to get the correct sharpening angle with these guides, the blade must extend a specific distance from the guide. If you change the distance the next time you use the guide, the sharpening angle will change.

This setup jig does two things for me. It saves time by making it easy to set the blade extension. It also helps me to be sure the blade is square to the guide.

Make the jig from hardwood. The V-groove positions the wheel of the honing guide and the block locates the end of the chisel or plane iron. The groove and block must be parallel to each other.

To use, set the wheel of the honing guide in the V-groove and slide the plane iron or chisel into the guide until it is square against the block. Then tighten the honing guide's clamping screw. You need a jig for each sharpening angle you use.

—MATT DANNING, Piedmont, Calif.

Fixed-angle honing jig

Traditionally, a blade for a scraper plane such as the Stanley No. 80 is prepared by filing a 45° bevel followed by stoning, burnishing, and, finally, turning a hook. I've found it difficult to maintain the 45° bevel through all of those steps freehand, so I made a jig to help. Construction of the jig is fairly straightforward. You want a platform that places the blade at the desired angle to the stone. My jig uses 10-in. by 4-in. DMT brand diamond stones, but with slight changes, the jig could accommodate any sharpening stone. To use this jig, rub the bevel against the coarse diamond stone until you raise an even burr; then work up through the grits and remove the wire edge. Don't forget to polish the back of the blade, too. Finally, burnish the edge, turn the hook, and prepare to be amazed at your scraper plane's performance.

This concept could be adapted for sharpening plane irons, chisels, or any other straight blade that has a flat back. You will, of course, need a separate jig for each sharpening angle.

—ED MULLIGAN, S. Yarmouth, Mass.

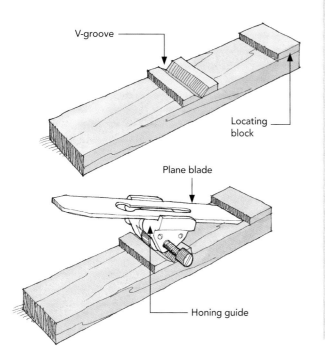

V-groove

Locating block

Plane blade

Honing guide

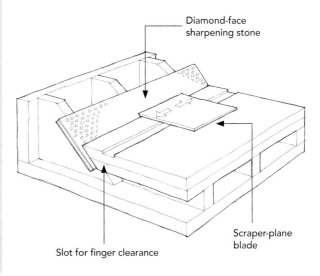

Diamond-face sharpening stone

Scraper-plane blade

Slot for finger clearance

Honing gauge ensures correct bevel angle

Here's a gauge that I use to set my honing guide consistently to the correct sharpening bevel for chisels and plane irons. It eliminates the tedious measuring and squaring that accompanies most honing-guide setups. The gauge is just a piece of plywood with a wood fence attached to each edge. Make sure the fences are perpendicular to the top and bottom edges of the plywood. I use one side of the gauge for plane irons and the other for chisels. Marks on the gauge show the correct projection for 25° and 30°. Intermediate marks would allow setting precise microbevels.

To use this gauge, butt the honing guide against the bottom edge of the plywood and extend the cutting iron to match the line you've marked for the sharpening angle needed. The side fences automatically square the blade to the honing guide.

—THOM TRAIL, Powder Springs, Ga.

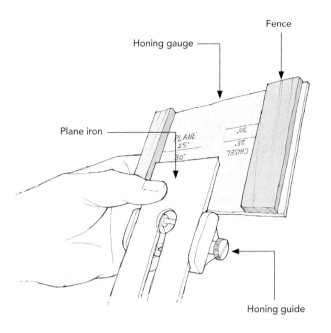

Angle gauge adds precision to honing-guide setup

Here is an easy way to get consistent and fast results when sharpening plane blades and chisels. Creating a microbevel using a stone or abrasive paper on glass takes only a few strokes if the blade is set to the exact right angle. To set the blade at the right angle consistently, I now use a magnetic digital angle gauge.

To use the gauge, I zero it on the same flat surface that the blade will be honed on. Then I place the magnetic base on the blade in the honing guide and move the blade in and out of the guide to set the angle. The gauge shows the angle to one-tenth of a degree. When the angle is right, I write it on the plane blade with a fine-tip felt pen so that there is no guesswork next time I need to hone.

—A.D. (TONY) IRWIN, Duncan, B.C., Canada

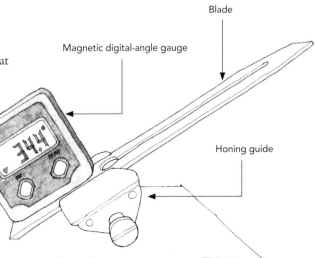

Angle gauges for bench grinders

I get excellent results sharpening my various turning tools using nothing more than the standard tool rest on my bench grinder. The secret, I've learned, is to set the tool rest to the exact same angle each time I regrind a tool. To do that, I use a shopmade angle gauge for each of the common grinding angles.

The gauges are nothing more than galvanized-steel flashing cut into 1-in.-wide rectangles. One corner of the rectangle is clipped to the desired sharpening angle for a given tool.

To use the gauge, place one edge on the tool rest. Then adjust the angle of the tool rest until the clipped corner of the gauge is tangent to the grinding wheel. The clipped corner is properly positioned when the wheel touches it near the bottom of its length, about where a tool's edge would hit the wheel. Once the tool rest is locked in place, you're ready to start sharpening.

—PHILIP THULLEN, Los Alamos, N.M.

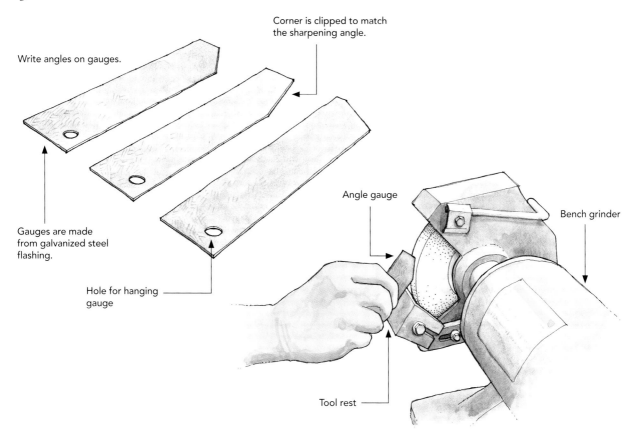

Write angles on gauges.

Corner is clipped to match the sharpening angle.

Gauges are made from galvanized steel flashing.

Hole for hanging gauge

Angle gauge

Bench grinder

Tool rest

Double-checking the bevel angle

To see if you're sharpening a tool at the proper bevel angle, color the edge with a felt-tipped marker. After you touch the tool to the stone, you can see where the color has been worn off and make adjustments to correct the bevel angle as necessary.

—RICHARD HEINES JR., Wood River Jct., R.I.

HANDPLANES AND CHISELS

Flatten the back of chisels or plane irons to control cuts

Creating a sharp edge involves making two polished surfaces intersect. For chisels and plane irons, these two surfaces are the tool's beveled tip and flat back. For chisels, a flat back is doubly important for controlling cuts, because it acts as a reference surface that keeps the chisel on a straight, predictable path.

To flatten a blade or chisel, rub the last inch or so of the tool's back on a flat abrasive surface such as a water-stone. Sandpaper glued to a flat surface works, too. Be sure to hold the back dead flat to ensure that the polishing abrasive will reach all the way to the cutting edge, where it matters most. The good news is that once it's polished, all you'll ever have to do with the back is rub it with your finest abrasive to remove the burr created by honing the bevel.

—GARY ROGOWSKI, Portland, Ore.

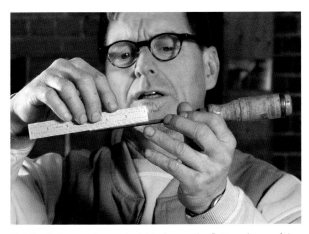

Test for flatness. Place a straightedge on the flattened area of the blade's back and look for gaps. With a truly flat back, you won't see light between the straightedge and the blade back.

Rub the back. Flattening and then polishing the back is tedious but crucial work that, thankfully, has to be done only once.

Thumbnail test for plane blade sharpness

Here's an easy way to check how sharp your plane blade is before you put it in the tool. Hold the blade lightly between your thumb and forefinger and lower the edge gently onto the thumbnail of your other hand. A sharp blade will catch on the nail immediately. A not-quite-sharp blade will skid a little and then catch, but not very solidly. A dull one will slide.

—AIMÉ FRASER, Westport, Conn.

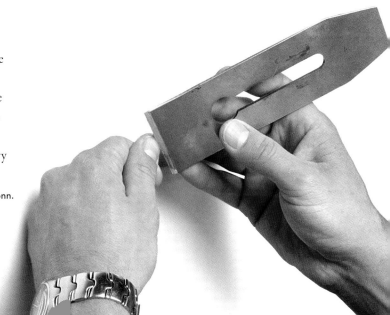

Keep a square edge as you grind a bevel

Each time the honed portion of the bevel of a chisel or plane iron becomes too wide to polish efficiently, prepare the bevel for honing by grinding it to the proper angle. I use a hollow-ground bevel, where the grinder wheel's radius scoops out steel between the bevel's heel and the edge.

Two common errors occur here. First, you need to be sure the tool is presented squarely to the wheel. Ride the outside of your right index finger under the bottom edge of the tool rest to act both as a depth stop and a brace, keeping the iron square to the wheel. Use your left hand to control the tool's side-to-side movement,

pressing down lightly on the tool with your thumbs. This grip allows you to keep the tool flat against the tool rest, pressed lightly against the wheel, and tracking in a straight line.

The second error is grinding the hollow all the way to the tip, until all that's left is a consistent wire edge across the back. Don't do this. Leave a thin band, about $\frac{1}{64}$ in. wide, of unground steel at the tip. This provides a visual reference to help ensure a square, consistent grind and helps prevent the thin edge from burning on a high-speed grinder.

—GARY ROGOWSKI, Portland, Ore.

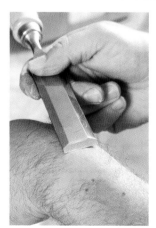

Positive grip. Hold the blade flat on the tool rest with your thumbs. Run the index finger of one hand along the bottom of the tool rest to help keep the blade square to the wheel.

Good grind. Leave a very thin band of the old bevel to ensure an even grind and avoid burning the tip.

Shave test for chisel sharpness

To ensure your chisels are sharp before using them, perform a "shave test": Take a thin layer of end grain from a piece of pine. Or, run it over the hair on your forearm—safely! A keenly honed chisel will cleanly slice the hair.

—HENDRIK VARJU, Acton, Ont., Canada

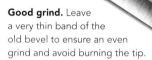

Use a jig to hone the beveled edge of a chisel or handplane

Hone the tip of the bevel with successively finer abrasives until it is as polished as the back. Some folks sharpen using sandpaper and plate glass; others use sharpening stones. Whatever method you prefer, I'd recommend using a honing guide, which helps you maintain a precise, consistent angle from grit to grit and gives you peace of mind, knowing that the finest abrasives are reaching the very tip of the tool.

—GARY ROGOWSKI, Portland, Ore.

Precision honing. By setting the jig slightly steeper than the grinding angle, you polish just the tip of the tool.

The right angle every time. For any given honing angle, the blade must extend a specific distance from the guide. For consistency, use an angle-setting jig.

Honing a beveled edge freehand

You save setup time when honing a bevel freehand, but it takes practice to maintain the angle.

When honing without a guide, keep a consistent angle by riding both the heel and tip on the stone. Start with the tool resting on the bevel's heel and rock the bevel forward until both heel and tip are in solid contact with the stone.

—GARY ROGOWSKI, Portland, Ore.

The result. An edge honed by hand will show two polished bands where the heel and tip meet the stone.

Use a strop to get a super-fine edge

Here's a great way to take a sharpened blade a step further for the most demanding tasks, such as planing difficult grain. Take a few final honing passes on a leather strop charged with very fine abrasive compound. My strop is a simple 2½-in.-wide strip of thin leather, mounted suede-side-up on a piece of ¾-in.-thick hardwood.

Keep the back of the tool flat. Pull it toward you for several strokes. Don't push the tool along the strop or you will dig it into the leather.

When sharpening the bevel, maintain a proper angle on the strop. Once again, pull the blade toward you. The finished edge will be amazingly sharp.

—GARY ROGOWSKI, Portland, Ore.

Keep the back flat. Pull the tool toward you for several strokes. Don't push: This will dig the tool into the leather.

Maintain a proper angle on the bevel. Again, pull the blade toward you. The finished edge will be amazingly sharp.

Sharpening a scrub plane

A scrub plane has a blade with a pronounced curve and works something like a gouge, removing lots of wood in a hurry. However, you sharpen the blade much the same way that you sharpen a blade with a straight edge.

Begin by flattening and polishing the back, then work from coarse to fine stones to hone the bevel to about 25°. Do this freehand.

To be sure you keep a uniform bevel on the curve, use your wrists to rock the blade from side to side as you move it forward and back on the stone. That way, you'll hone progressively along the entire curved edge.

—GARRETT HACK, Thetford Center, Vt.

Rock and hone. To sharpen a scrub plane, begin with one edge against the stone (left), then rock it to the other side as you move it over the stone (right).

Jig for sharpening skew chisels

This inverted T-shaped jig makes it easier to sharpen skew chisels with a disc sander and a resin-bonded, 120-grit aluminum-oxide sanding disc. To make the jig, use a large scrap of hardwood as a stable base. Cut a 75° miter on both sides so the jig can hold the blade to the disc at the correct grinding angle. Attach a center upright to the base and add 20° ramps to both sides of it for blade rests.

Align the edge of the base with the edge of the disc-sander table. Clamp the chisel to one side of the upright with a small C-clamp and gently hold it to the disc to produce the skew on one side. Then move the chisel to the other side of the upright and repeat.

Hone the chisel using 280-grit wet-and-dry paper glued to medium-density fiberboard to polish the bevels and remove the slight burr left by the disc.

—BRIAN J. GERRATY, Canterbury, Victoria, Australia

Modifying a grinder to sharpen carving gouges

To sharpen carving chisels and gouges, start with a common grinder motor and turn around the grinder so that the wheels rotate away from you at the top and give you more control. Mount the grinder on a platform supported by four springs to remove vibration. Mount a plywood sharpening wheel (described below) on the right side of the grinder and sandwich two 1-in.-thick cloth buffing discs on the left side to make an oversize buffing wheel.

To make the sharpening wheel, laminate plywood to produce a 6-in.-dia., 1-in.-thick disc. If you don't have a lathe, saw the disc to rough shape on a bandsaw, mount it on the grinder and turn it to final shape in place. Mount a disc of fine sandpaper (150-grit or 180-grit) to each side of the disc and a ribbon of sandpaper to the rim. Don't glue the side pieces to the wheel: Allow them to float on a film of air as the wheel rotates so you can apply a very gentle pressure with the gouge and remove the risk of overheating the blade being sharpened. After you sharpen the tool on the wheel, move to the cloth buffing wheel to polish and hone the edge.

—ALEX CAMERON, Golden Grove, South Australia

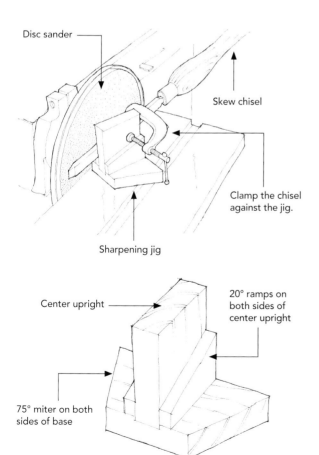

Disc sander

Skew chisel

Clamp the chisel against the jig.

Sharpening jig

Center upright

20° ramps on both sides of center upright

75° miter on both sides of base

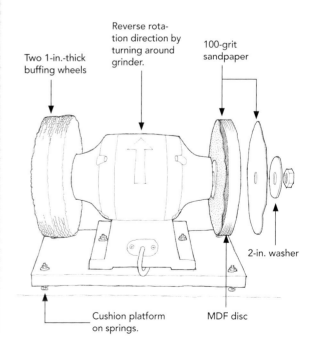

Two 1-in.-thick buffing wheels

Reverse rotation direction by turning around grinder.

100-grit sandpaper

2-in. washer

Cushion platform on springs.

MDF disc

SCRAPERS, AWLS, AND SPOKESHAVES

A quick, precise method for sharpening scrapers

Here is a fast and accurate method for sharpening a card scraper. It requires only a mill file, a burnisher, and a worktable. The secret is controlling the angle of the burnishing tool using the thickness of your worktable.

First, file off the old burrs. Lay the scraper flat on the worktable and run the flat side of a sharp mill file down the length of each burr. Tap or brush the file clean and wipe off the scraper after every few strokes. Now, square up the cutting edge. Hold the mill file against the side of the worktable and push the scraper against it. A few strokes are all that is needed.

Next, burnish the edge to the desired angle. I use the thickness of the worktable top as an angle gauge. Place the scraper on the worktable, overhanging the edge by just a fraction of an inch. Put the burnishing tool against the bottom edge of the worktable and against the scraper edge to be burnished; this is the final angle. But start with the burnisher held at an angle less than that final angle, and make a few swipes to start the burr. Continue increasing the angle of the burnisher until it is swiping at the final angle against the worktable's bottom edge. The larger the overhang, the larger the burr angle on the scraper. For fine work, I like a burnishing angle of about 4°. For rough work, a burnishing angle of 7° or so is best. My worktable top is 2¼ in. thick, and an overhang of ⁵⁄₃₂ in. leaves a 4° burr angle. An overhang of ⁷⁄₁₆ in. leaves a 7° burr angle.

—PETER LORING, Robbinsdale, Minn.

First, file the burr off the side of the scraper.

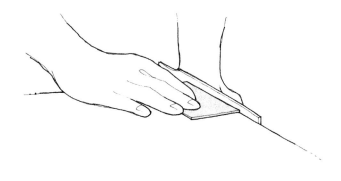

Then, slide the scraper against the file to square up the cutting edge.

Finally, burnish the edge. How much you overhang the scraper determines the burnishing angle.

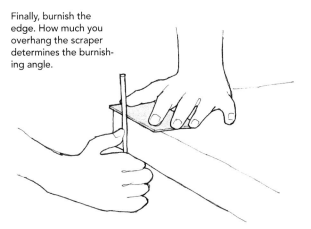

Sharpening jig for scraper blades

Blades for scraper planes are wide, thin, and difficult to grind to the correct angle consistently by hand. So I built two jigs like the one in the sketch, one for my 60° Lie-Nielsen® scraper and another for my 45° Stanley scraper. The jigs are just like the back half of a Krenov-style plane. To make the jig, first laminate the middle section with a few pieces of white pine and cut it to the appropriate sharpening angle. Then add the maple sides and pin and make a maple wedge. The construction shouldn't take a lot of time, perhaps an hour or two.

To use the jig, wedge the scraper blade into it so that the cutting edge is just proud of the bottom. Turn the jig upside down on the bench and tap with a piece of soft pine until the blade is flush with the bottom of the jig. Now clamp the jig in the vise and grind away. Start with a fine silicon-carbide stone flat on the jig, then move to a hard black Arkansas stone. To finish, take the blade out of the jig and gently grind off any wire edge that may have formed.

—**CHARLIE CHAMBERS**, Annandale, Va.

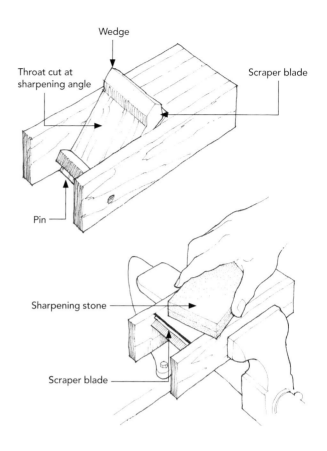

Wedge

Throat cut at sharpening angle

Scraper blade

Pin

Sharpening stone

Scraper blade

Get a square edge on any scraper

This jig makes it quick and easy to put a 90° edge on a scraper. To make it, cut a rabbet along one edge of a piece of hardwood. The rabbet should be just wide enough to accept the file thickness, and just deep enough to be one-third to one-half the width of the file. A bevel in the top corner of the rabbet allows metal shavings to clear. Now, screw a second hardwood piece to the rabbeted edge, as shown. The same concept could be used to hold a diamond stone. To use the jig, just lay the scraper on it and rub the scraper's edge against the file.

—**JIM CRAWFORD**, Brownstown, Mich.

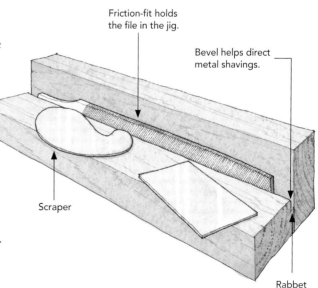

Friction-fit holds the file in the jig.

Bevel helps direct metal shavings.

Scraper

Rabbet

Sharpening curved scrapers

Sharpening a curved scraper uses the same techniques as sharpening a flat one, though a couple of additional tools are needed to handle the concave areas. To sharpen these parts of the scraper, you'll need a round or a half-round mill file and a cone-shaped slip stone.

File and hone the convex edges with a flat file and stone, just like you would file a straight-edge scraper. Use the same draw-filing technique, with the file square to the edge but skewed at an angle to the direction of the stroke. The trick is to make your stroke follow the curve. To hone the convex areas, hold the scraper upright and drag it across the stone while rolling it to follow the curve.

To joint the concave areas, use a round or half-round file, and perform the same draw-filing technique. Then use the cone-shaped slip stone to hone these areas. The goal is the same with all scrapers: to get a square edge, free of file marks, before burnishing.

There's nothing different about the burnishing of a curved scraper. A standard round or triangular burnishing rod will follow almost any contour, and the idea of turning over the edge to create a fine burr is the same. Start the bur-nisher nearly level for the first stroke, then bring it down to about 10° off level in subsequent strokes. If the burr, or hook, gets bent over too far, it can be straightened with the point of the burnisher.

—PHILIP LOWE, Beverly, Mass.

1. JOINT THE EDGE

Keep the file level and follow the curve. Use a round file for the concave areas (left) and a flat mill file for the convex areas (right). Make your strokes diagonally—moving across the edge and along it at the same time.

2. HONE THE EDGE

Again, keep the stone square to the scraper. A rounded stone is necessary for the concave areas (left). Use a standard waterstone for the other curves, holding the scraper instead of the stone (right).

3. CREATE A FINE BURR

Concave, convex, or straight, burnishing is the same. Use a standard burnishing rod and follow the scraper profile. Just as with straight edges, start the burnishing rod level, then tilt it for a bit for each subsequent stroke, ending at about 10° off level.

Sharpening a spokeshave blade

The short blade of a high-angle, cast-iron spokeshave is sharpened as you would any plane blade—at a 25° bevel with a flat back. Put a slight curve on the edge if you want to use the shave for smoothing.

To hold this small blade in a honing guide, tape the blade to the end of a standard plane iron—or to a ¼-in.-thick scrap of wood the same size as one. The idea is to "lengthen" the blade so it fits in the jig. Then you can sharpen it as you would a plane iron.

—GARRETT HACK, Thetford Center, Vt.

Tape two blades together. To sharpen the blade of an all-metal spokeshave, begin by taping it just ahead of the front edge of a plane blade, with the bevel facing outward. Place the assembly into a sharpening jig and work the shave's blade over a stone as you would a standard plane blade.

Sharpening to a point

Here's a simple way to sharpen awls, scribes, and round-leg dividers or compass legs. Stabilize the tool against the grinder's rest, and grind the tip. Rotate the tool, removing enough material for an even and balanced tip. The tip may be honed further with a coarse slip stone, sandpaper, or other abrasive surface.

—MARIO RODRIGUEZ, Cherry Hill, N.J.

Keep the tool moving. For a balanced grind, roll the tool under your thumb as you hold it against the wheel.

Refine the point. Use a bench-stone, sandpaper, or other abrasive surface to smooth and sharpen the tip.

MILLING LUMBER

JOINTING AND PLANING

Avoid planer snipe on short stock

When you put a short piece of wood through the thickness planer, here's how to eliminate snipe at each end of the workpiece. Cut 1-in.-wide wood strips about 8 in. longer than the workpiece, and glue one to each edge.

Run the setup through the planer, taking thin cuts until it is the desired thickness. Snipe will appear at the ends of the strips, not the workpiece. Use yellow glue. Cyanoacrylate glues will mess up your jointer blades when you smooth the edges after removing the strips. This technique also works well with a jointer.

—ROGER RUSSELL, Anderson Island, Wash.

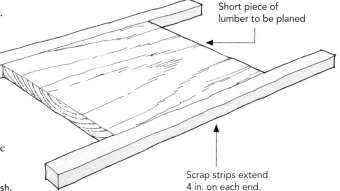

Short piece of lumber to be planed

Scrap strips extend 4 in. on each end.

Prevent tearout while planing figured wood

Highly figured woods, like curly maple, are prone to tearout, especially when they are being put through the planer, but there are a few things you can do to lessen it. First, make sure that your planer blades are razor sharp. If you haven't changed them out in a while, now is the time.

Second, feed your wood into the planer at an angle. Angling the board allows the planer's cutterhead to slice shavings on the bias to the direction of the grain rather than shearing along the grain. This is important for planing curl, because the grain is compacted vertically like ribbon candy along its length.

Third, take light passes or else you'll gouge the wood. If your planer has a variable-speed feed rate, put it on the slowest setting to get the most cuts per inch while planing.

Finally, dampen the surface to be planed before feeding it into the machine. This gets the wood fibers to stand up and be clipped.

—BRAD GORDON, York, Maine

Figured wood, like this curly maple, tends to chip out when put through a planer. If the face of the board is dry, and it is fed into the machine perpendicular to the cutterhead, tearout can be so bad that it renders the piece useless.

Dampen the board first. Dampening will swell surface fibers slightly, raising short fibers while keeping longer ones flexible.

Feed at an angle. Angling the board, even slightly, will keep cutterhead blades from lifting the long, undulating wood fibers along the grain.

Jointing roughsawn lumber

After you cut roughsawn stock to an approximate length and width (see pp. 118 and 121), it must rest overnight before it can be jointed and planed. The very next step is to joint one face flat. A thickness planer cannot do this job—it can only mill one side of a board parallel with the other. Inspect the stock for grain orientation and pass it over the jointer (cup side down).

Sometimes the grain direction isn't obvious, so take several light passes rather than one heavy cut. If particularly bad tearout occurs in one area, you can flip it end for end to reorient the grain and try again.

Next, if you haven't done so already, joint one edge, using the freshly jointed face as a reference surface against the fence of your jointer.

—MICHAEL FORTUNE, Lakefield, Ont., Canada

Joint a face. Joint with the cupped side down. Take light passes until the face is flat.

Joint an edge. Register the freshly jointed face against the fence and again take light passes until the edge is flat. If the fence is set at 90° to the jointer table, the two jointed surfaces should now be square to one another.

Feeding a board through the jointer

To reduce tearout, consider the rotation of the cutterhead and the direction of the grain when deciding which way to feed a board. Mark the jointer near the cutterhead for easy reference. The diagonal lines on this jointer represent proper grain orientation.

—MICHAEL FORTUNE, Lakefield, Ont., Canada

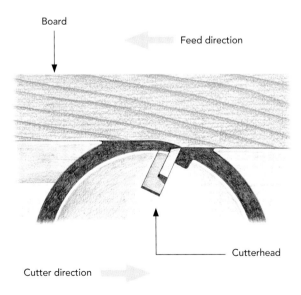

Board

Feed direction

Cutterhead

Cutter direction

Planing twisted boards

I needed to recover a short, wide piece of walnut that was twisted. My small jointer is very narrow, so I couldn't use it to flatten one face. Finally, the thought came to me to add a couple of leveling strips, one on each side of the board, and then put the board through my thickness planer. I cut the leveling strips as long as and a bit thicker than the twisted board. I then screwed one leveling strip to each side, adjusting the twist in the board equally between them. Using hot-melt glue to attach the strips to the workpiece also would work and would reduce the possibility of nicking your planer knives with a screw.

I ran the resulting assembly through my planer until the board was flat on one side. Then I removed the strips and surfaced the other side. Finally, I squared up the board on the tablesaw. The whole process worked great.

—WAYNE JOHNSON, Grand Ledge, Mich.

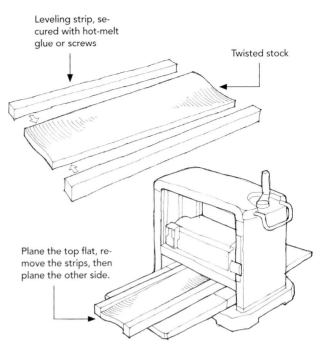

Leveling strip, secured with hot-melt glue or screws

Twisted stock

Plane the top flat, remove the strips, then plane the other side.

Engineer's squares for checking flatness of boards

Winding sticks are commonly used to check whether the face of a board is true along its length. This involves visually judging the alignment of two sticks, something that some woodworkers find difficult.

A simple and reliable alternative is to use a pair of engineer's steel squares. Place one square blade-up on one end of the workpiece and the other square blade-up on the other end. Sight along the two blades, moving your head until there is a small gap between the blades. If the gap between the blades is parallel, the face is true.

It is best to use engineer's steel squares, as they are certified true inside and out. Traditional carpenter's squares are not always true on the inside. A pair of 4-in. squares is ideal for most purposes, though larger sizes may be better for very long boards.

—BOB HULLEY, Sonning, Berkshire, England

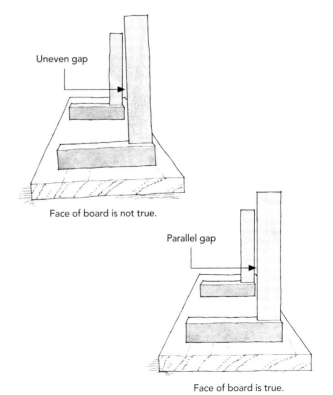

Uneven gap

Face of board is not true.

Parallel gap

Face of board is true.

Checking board flatness with MDF winding sticks

Winding sticks are invaluable for helping to check the flatness of large boards, but they are useless if they warp from humidity. I avoided that problem by making a pair of winding sticks out of MDF and hardboard, which will remain accurate despite varying humidity conditions.

The MDF strips, ¾ in. thick by 1½ in. wide by 2 ft. long, have ¾-in.-deep grooves to fit the ¼-in.-thick by 1½-in.-wide hardboard strips. Before gluing up the winding sticks, I chamfered the top edges of the MDF supports.

Chamfers help deflect bumps or dings and make handling the sticks more comfortable. I glued the strips in the grooves and clamped the top edges of the sticks together to keep them parallel, as shown below.

Finally, I lightly sanded all sharp edges and, using a permanent black marker, drew a fine line along the corner of the top edge of each hardboard strip to make it easier to read the sticks when at work.

—SERGE DUCLOS, Delson, Que., Canada

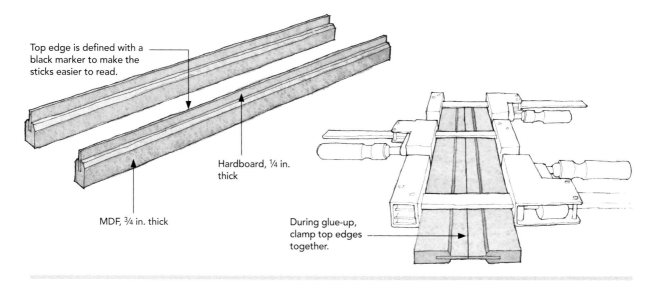

Top edge is defined with a black marker to make the sticks easier to read.

Hardboard, ¼ in. thick

MDF, ¾ in. thick

During glue-up, clamp top edges together.

Jointer knife-setting jig

This knife-setting jig is as simple as it gets. Inlay two large, round rare-earth magnets near the end of a length of a ¾-in.-thick plywood scrap. Inlay the magnets just below the surface of the wood so that they will hold the knife without damaging a freshly honed edge. My jig, made for a 6-in. jointer, is about 4 in. wide and 12 in. long. To use it, place the jig on the outfeed table and hold it down with hand pressure. The magnets will hold the jointer blade at the outfeed-table height while you snug up the knife-holding bolts. When done, just slap the magnetic board against the outside of the jointer cabinet to store it.

—J. PRENDERGAST, Surrey, B.C., Canada

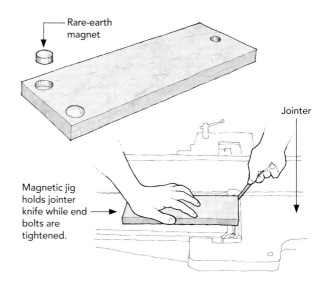

Rare-earth magnet

Jointer

Magnetic jig holds jointer knife while end bolts are tightened.

Jointing without a jointer

You don't need a jointer to mill rough stock. I use this pair of jigs to mill stock straight and flat. The only machines I need are a thickness planer and a tablesaw.

—MIKE BIELSKI, Waterville, Ohio

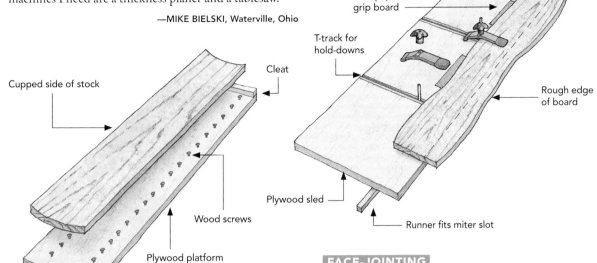

Cupped side of stock

Cleat

T-track for hold-downs

Push handle

Sandpaper to grip board

Rough edge of board

Wood screws

Plywood platform

Plywood sled

Runner fits miter slot

FACE-JOINTING

EDGE-JOINTING

The thickness planer can flatten a board's face. On this simple jig, the stock is supported by twin rows of wood screws driven into a platform and adjusted to meet the varying clearances on the underside of the board. The stock rides the sled cup side up. Slide the board slightly sideways to adjust the screws, then seat it firmly on the screw heads for planing.

Use the tablesaw to straighten a wavy edge. The jig's plywood sled rides on a long runner that fits in the miter slot. Make sure the blade is parallel to the slot. Secure the rough lumber with hold-downs so that the rough edge overhangs the sled slightly along its length.

Plane roughsawn stock to final thickness

After jointing one face and an edge of your roughsawn stock (see p. 112), you'll want to bring the piece to final thickness. To do this, mill the unjointed face in the planer to make it parallel with the opposite surface. Light passes are best. Roughsawn lumber can vary in thickness; you don't want your planer to bog down if the wood increases in thickness down the length. Also, a heavy cut will yield a rough surface and promote snipe at the ends.

When jointing and planing the faces, try to remove the same amount of material from each face. This will help prevent an unbalanced release of tension in the wood, which would cause twist or cup. If you have a lot of material to remove, make a bandsaw cut to get closer to final thickness.

—MICHAEL FORTUNE, Lakefield, Ont., Canada

Bandsaw first? If you still have a fair amount of material to remove, a thin bandsaw cut lets you approach final thickness quickly and avoid repeated passes in the planer, saving the blades.

Plane to final thickness. Take passes of no more than 1/16 in. The planed surface will now be parallel to the previously jointed face.

Thicknessing small pieces with an oscillating spindle sander

My projects typically require small, thin pieces (1/8 in. to 3/8 in. thick) of highly figured wood. Even the sharpest of planer blades can chip and ruin a workpiece with this type of wild grain. To eliminate chipping, I built a jig that converts my oscillating spindle sander into a mini thickness sander. The jig, which is a tall fence that can be clamped to the sander table, can be made from any material—3/4-in.-thick scrap MDF in my case.

It is important for the fence to be parallel to the sander's spindle. To accomplish this, add masking-tape shims, if needed, under the fence legs. It also is important to position the jig on the table so that the spindle is rotating into the workpiece. In my case, this puts the jig on the left side of the counterclockwise-turning spindle.

To use, set the distance from the spindle to the fence at slightly less than the rough thickness of the workpiece, and clamp the fence in this position. If you wish, install a featherboard on the outfeed side of the fence. You will get better results if you make multiple passes. Using a push stick of equal or lesser thickness than the workpiece, feed the wood into the gap between the fence and spindle. After the first pass, adjust the fence closer to the spindle and take another pass. Slow and steady pressure will ensure even surfacing on any type of highly figured wood, even bird's-eye maple.

—GEOFFREY CARSON, Issaquah, Wash.

RIPPING AND CROSSCUTTING

Align bandsaw fence and blade to achieve consistent resaw thickness

If you're having trouble getting a consistent thickness while resawing, more than likely the fence is not parallel to the blade. On a well-tuned bandsaw with a good sharp resaw blade (3 tpi) and a tall fence, the thickness of the resawn piece should vary only by a few thousandths of an inch between the thickest and the thinnest areas.

When resawing, it's best to use a tall auxiliary fence with a support brace; a screw on the bottom makes the brace adjustable. To check whether the fence is parallel to the blade top to bottom, bring the fence right up to the blade. Adjust the screw on the bottom of the brace until the fence is set parallel. The outfeed end of the fence must be locked to the table to prevent it from lifting and shifting sideways.

To prevent tension in the wood from causing the offcut to twist and push the stock away from the fence, use a fence that is short in length. A shorter fence allows the offcut to move without affecting the blade and the stock.

In addition, the face of the stock going against the fence should be flat. Joint the face of the resawn stock before starting each cut.

—JOHN WHITE, Rochester, Vt.

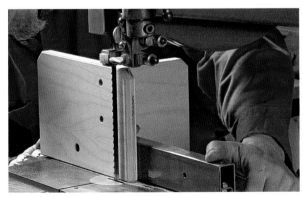

Use a tall fence that's parallel to the blade. A brace on the back prevents the fence from tilting. An adjustment screw on the bottom of the brace (top) helps set the fence parallel to the blade (above).

Lock the fence into place. First, clamp down the fence at the outfeed end. Then clamp a block at the outfeed end to stop the fence from shifting sideways. Note that the auxiliary fence stops just past the blade, to allow off-cuts to twist away freely.

Cut roughsawn lumber to approximate length with a jigsaw

Rough lumber that is twisted or cupped won't sit flat on a chopsaw. As you cut, the stock can drop into the blade, pinching and binding. For this reason, use a jigsaw with the stock set across three or four sawhorses. A jigsaw with an oscillating cutting action and a very coarse blade will cut through the hardest wood up to 2 in. thick.

Always cut off the rough ends of the boards, which may be checked (cracked) and embedded with grit, staples, and other debris that could nick your jointer and planer knives. Then use the jigsaw to cut boards into pieces that are 1 in. or 2 in. over the finished length.

—MICHAEL FORTUNE, Lakefield, Ont., Canada

Four sawhorses. Position sawhorses so that stock on both sides of each cut is fully supported.

Push stick aids in ripping thin stock on the tablesaw

This push stick rides in the channel on top of a Biesemeyer-style rip fence. Though ideal for any ripcut, the design is especially useful when I need to rip thin strips of a consistent width.

The push stick consists of three main parts: the sliding block, the handle block, and the push finger. The sliding block should be milled so that it is slightly proud of the fence faces. The handle block is flush with the fence face that's close to the blade. The notched push finger is ¼-in.-thick hardwood, but a ⅛-in.-thick piece of aluminum would work as well. Attach the finger to the handle block with a screw and a large washer. The finger should slide against the rip fence.

To use, simply engage the workpiece with the finger and push through. When you're not using the push stick, just pop it off the rip fence.

—JERRY OBERWAGER, Great Neck, N.Y.

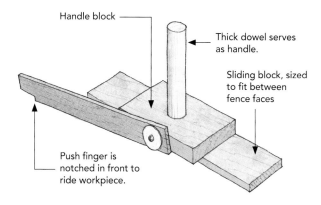

Handle block

Thick dowel serves as handle.

Sliding block, sized to fit between fence faces

Push finger is notched in front to ride workpiece.

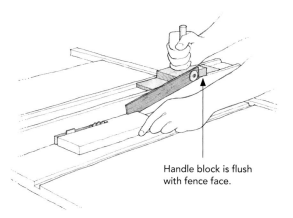

Handle block is flush with fence face.

Resawing logs into lumber with a bandsaw

You can saw small logs into lumber with your bandsaw, but this is a labor-intensive process. Green logs are heavy with sap, so don't expect to saw big logs for large woodworking projects. However, depending on the size of your bandsaw, you can saw planks that are suitable for many smaller projects.

Once you've acquired the logs, set up your bandsaw with the proper blade and a simple jig to guide the log safely past the blade. Also, if you own one of the many 14-in. bandsaws on the market, adding a riser block to the column will double your saw's cutting capacity.

The best blade for this job is one with large gullets and few teeth. The gullets will haul the sawdust out of the kerf and prevent the motor from bogging down. A 3-pitch, ½-in.-wide, 0.025-in.-thick hook-tooth blade is a good choice; most 14-in. bandsaws can't adequately tension anything wider.

The jig is simply an L-shaped platform made of inexpensive plywood or medium-density fiberboard. Fasten the log to the jig with two or three lag screws. It's important that the screws penetrate the soft bark and bite into the fibrous sapwood. The jig runs against the bandsaw fence to guide the log in a straight path. You can also attach a U-shaped channel to slip over the fence for additional support.

After you saw the planks, be sure to dry them before you use them.

—LONNIE BIRD, Dandridge, Tenn.

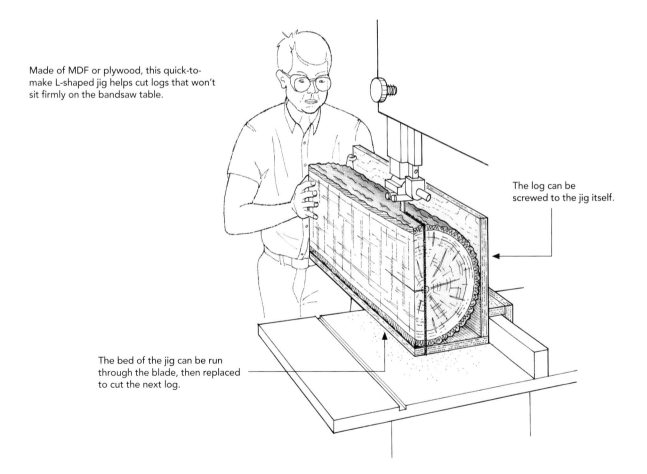

Made of MDF or plywood, this quick-to-make L-shaped jig helps cut logs that won't sit firmly on the bandsaw table.

The log can be screwed to the jig itself.

The bed of the jig can be run through the blade, then replaced to cut the next log.

Three approaches to cutting your own lumber

When I saw logs into lumber, I shoot for four qualities: consistent, even grain; no internal stress; no knots or other defects; and as much width as possible. Success depends mostly on the initial quality of the log, but the sawing method is also a key.

The first approach to cutting your own lumber is a common method called through-and-through sawing—one cut after another from one side to the other. It's the most efficient method. But the outside boards are flatsawn and prone to warping, while the center boards often contain knots and defects from when the tree was young. You will get wide boards this way, but of potluck quality.

Far better is sawing for grade: basically, taking off boards while rolling the log to expose the best faces to the saw, or the second approach to self-cutting lumber, best-face sawing. This takes more time and effort than cutting the log through and through.

Place the log on the mill with the best side of the log facing the saw for the first cut. It is important to saw with the grain, whenever possible. For example, if the log has any curvature, saw in the same plane as the sweep. This will reduce the built-in tension, and you'll be able to correct some of the crooked grain later in the ripping process. If the log has a lot of taper, wedge up the smaller end so that you saw parallel with the center of the log.

Take off a board or two and then roll the log and make cuts until all four faces are exposed. Then simply find the best face and take off boards until the quality changes. Then roll again to your next-best face, and so on. You won't get the widest boards, but you will get fewer defects and more consistent grain.

More time-consuming still is quartersawing, the third method of cutting logs to lumber. Quartersawing yields very stable material and, in the case of species such as oak and sycamore, beautiful fleck patterns as well. The first cut is through the center of the tree, and then these halves are quartered. Each cut after that is parallel to one of these sawn faces, or close to radial from the center of the tree. Quartersawn boards are not very wide but offer vertical grain and stability that are very desirable for certain applications.

—GARRETT HACK, Thetford Center, Vt.

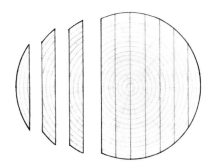
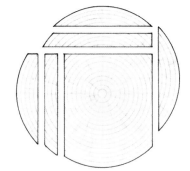
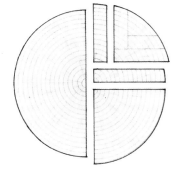

Through-and-through sawing. Also called flitchsawing, this is the simplest method and delivers the widest boards. However, the overall quality is random, and the boards that pass through the center, or pith, of the log often contain defects.

Best-face sawing. This approach is more time-consuming because it involves rotating the squared log a number of times during the process to find the best faces. It produces the best figure and grain for most furniture uses.

Quartersawing. The goal here is to cut boards perpendicular to the growth rings, so the grain is as vertical as possible. This process involves quartering the log before sawing boards. The downside is their stock can be narrow.

Two ways to make a straight edge on a rough board

When working with oddly shaped or roughsawn lumber, making a straight edge can be a difficult task. Here are two ways to simplify the feat.

Use a carpenter's chalk line (see the photo, left) to produce a bright, straight line on stock that's too long for marking with a straightedge. Cut along the line freehand (see photo, center).

A surer path to a straight rip is to attach a piece of edge-jointed stock, nailing into the waste area of the rough board (see photo, right). The jointed edge rides the bandsaw fence and guides the stock in a straight path through the blade. Don't sink the nails flush; you'll pull them out when you are done.

—MICHAEL FORTUNE, Lakefield, Ont., Canada

Rip roughsawn lumber to approximate width using a bandsaw

Many woodworkers use the tablesaw to cut stock to rough width, but the bandsaw is a safer tool for the job because there's less chance of kickback. Set up the bandsaw with a coarse, 3-tpi skip-tooth blade, and make sure the blade is centered on the upper wheel of the saw.

The first step is to straighten one edge. You can do that by tacking a wooden fence to the board, then running that fence along the bandsaw fence. I've also cut the board to rough width freehand, following a layout line.

Joint the edge, then rip the board about ⅛ in. oversize, running the clean edge against the bandsaw fence, to accommodate any unevenness in your straight edge and the release of any tension in the wood. Let the stock rest overnight before milling to final dimension (see p. 122, top).

—MICHAEL FORTUNE, Lakefield, Ont., Canada

Safe ripping. To provide adequate support to long or heavy stock, mount an outfeed roller on an adjustable stand modified to mount directly to the saw's housing (right). This provides a sturdy outfeed that stays level and doesn't tip.

Cut roughsawn lumber to final width and length

I usually bring a roughsawn piece to finished width on a benchtop planer; this method leaves a clean, square edge that's parallel to the opposite edge. Before you do that, make a final ripcut on the bandsaw, bringing the piece to about 1⁄16 in. over its finished width. This lets you take the lightest possible passes on the planer, saving wear and tear on the knives and ensuring the best performance.

Mill the piece to final width, standing the piece on its jointed edge and passing it through the planer. Use the 1-to-5 rule here. If the stock is 1 in. thick, you can plane a board up to 5 in. wide. If it is 1⁄2 in. thick, then the maximum width is 2 1⁄2 in., and so on. Always use the center portion of the planer to avoid tilting the wood.

If the dimensions exceed the 1-to-5 rule, then trim the piece to final width on the tablesaw.

The last step is to cut the ends on the chopsaw. If the pieces are too wide for the chopsaw, or if you aren't getting a clean cut there, cut them to length using a tablesaw and crosscut sled.

—MICHAEL FORTUNE, Lakefield, Ont., Canada

Planer makes a clean cut. Take light passes, and use the center portion of the planer.

Tablesaw works, too. If a board is too narrow or tall to fit in the planer, rip it to final width at the tablesaw.

Cut one end square, then cut the other to length. Make the final crosscuts on the chopsaw (left). If the stock is too wide (right), use a crosscut sled on the tablesaw.

Carriage for milling wood on the bandsaw

Hand-feeding hardwood scraps, split firewood, and small logs through the bandsaw to cut them into usable pieces isn't safe. I developed a solution based on a rolling log carriage used in sawmills. I used the same basic idea but scaled down the carriage.

Mount a 3-ft.-long pipe clamp to a 2-ft.-long U-shaped maple bracket. To allow lateral adjustment, slot the bracket's bottom and fasten it to the base with bolts and wing nuts. A maple track glued to the bottom of the base slides in the saw's miter-gauge slot. When making the carriage, be sure the clamp jaws clear the bandsaw blade with the bracket at its closest setting. To use the carriage, tighten the log in the clamp, adjust the bracket for the width of cut, and feed the log past the blade.

—E.G. LINCOLN, Parsippany, N.J.

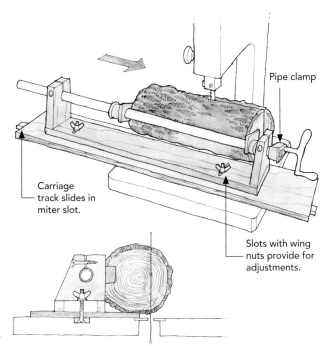

Pipe clamp

Carriage track slides in miter slot.

Slots with wing nuts provide for adjustments.

Improve ray-fleck pattern in oak

Rays in a tree contribute to the figure of a piece of wood. They radiate out from the center of the tree, perpendicular to the growth rings. Ideally, when lumber is quartersawn, the growth rings are perpendicular to the surface of the board and the rays end up parallel to the surface. The split and exposed rays create what is known as ray fleck. The effect occurs in a few wood species, but it's more commonly seen in oak. Not every piece of quartersawn lumber has rays parallel to the board surface, but by resawing the board's surface relative to the rays and growth rings, you can make the ray fleck in your wood look spectacular.

To accomplish this, I use a 14-in. bandsaw, which lets me cut at the proper angle on boards as wide as 6 in. (or even 12 in. with a riser kit installed on the saw). First, tilt the table to an angle so that when the board is placed on its edge, the rays are parallel to the blade. Then set up the fence so that the blade cuts to the corner of the board, maximizing the final thickness.

Now the face of the board is parallel to the rays. Use that new face as your reference to mill the remaining sides of the board.

Although this process generates a large amount of waste, it gives me the option to build furniture that has a stunning ray-fleck pattern.

—HENDRIK VARJU,
Acton, Ont., Canada

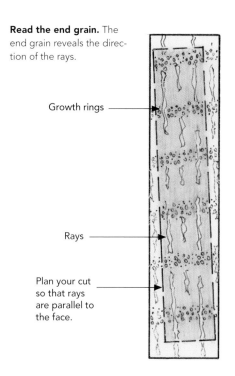

Read the end grain. The end grain reveals the direction of the rays.

Growth rings

Rays

Plan your cut so that rays are parallel to the face.

Improving mediocre ray-fleck stock. Quartersawn stock doesn't always have growth rings that are perfectly perpendicular or rays that are perfectly parallel to the face of a board (top). But slicing through the rays closest to the face of the board will reveal classic ray-fleck figure (bottom).

Resaw for stunning ray fleck. Place the stock against the fence and tilt the table to align the rays parallel to the blade. Position the rip fence so the blade just clears the top corner of the board.

Chop mitered pieces to precise lengths

It's easy to cut mitered stock to the right length with this registration block. To make it, drill a ¼-in.-dia. hole through a scrap of hardwood. With a portable drill, transfer that hole through the block into the left and right fences. Next, press a ¼-in.-dia. steel pin into the block, leaving about ½ in. of the pin above the surface. After engaging the pin in the hole in the left fence, swing the chopsaw to 45° on the right side and cut partway into the block. Remove the block from the saw and mark a square pencil line across it, beginning where the kerf intersects its back edge. Return the block to the left fence and complete the 45° cutoff. Finally, set the saw at 0°, remove the pin, and cut off the waste up to, but not including, the pencil line on both ends. Then swing the saw to the 45° left setting and repeat with the block on the right fence.

Reinsert the pin, and the registration block is ready for use. To use it, first chop the workpieces to the desired length. Then set the blade to 45°, install the registration block, and trim a miter from one end. The block ensures that the mitered workpiece will measure exactly the same length as the square-cut workpiece. To miter the other end accurately, install the block on the other side of the blade.

—THOMAS KOSZALKA, Hicksville, N.Y.

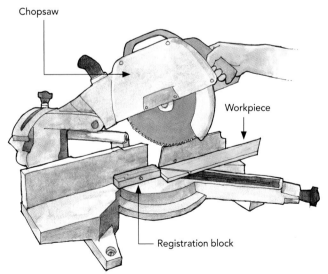

Chopsaw

Workpiece

Registration block

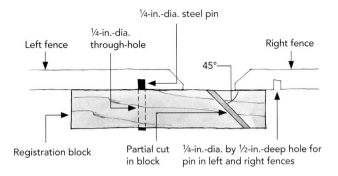

¼-in.-dia. steel pin

¼-in.-dia. through-hole

Left fence

Right fence

45°

Registration block

Partial cut in block

¼-in.-dia. by ½-in.-deep hole for pin in left and right fences

1. To make the registration block, drill a ¼-in.-dia. hole into a piece of hardwood. Then drill into the chopsaw fence through this hole. The exact distance from the sawblade to the hole is not important; just be sure to start with a wood block that is long enough on each side to overlap the saw's cut line. Affix the block to the fence by inserting a metal pin into the hole, and make a partial cut at 45° in the block.

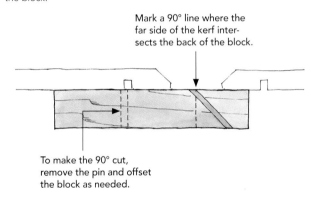

Mark a 90° line where the far side of the kerf intersects the back of the block.

To make the 90° cut, remove the pin and offset the block as needed.

2. Mark a line on the block that intersects the sawkerf at the back edge, remove the pin, and trim the block to that line.

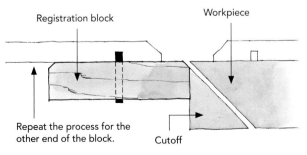

Registration block

Workpiece

Repeat the process for the other end of the block.

Cutoff

3. For precise miters, first cut the workpiece to length, then butt the workpiece against the registration block and cut the miter.

Safer, cleaner cuts on the miter saw

It is difficult to cut small pieces of mitered trim on a power miter saw. The short sections often get eaten up between the blade and the fence or the blade and the guard. Or, if the piece survives, you have to mount a search mission underneath the saw to find it. Also, you can get tearout, which will destroy a small molding, leaving scarcely any smooth, flat surface for a good glue joint.

To solve all of these problems, support small pieces of molding by adding an auxiliary wooden fence to your miter-saw table. I've made many fences of different sizes to fit whatever molding I need to miter. First, cut a rabbet in the front edge of the auxiliary fence to accommodate the size of the molding. Then make three registration cuts in the fence—one at each 45° angle and one at 90°. To keep from cutting the auxiliary fence in two, make the registration cuts only as deep as necessary to crosscut the molding.

Because the auxiliary fence supports the molding on both sides, you get cleaner cuts. You'll find the auxiliary fence especially useful on really short pieces, and the sawkerfs in the fence serve as reference points for your cuts. Mark the cut, slide the line to the edge of the kerf, and cut away. All of the guesswork is eliminated.

—STEVE LATTA, Gap, Pa.

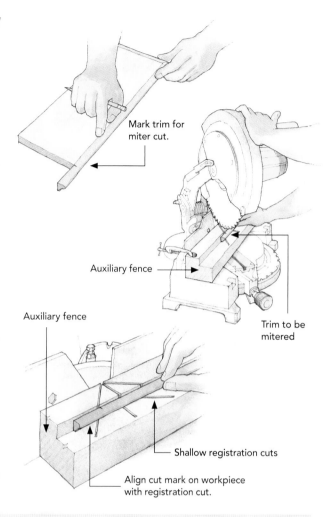

Mark trim for miter cut.

Auxiliary fence

Trim to be mitered

Auxiliary fence

Shallow registration cuts

Align cut mark on workpiece with registration cut.

Sawhorse crosscutting aids

These two hold-down arms are mounted on sawhorses to enable clamp-free crosscutting of long boards. To make them, screw together two arms from scrap offcuts the same thickness as the stock to be cut. Mount the arms to your sawhorses with a thin shim under each one, so that the workpiece will slide under the arms easily. The arms should be mounted in opposite directions—open to you on the near end and closed on the far end (as shown). Properly set up, these arms will lock the board in place and prevent it from pivoting or lifting.

—LOUIS PENNACCHIA JR., Syracuse, N.Y.

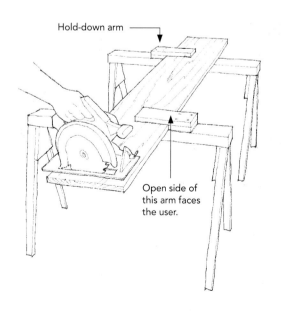

Hold-down arm

Open side of this arm faces the user.

Stop blocks for precise crosscuts

A stop block makes it easy to crosscut multiple pieces to the same length. I use two versions: a short, hinged block and one for pieces that are longer than the miter gauge. With either method, be sure to hold the workpiece tight against the fence and stop block. The hinged block is designed to work with my 3-in.-tall auxiliary fence. A small piece of ¼-in. plywood fastened at the top of the block keeps it about ⅛ in. off the saw table. This gap prevents dust buildup, which can hinder accuracy. The plywood also keeps the stop perpendicular to the table. If a stop block is clamped at an angle, there will be discrepancies in length between pieces of different thickness.

—STEVE LATTA, Gap, Pa.

A hinged block is nice. It lets you trim both ends of a board without changing the setting.

For longer work, a longer stop block. A hooked block, held in place with a pair of clamps, works for even the longest workpieces.

Using the hinge. With the block flipped up, trim one end square (top). Then butt the square end against the block and cut to length (above). Cutting multiples will be quick and accurate.

Tablesaw push sled makes ripping thin strips simple

This sled easily rips thin strips of consistent width without having to reset the fence for every cut. The sled is a piece of ¾-in.-thick hardwood, 6¼ in. wide, with a ¼-in.-deep notch at one end. Install a 1-in.-dia. dowel handle about a third of the way from the back end and add a thin, 2-in.-wide hardboard hold-down strip to help prevent kickback. If your workpiece is thicker than the sled, shim up the safety strip with washers.

To use the sled, set the rip fence so that the desired strip thickness is left between the sled and the blade. Hold the workpiece with your left hand and slide it through. If desired, you can joint the freshly cut workpiece to get a smooth side on the next strip.

—DAVID KILDAHL, Crookston, Minn.

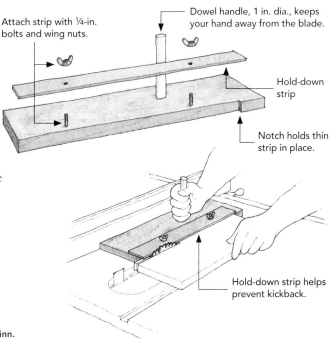

Attach strip with ¼-in. bolts and wing nuts.

Dowel handle, 1 in. dia., keeps your hand away from the blade.

Hold-down strip

Notch holds thin strip in place.

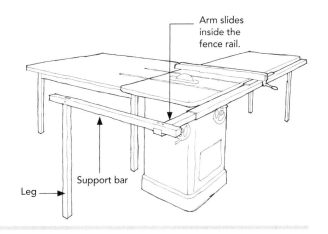

Hold-down strip helps prevent kickback.

SHEET GOODS

Support for ripping plywood

I use this simple support to aid in cutting full sheets of plywood on the tablesaw. It consists of an arm, a support bar, and a leg. Size the arm to fit inside the square tubing of the fence rail on your tablesaw and join the parts so that the support bar is the same height as the saw table. When it is in use, the support rests against the saw table; just pull it out to the width you need.

—VERN TATOR, Friday Harbor, Wash.

Arm slides inside the fence rail.

Support bar

Leg

Clean crosscuts in plywood

Ripping cuts in plywood tend to be clean, but crosscuts are prone to tearout. To eliminate tearout, raise the blade well above the sheet and put the most important face up. Then wrap tape across the bottom and around the ends.

—MARK EDMUNDSON, Sandpoint, Idaho

Folding panel-saw frame saves space

Cutting down full sheets of plywood has always been a hassle. I don't have room in my shop for a commercial panel saw, so I built a version of one that works well and folds flat against the wall when not in use.

To make the fixture, first build a grid by butting and screwing 1×4s on edge. Half-lap joints connect the grid parts. The ends of the grid parts are screwed to the frame. In use, the saw cuts into the front edges of the grid, so keep any screws well back from those edges. Use lag screws to mount a 2×4 ledge to the bottom edge of the grid and drill holes for six rollers—I salvaged wheels from a pair of kid's roller-skates found at a yard sale—to support the sheet.

Next, build the folding A-frame legs by gluing and screwing 1×4s to a 2×4 base. The legs should support the grid at about 80° to the ground. Size the legs so they don't overlap each other when folded flat. Also, extend the feet forward of the rollers for stability.

Before the legs can be mounted, you need to attach a pair of 2×4 cleats to the frame and screw a filler block to the ledge to help transfer the weight of the sheet to the legs without stressing the grid. Use door hinges to mount the A-frame legs to the cleats and the filler block.

A pair of cutting guides—a 5-footer and a 10-footer—completes the project. Each guide is made of a 1×4 glued to ¼-in.-thick hardwood plywood. Cut the plywood wider

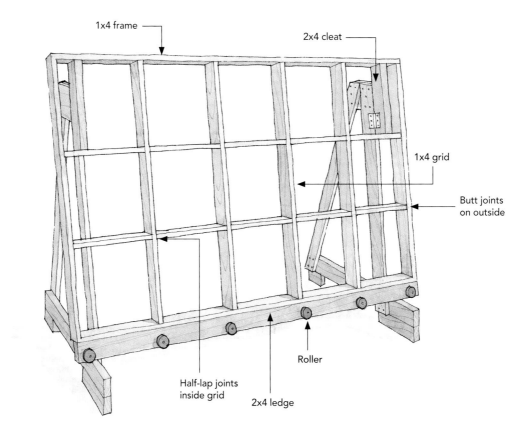

1x4 frame

2x4 cleat

1x4 grid

Butt joints on outside

Half-lap joints inside grid

2x4 ledge

Roller

than necessary and let the first cut with your portable circular saw clean up the edge.

To use, mark both ends of the cut line on the sheet and clamp one end of the guide close to the line. Carefully line the other end right to the other mark. Then go back to the first mark and put the edge of the guide right on it. Secure the sheet to the grid below the cut line with a third clamp to keep the sheet from moving during the cut. Then add a clamp above the cut line to prevent the upper piece of plywood from pinching the blade during the cut. Finally, set your saw depth to no more than ¼ in. more than the sheet thickness and make your cut.

—IVAN HELMRICH, Kansas City, Mo.

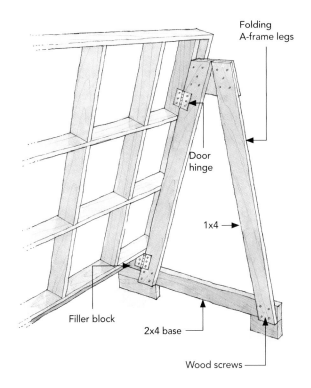

Folding A-frame legs

Door hinge

1x4

Filler block

2x4 base

Wood screws

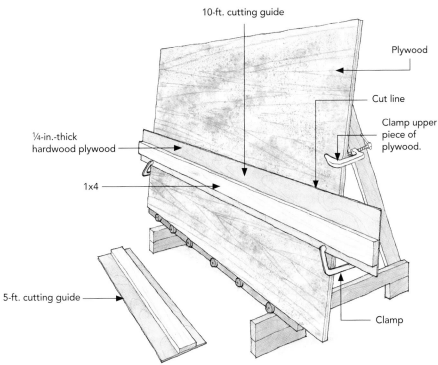

10-ft. cutting guide

Plywood

Cut line

Clamp upper piece of plywood.

¼-in.-thick hardwood plywood

1x4

5-ft. cutting guide

Clamp

Tablesaw fence extension supports a full sheet of plywood

On most tablesaws, cutting a 4×8 sheet of plywood is, at best, a dicey proposition. The sheet is heavy, the rip fence is too short, and, at the beginning of the cut, most of the sheet hangs unsupported in front of the saw.

As a solution, I added a rip-fence extension to my tablesaw. It helps support the right side of the plywood when it's overhanging the front of the saw table.

The extension has just three parts: an auxiliary fence, a ledge, and a clamping block. The auxiliary fence serves as a substitute for the rip fence, extending forward to provide a longer, more positive reference for the right edge of the plywood. The ledge provides vertical support for the overhanging plywood. And the clamping block provides a means to clamp the extension securely to the rip fence.

When cutting the auxiliary fence, make sure its two edges are straight and parallel. The clamping block and ledge attach to the auxiliary fence with glue and a few screws. To use it, clamp the auxiliary fence tightly to the rip fence. Establish the cut width by measuring the distance from the blade to the edge of the auxiliary fence, and lock the rip fence in place. Place the front of the plywood on the saw table, and keep the right-hand edge of the plywood against the auxiliary fence during the cut.

—PHILIP A. HOUCK, Boston, Mass.

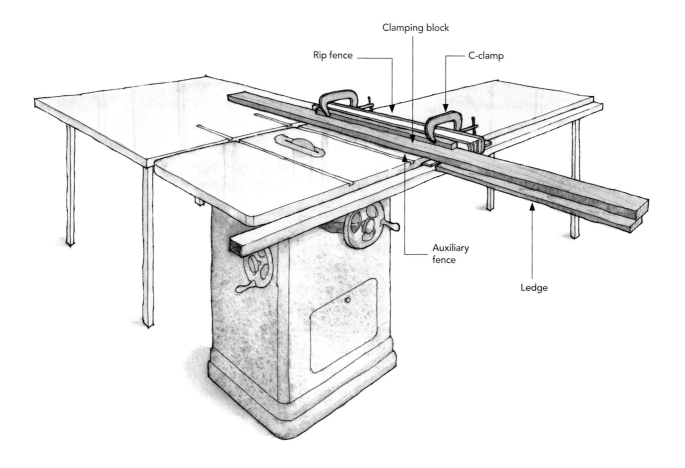

Clamping block

Rip fence

C-clamp

Auxiliary fence

Ledge

TAPERS AND BEVELS

Taper jig combines bandsaw and planer

This jig makes tapered parts accurately and safely. To begin, cut the workpiece to size, making sure all the face and end surfaces are planed flat and square. Then cut the jig from a piece of scrap that's about the same thickness as the workpiece. Cut the scrap about 3 in. longer and 1 in. wider than the workpiece.

Next, mark the taper on the workpiece. Place the workpiece on the jig, centered end to end. Line up the taper marks along the edge of the jig, then trace around the workpiece with a sharp pencil.

Use a bandsaw to cut the jig along the marked line. As you cut, stay slightly on the waste side of the mark. Use a block plane, or sandpaper wrapped around a hardwood block, to straighten and smooth the cut until it meets the line exactly. The workpiece should fit snugly into the cavity.

With the workpiece removed from the jig, use the bandsaw to trim about 1⁄16 in. from the face of the jig's two end sections. This provides clearance for the jig as the workpiece is run through the bandsaw and will help you set up the planer for the final cut.

On the bandsaw, set the fence to make a cut about 1⁄8 in. wider than the jig, then run the jig and workpiece through the blade. For a workpiece with a taper on two adjacent sides, rotate the part 90° and cut again.

The next step is to run the same jig through a thickness planer with the depth set to clear the jig by 1⁄16 in., giving the desired dimension. To minimize tearout along the taper, the thicker end of the workpiece should go into the planer first. If the workpiece has adjacent tapers, rotate the stock 90° and send them through the planer again.

—**MICHAEL FORTUNE**, Lakefield, Ont., Canada

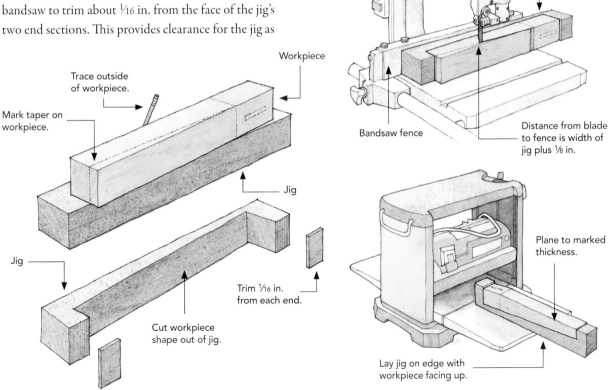

Trace outside of workpiece.

Mark taper on workpiece.

Workpiece

Jig

Jig

Cut workpiece shape out of jig.

Trim 1⁄16 in. from each end.

Lay jig on side.

Bandsaw fence

Distance from blade to fence is width of jig plus 1⁄8 in.

Plane to marked thickness.

Lay jig on edge with workpiece facing up.

Safer bevel cuts on the tablesaw

Most references to cutting bevels on the tablesaw I've seen have the sawblade tilted away from the fence with the workpiece between the fence and the blade. I think this arrangement increases the possibility of burning or gouging the work, and also poses a risk of kickback.

To avoid those problems, I moved the rip fence to the other side of the blade, made an auxiliary fence, and cut bevels a different way. The offcut falls into the large space under the auxiliary fence where it can't bind and kick back, and any wayward movement of the workpiece during the cut produces not a gouge but a high spot, and can be corrected by running the piece through again. It isn't possible to cut too deeply because the fence keeps the workpiece a fixed distance from the blade.

The method also works well at beveling long workpieces lying flat on the saw table, such as cutting octagonal posts from square blanks. By adding a tall fence you can easily and safely use this setup for raising panels.

—TOM LATHROP, Oriental, N.C.

Improved tapering jig for a tablesaw

The tapering jig I use is quick to make, handles longer workpieces, and provides more control and safety.

I simply cut three notches into a scrap piece that's 6 in. or so longer than the workpiece to be tapered, as shown in the drawings below. The width of each notch is one-half the taper. For longer runs or if the final taper is too small to hold securely and safely, I attach the jig to a substrate and use De-Sta-Co toggle clamps to hold the workpiece firmly. The method works great for making tapered back splats.

—TAI LAKE, Holualoa, Hawaii

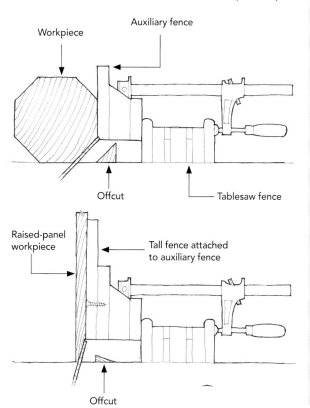

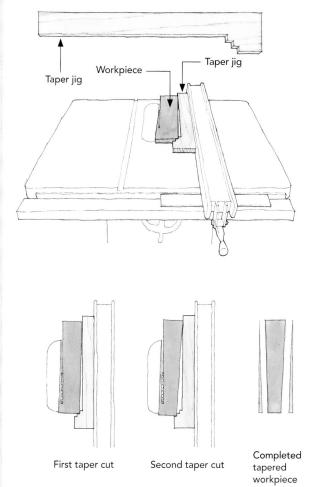

First taper cut   Second taper cut   Completed tapered workpiece

Adjustable jig for cutting tapers

This adjustable tapering jig for the tablesaw is easy to make and sets up in a flash. It replaces all of those dedicated one-time jigs, and it's more reliable than a jig that puts the blank directly on the tabletop.

The fixture is basically a sled with a runner on the bottom that slides in the miter-gauge slot. This arrangement ensures that the edge of the sled is snug against the blade every time. No fence adjustments are required. The jig consists of five main parts: The sled, the runner, a fence at the front that incorporates an adjustable stop block, a hold-down, and a cam-action disk at the back that sets the taper angle.

To make the fixture, cut the 30-in.-long sled from ¾-in.-thick plywood, and cut an equally long hardwood runner to fit the miter-gauge slot. Put the runner in the miter slot, raise the sawblade all the way up, and, with the edge of the sled square against the blade, nail two brads through the sled into the runner to attach it temporarily.

Remove the sled, flip it over, and secure the runner with four countersunk screws. Now attach the fence assembly to the front and the disk to the back. Secure the 3½-in.-dia. disk with a wood screw ¾ in. off center. This creates a cam action that will vary the depth of the taper cut.

To use the jig, first adjust and lock the stop block on the fence to set where the taper will end. Then, with one end of the workpiece against the stop block and the other end against the disk, turn the disk until the finished width of the leg is in line with the edge of the sled. Readjust both stops, if necessary, until everything is perfect. Now push the workpiece blank against the two stops, lock it down, and cut the taper. Turn the blank 90° clockwise and make a second cut. This will produce a leg that is beautifully tapered on two sides. To make a leg that is tapered on four sides, you will need to readjust the disk for cuts three and four.

—DAVID HASTINGS, Haverford, Pa.

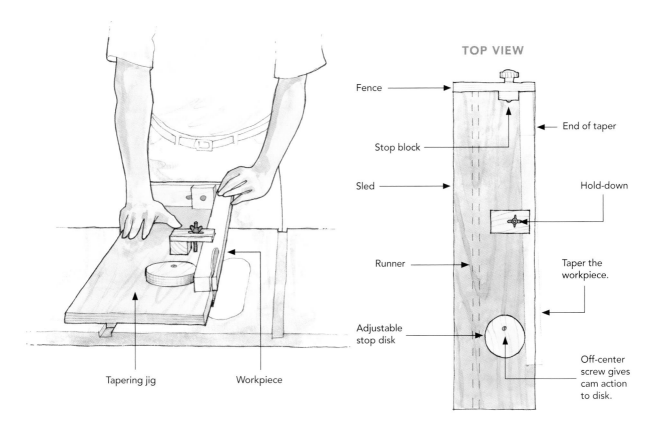

Tapering jig   Workpiece

TOP VIEW

Fence

End of taper

Stop block

Sled

Hold-down

Runner

Taper the workpiece.

Adjustable stop disk

Off-center screw gives cam action to disk.

JOINERY

REPAIRS

Shim a miscut tenon cheek

The cheeks, or faces, of a tenon can be miscut in several ways. Planing a tenon too thin is probably the most common mistake, but you also can create tenons that are twisted or trimmed narrower at one end than the other. The strategy for repairing any of these problems is to glue a slightly oversize shim to the offending side of the tenon and plane away the excess wood until the tenon is square and fits the mortise.

Make sure that the surface to be corrected is flat so that the added piece will have an adequate glue joint. For shim stock, I typically use a thin cutoff of the workpiece material. The grain of the shim should run in the same direction as the tenon so that it will shrink and swell in the same way.

When gluing, I use a thick block as a caul to distribute the clamping pressure evenly. If the shim is very thin, glue can seep through, so I use a sheet of waxed paper to prevent the caul from sticking to the work.

—PHILIP C. LOWE, Beverly, Mass.

A too-slender tenon. A tenon that has been cut or trimmed too narrow creates a weak joint.

Add a shim. Make a shim from the material used for the workpiece and glue it to the tenon. Make sure that the grain runs in the same direction on both pieces.

Trim the excess. After the glue has set, use a shoulder plane to pare the tenon to proper size. Check your progress frequently as you plane away the excess material. Stop when you have a snug fit.

Glues for joinery repairs

For repair work, I typically use the quickest-setting glue I can. Instant glues such as cyanoacrylate can get you working again in a few minutes, but they tend to darken the area around the repair.

Yellow glue works fine for most repairs, but it needs to set for an hour or so. Hide glue is the slowest option; however, its dark color helps some repairs disappear. It's also water soluble, so you can redo the work, if needed.

—PHILIP C. LOWE, Beverly, Mass.

Trim a damaged tenon shoulder

When cutting a tenon shoulder, a common mistake is going too far when sawing it, or making a bad cut with a shoulder plane when trimming it. The best correction is to scribe another line and pare the shoulder to it. Remember that the corresponding tenon shoulders on an opposite rail (or rails) should be trimmed to the same length; otherwise, you will build the frame out of square. You won't always have the room to fix errors in this way because it will change the finished dimensions of the piece.

—PHILIP C. LOWE, Beverly, Mass.

An ugly result. Slips with the shoulder plane can leave unattractive gaps.

Mark out the repair. Scribe a line for a new shoulder just behind the damaged edge (above). Don't forget corresponding parts. You'll need to trim the opposite apron to match the length of the piece you're repairing, so transfer your newly scribed line to the second piece (right).

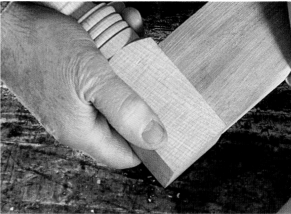

Cut a new shoulder and check the fit. Use the new line as a guide to pare away the waste and create a new surface (left). Careful work with the chisel yields a clean line at the joint (above).

Patch and recut a dado

A dado is cut across the grain and a groove is cut with the grain; both are set in from the end of the board. A rabbet is a dado or groove that is open on one side, such as on the end of a panel. If you cut these joints too wide or deep, fill the cavity, plane it smooth, and cut it again.

Fill a dado with a piece that runs across the grain so that the infill piece will shrink and swell along with the panel. To make an invisible glueline, use cutoff from the end of the panel as the filler. A miscut groove can be fixed the same way, but the grain should run with the length of the groove. For this repair, use cutoff from the edge of the panel if it's large enough; it'll be less visible because the long grain aligns with the edges of the groove.

—PHILIP C. LOWE, Beverly, Mass.

That sinking feeling. The wrong end of the workpiece was against the fence, so the center dado is in the wrong place.

Save your cutoffs. A crosscut scrap from the end of the board is trimmed to fit and glued in place (left). Plane the repair piece flush (right) for a barely detectable repair. The dado can now be recut in the right place.

Fill gaps in dovetails

A number of mishaps can occur when cutting dovetails by hand. If you cut the pins first, like I do, you can wind up miscutting the tails so that they don't mate snugly with the pins. It's also possible to pare a pin too aggressively, causing a poor fit or a weak joint.

If you miscut a tail, go ahead and glue up the work and then fill the gaps by gluing in wedges made from cutoff stock from the pin board. When choosing wood for this repair, look closely at the end grain and try to match the annual growth rings of the pins as closely as possible.

For wedge stock to repair through-dovetails, use waste material that was sawn away from between the pins when you roughed out the work with a coping saw.

Set aside these waste pieces as you cut them.

—PHILIP C. LOWE, Beverly, Mass.

A little too roomy. A mistake with the saw or chisel has resulted in a loose fit around one of the pins.

Fill the gap. Use a chisel to pare a short, thin wedge from a cutoff of the drawer-front material. Orient the grain in the same direction, dab one end in glue, and tap the wedge home between the pin and tail (left). Cut the wedge flush with the surface of the drawer side. After planing the surface, the finished repair disappears (right).

Replace a broken dovetail pin

If you've pared a dovetail pin at an angle, you can repair the mistake with a shim. Glue a piece of small, thin stock to the side of the pin, then trim it flush to the inside face of the board and to the end. Pare the restored pin carefully with a chisel for a tight fit.

It's also possible to salvage a pin that you've broken off or weakened by paring it too small. To do this, I begin by chiseling away the broken pin altogether. Continuing with the chisel, I then cut an open-ended mortise immediately behind the pin location. This mortise will accept an oversize, rectangular replacement piece from which I'll cut a new pin.

The piece, milled from cutoff stock, is glued in place and then sawn, planed, and pared to fit. Use the tail board as a template to mark out the sides of the new pin.

—PHILIP C. LOWE, Beverly, Mass.

This can't be shimmed. A slip with the chisel broke a pin.

Mark out for pin removal. Scribe lines to create a rectangular mortise matching the maximum width of the pin (left). Remove material by making angled chisel cuts to create a ramp to the baseline at the front of the pin. Then pare from the front (right) until the bottom is square.

Use cutoff stock for the repair. Fit and glue in the rectangular repair piece (left). Trim it flush with a saw and handplane. Use the tail board to mark out the sides of the new pin. Then trim it to fit (above).

BISCUITS

Fast-action biscuiting jig

I embraced biscuit joinery years ago, but I never seem to have a flat, usable space to register the base of the joinery while making cuts. This is mainly because my workbench tends to be covered with dried glue, shavings, etc.

A simple, modified bench hook solved the problem. It provides a flat, smooth registration surface and has a pair of fences to hold the work. The best is the split fence, which simplifies cutting biscuit slots in the ends of mitered frames.

The jig is made from ¾-in.-thick melamine. Cut the base to 12 in. wide by 16 in. long and each plywood fence to 2 in. wide by 18 in. long.

Start by cutting a ¼-in. by ¼-in. rabbet along one edge of both fences. The rabbets provide a place for dust and shavings to collect, so they won't prevent the workpiece from butting tightly against the fence.

To install the split fence, first mount it in one piece by screwing from the top and bottom. Then, mark a 4-in.-long cutout in the center. Remove the fence and cut out the marked section. Sand a small radius on all four

corners of the gap. Sanding is important because you'll be wedging workpieces against the corners and you don't want them so sharp that they mar your material. Install all fences with glue and screws.

To cut a slot in the edge of a workpiece, simply hook the split fence on the edge of the workbench and place the workpiece against the straight fence. The melamine provides a smooth and true registration surface.

The jig really shines when cutting the end of a mitered joint. Place the workpiece in the opening of the split fence, then rotate it until it binds in the gap. As you make the cut, apply continuous sideways pressure to prevent the workpiece from moving.

—GORD GRAFF, Newmarket, Ont., Canada

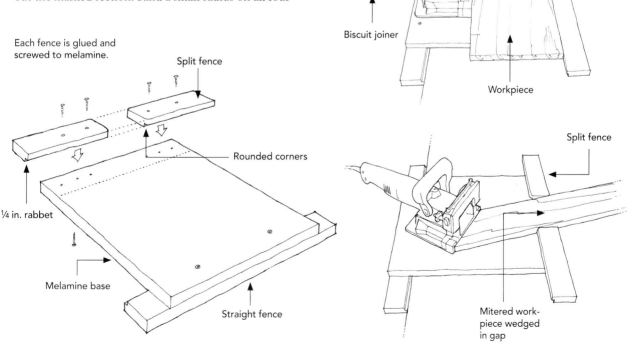

Each fence is glued and screwed to melamine.

Split fence

Rounded corners

¼ in. rabbet

Melamine base

Straight fence

Straight fence

Biscuit joiner

Workpiece

Split fence

Mitered workpiece wedged in gap

Remedying swollen biscuits— two methods

To compress a biscuit swollen with moisture, lay it on a solid surface and strike it a few times with a carpenter's claw hammer. Test it in the slot and strike again, if necessary. The biscuit will swell for a tight fit as soon as glue is applied.

—JIM MILLER, Milan, Ill.

Biscuits can swell in the summer due to humidity and thus become difficult to push into the slots. I solved this problem by throwing a couple of those little silica-gel desiccant packets into my biscuit-storage jars. The packets are commonly found in mail-order shipments.

—CHARLES T. JAMES, Williston Park, N.Y.

Nonslip fence for a biscuit joiner

The biscuit joiner is invaluable for making joints in a snap. However, the tool tends to shift as the blade enters the cut. To hold the joiner steady, manufacturers install pins in the fence, but the pins don't always work when a workpiece is narrow, hard, or slippery.

To improve the grip of the fence, I added a layer of fine-grit adhesive-backed sandpaper. This simple addition is like adding snow tires to your car.

—SERGE DUCLOS, Delson, Que., Canada

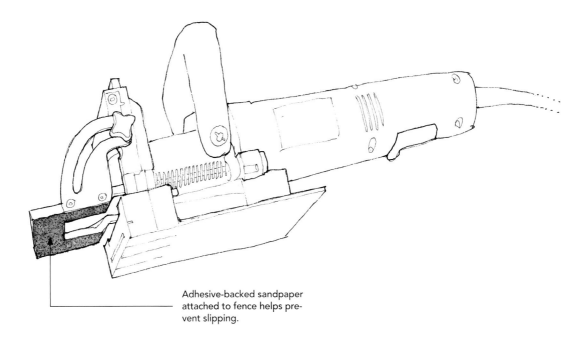

Adhesive-backed sandpaper attached to fence helps prevent slipping.

DADOES AND GROOVES

Jig for routing dadoes

The concept is simple, but this jig is indispensable for routing dadoes in carcase sides, especially when several dadoes are to be made in one board. Once the jig is clamped together, you can slide it quickly into position for the next cut.

Make up two L-shaped pieces with 4-in.-wide plywood strips. Cut the shorter pieces of the Ls 16 in. to 18 in. long (router base plus 8 in. to 10 in.) and the longer pieces 20 in. to 30 in. long (widest carcase plus 8 in.). Face-glue and screw the pieces together, taking care to maintain a 90° angle.

To use, place one L on the front edge of the board to be routed and one on the back edge so that the two Ls form a woven rectangle. Adjust both directions to give a slip fit against the router base and against the sides of the board. Then clamp the intersections of the two Ls. Pencil in an index mark on both sides of the jig to simplify lining up for a cut. Clamp the jig to the board before routing the dado.

—ROGER DEATHERAGE, Houston, Texas

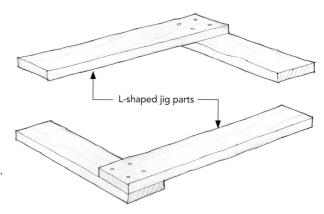

L-shaped jig parts

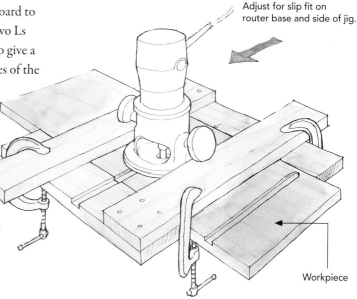

Adjust for slip fit on router base and side of jig.

Clamp jig parts together and clamp jig to workpiece.

Workpiece

Dado sizing board

A "sizing board" makes it easy to remember my stacked-dado setup for a given cut. Every time I cut a dado that has a width I've not used before, I take a minute to cut the same dado in my sizing board. Then, at the bottom of the dado, I note the arrangement of cutters and spacers. The next time I need to cut the same width, all of the pertinent information is there for the taking.

—WILL BRAUN, Lacombe, Alta., Canada

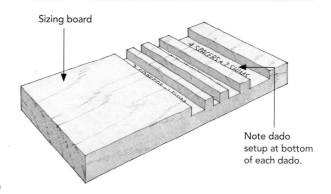

Sizing board

Note dado setup at bottom of each dado.

DOVETAILS

Two ways to lay out dovetails

The dovetail joint is the hallmark of finely crafted furniture. To make this joint as attractive and strong as possible, you need an accurate layout, but the process can be bedeviling. Here are two simple methods that I've used.

One common technique for drawers is to put half-pins at the edges of the board, then find the center and lay out a pin there. If the drawer is tall enough, two more pins are laid out halfway between the edge pins and the center pin, producing three full pins and two half-pins at each edge. If this method is used for a case, the spaces between the pins are split again until a pleasing effect is created and the joint's strength is sufficient (usually a pin every 2 in. to 2½ in.).

Another technique is to divide the width of the board into equal spaces by holding a ruler on a diagonal until the markings line up appropriately. Small marks are made on the inside face of the drawer or carcase and then transferred to the end. Again, the layout marks locate the centers of the full pins, and the two half-pins go at the edges.

—PHILIP C. LOWE, Beverly, Mass.

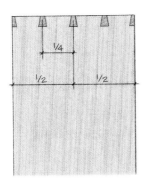
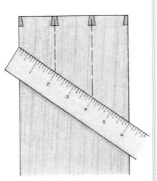

Trick of the eye. Divide the overall width in half by eye, then halve the spaces again as needed. Because the eye excels at dividing a space in half, this method can be done without measuring.

The slanted scale. Angle a scale until the appropriate number of increments line up with the edges of the board. If an inch scale doesn't work, try a metric one. This method will deliver an even or odd number of divisions.

Use graphite to check the fit

When test-fitting dovetails, here's a nifty trick to find the exact places the joint is binding. I mark the bottoms of the tails with a pencil. Then I put the workpieces together and assemble the joint as far as it will go, pound it firmly with my fist, and then take it apart. The graphite will rub off on the tight spots on the pins, indicating exactly where I still need to remove some material. I carefully shave away the pencil marks with a chisel, shaving from the top if the grain is parallel to the length of the pin, or shaving from the inside or the outside if the grain runs in the other direction.

—CHRISTIAN BECKSVOORT, New Gloucester, Maine

Mark the leading edge of all of the tails. A soft #2 pencil works best.

Test the fit. Use your fist to engage the two workpieces, and then pull them back apart.

Shave off the excess with a chisel. The graphite left on the sides of the pins will tell you where you still need to remove material to get the joint to fit perfectly.

Double-up dovetail boards

When it comes to cutting dovetail joints, I'm a firm believer in cutting the tails first. It's more efficient because you can lay out the dovetails on only one piece, then use those marks to cut the tails on two pieces at the same time. And when you transfer those longer layout lines across the end grain of two workpieces and use the lines to sight your saw, you get a more accurate cut. Also, when you cut two pieces at the same time, such as two drawer sides, the resulting joints match visually. So whether you are cutting case parts or drawer sides, lay out the tails, clamp the two workpieces together, and save yourself some time.

—CHRISTIAN BECKSVOORT, New Gloucester, Maine

First, stack and mark. Pencil the layout on the face of only one piece.

Second, transfer the tail marks. Use a pencil and a small square to lay out the tails across the ends of a pair of drawer sides.

Third, make the tail cuts in both workpieces. By cutting the tails in both pieces at the same time, it's actually easier to keep the sawkerf 90° to the face of the boards.

Depth stop for a dovetail saw

I found it difficult to saw exactly to the baseline consistently when making dovetail pins and tails. But this extremely simple jig guarantees absolute accuracy. It consists of a thin strip of wood, the width of which is determined by subtracting the depth of the dovetail from the width of the backsaw blade. Clamp the strip to the saw so that it is parallel to the sawteeth, and cut away until the strip bottoms out on the edge of the board. The result will be perfect stops at the baseline from front to back.

—OLLIVER RANSOME, Ramsgate, South Africa

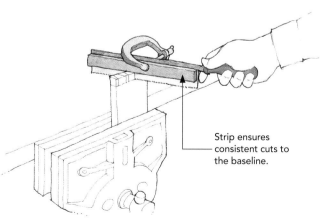

Strip ensures consistent cuts to the baseline.

Cutting a mitered box dovetail joint

A mitered dovetail joint is most commonly used in carcase construction when the edges aren't covered by a face frame, molded strip, or some other kind of decoration. At North Bennet Street School, where I have studied and taught, this is one of the first joints students learn. Many use it to give a more refined look to their toolboxes, the first project the students build.

The joint is more decorative than functional. With normal box dovetails, the exposed edges of a dovetailed carcase appear from the front to be butt-joined, a look that most woodworkers find undesirable. The intent of this mitered box dovetail joint is to make the top and bottom look as if they are joined to the sides with miters, which gives the piece a much more finished appearance.

The joint is made by removing half of the front pin and leaving half of the waste on the tail. Prior to fitting the dovetails, trim the two slightly oversized to approximately 45°. As the dovetails fit deeper and deeper, you will have to trim these mitered surfaces more and more. You can do this with a chisel, but I find it easier and more precise to pass a very fine dovetail saw between the two. The set of the saw's teeth will trim both surfaces at the same time and give you a perfect match.

After the two miters have been trimmed and mated, the joint should draw up tight. It's a simple joint to cut, and it lends a nice effect.

—DAN FAIA, East Wakefield, N.H.

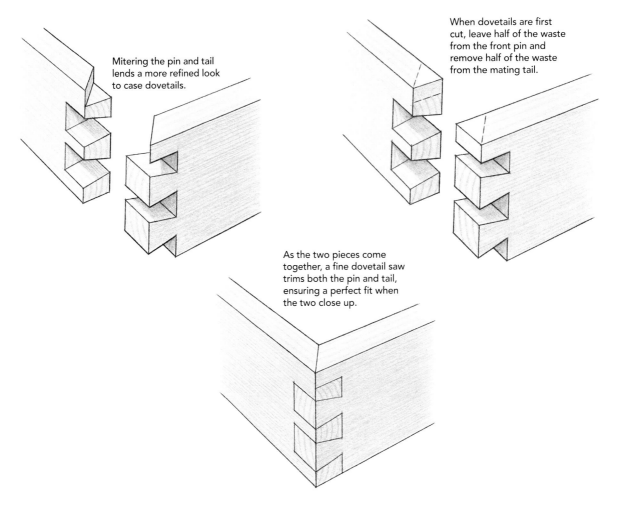

Mitering the pin and tail lends a more refined look to case dovetails.

When dovetails are first cut, leave half of the waste from the front pin and remove half of the waste from the mating tail.

As the two pieces come together, a fine dovetail saw trims both the pin and tail, ensuring a perfect fit when the two close up.

A faster way to make half-blind dovetails

I was fortunate to learn how to cut dovetails from one of the best in the craft. In 1987, I spent two weeks as Alan Peter's assistant at the Anderson Ranch Arts Center. After all of that training, I can cut a set of through-dovetails as fast as I can set up a router jig.

But cutting half-blind dovetails is another story. Although there are some tricks to speed up the process using a router, removing the bulk of the waste from between the pins is mostly a slow and tedious process using a chisel. My solution is to start with a thick drawer front and rip a fat, ⅛-in.-thick slab off the front. I do this while the drawer

front is still oversize in width and length. Then I plane both pieces and set aside the ⅛-in. piece. After that, I cut regular through-dovetails—front and back—and assemble the through-dovetailed drawer. Once the drawer is together, I simply laminate the ⅛-in.-thick piece back onto the drawer front. After trimming the front piece flush on all four sides, I have (from all appearances) a set of perfect half-blind dovetails.

Another advantage of this approach is that I can rip a set of drawer fronts in sequential order from one thick board, resulting in a nicely matched flitch pattern on the fronts of all of the drawers.

—ROB COSMAN, Grand Bay, N.B., Canada

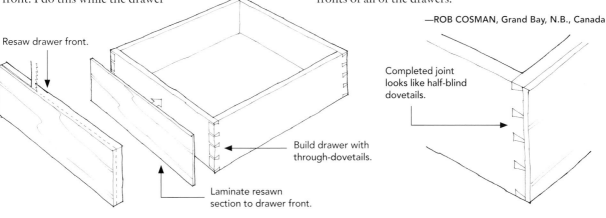

Resaw drawer front.

Build drawer with through-dovetails.

Laminate resawn section to drawer front.

Completed joint looks like half-blind dovetails.

Picture-frame clamps hold dovetail parts for marking

Holding boards in alignment while marking dovetails can be a challenge. Whether you mark with a pencil or a knife, any movement during marking will ruin your work. I solved the problem by using two 90° picture-frame clamps.

Place one on each side of the joint, adjusting the workpieces until they are in perfect registration. Tighten the clamps and mark the pins from the tails (or vice versa). The clamps hold the work firmly and will allow precise adjustments for perfect registration. With proper support, you can even use this method to hold and mark large casework.

—DAVID RAY, Coupland, Texas

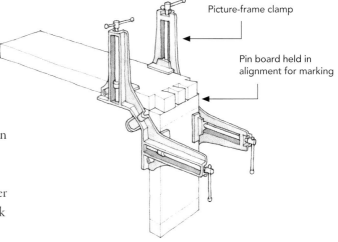

Picture-frame clamp

Pin board held in alignment for marking

Jig for hand-chopping dovetails

This jig puts your chisel exactly where you want it when chopping dovetails. It guarantees that shoulder lines will be perfect on both sides of the pins and tails and will be consistent from one workpiece to another.

The jig consists of a ¾-in.-thick wood or plywood base, two side fences, an adjustable stop, and a hold-down. Cut the side fences from ⅜-in.-thick stock or stock that is thinner than any lumber you will be working. One pair of wing nuts tightens the hold-down onto the workpiece, and another pair of wing nuts, fit over slots, allows adjustment of the stop.

To use the jig, adjust the stop so that the shoulder line of the pins or tails is directly under the edge of the hold-down. Insert the dovetail workpiece by sliding it against one of the side fences, then tighten the hold-down in place. Once the workpiece is secured, hold the chisel against the edge of the hold-down, where it is registered at a perfect 90°, and chop down halfway through the waste. Flip the workpiece to complete the other side.

—JACQUE L. DUPUY, Ft. Leavenworth, Kan.

Flared chisel for dovetail sockets

When I began making half-blind dovetails, I found it difficult to pare the deepest corners of the tail sockets with a regular chisel. So I made a special flared chisel for that purpose by grinding the edges off a regular ⅝-in. paring chisel. The flare at the cutting end should be a bit steeper than the dovetail angle so that you can easily get the tool into the corner of the socket.

You can use a bench grinder to remove the metal, but be sure to dip the chisel in water frequently to keep the cutting edge from overheating. It takes some patience to grind away all of the steel, but your reward will be a tool that makes an awkward job easier to do.

I try not to use the chisel for other tasks when a regular paring chisel will suffice. Each successive sharpening removes a bit of length from the chisel and therefore reduces the width of the flare. I should say, however, that I've been using and sharpening this tool for more than 20 years, and it still does the job well.

—RANDY LEAVITT, South Royalton, Vt.

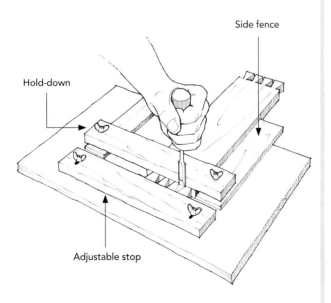

Hold-down

Side fence

Adjustable stop

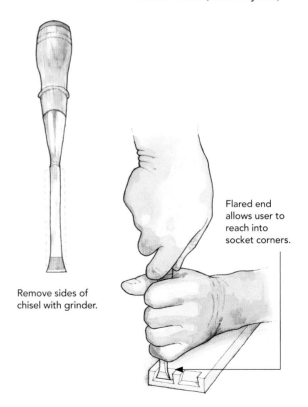

Remove sides of chisel with grinder.

Flared end allows user to reach into socket corners.

Custom-ground blade for tablesawn dovetails

I often cut the tails of a dovetail joint using a tablesaw. But instead of a standard blade, which can't reach all the way into the corner, I use an old thin-kerf blade custom-sharpened for the job. When tilted to the proper angle, the top edges of the teeth are parallel to the surface of the table. The blade cuts a perfect corner, leaving only the small triangle of waste between the cuts that I remove with a scrollsaw or chisel.

You can have a blade ground to your favorite dovetail angle. I chose a 5:1 angle, which works out to $11\frac{1}{2}°$, but you might prefer a 6:1 ($9\frac{1}{2}°$) or an 8:1 ratio ($7°$). The cost of having a blade custom ground is relatively inexpensive. A couple of grinding sources are Forrest Manufacturing (www.forrestblades.com) and Freud Manufacturing (www.freudtools.com/t-sharpen.aspx). The blade will handle its light task for many years without resharpening.

I recommend using a carbide-tipped blade that has a flat-top grind. Square-tipped teeth like this are common on older blades and blades designed for ripping. The problem with alternate-top-bevel (ATB) teeth is that too much of the carbide may have to be removed to get each tooth down to a common angle, and then the blade may not cut properly. Try telling your local sharpening service what you want; they may be able to work with almost any blade.

—STEVE LATTA, Gap, Pa.

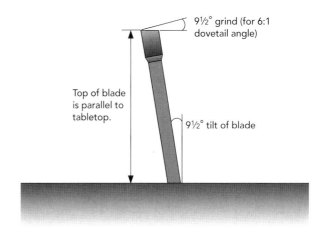

9½° grind (for 6:1 dovetail angle)

Top of blade is parallel to tabletop.

9½° tilt of blade

Tablesaw setup. Use a tall support board attached between two miter gauges. A simple stop and clamp allow for accurate repeat cuts.

Angled teeth make for perfect tail cuts. With the sawteeth ground to the dovetail angle, the blade can be tilted to the same angle, making the top of the cut flush with the scribe line. Only a small triangle of waste stock is left.

Routing dovetails on turned posts

I made a round Shaker stand and used a different technique for cutting the sliding dovetails into the base of the post. The usual approach is to index the post between centers on the lathe and build a box above the lathe ways that allows a sliding router to cut the dovetails. Being a one-armed woodworker, I didn't feel comfortable with this approach.

Instead, I made a fixture that is a triangular box. The post is locked into the box by stub tenons turned on both ends of the post that fit tightly into holes in the triangular ends of the fixture. To cut the dovetails I slid the fixture along the router-table fence, then I removed the stub tenon on the bottom of the post.

To cut the slots, I used three router bits: A ¾-in. straight bit to mill a flat (the base of the turned post protrudes slightly from the triangular box before you make this cut), a ½-in. straight bit to hog out the waste, and a dovetail bit to rout the dovetail slot. It's essential to use a stop block to control the length of the router-bit cuts.

—LESLIE DAVIS, Tottenham, Ont., Canada

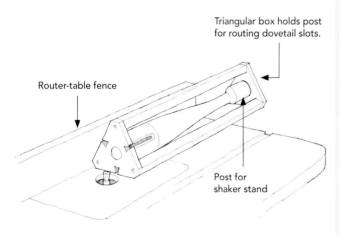

Router-table fence

Triangular box holds post for routing dovetail slots.

Post for shaker stand

Remove stub on bottom after routing slots.

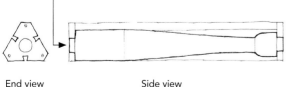

End view   Side view

Bandsaw dovetail fixture

To cut dovetail joints, I start with the pins, cutting everything on my bandsaw. One problem that I ran into was that the table on my bandsaw—like that on most bandsaws—tilts in only one direction, limiting me to cut only one side of the pins. To overcome this problem, I built a small platform of laminated plywood that is angled at the correct dovetail slope.

I simply place the platform in front of the bandsaw blade, pushing it into the blade slightly to keep the blade from wandering. I cut one side of all of the pins, flip the platform around, and cut the other sides. I then remove the waste with a chisel, mark the tails from the pins, and saw the tails on the regular bandsaw table. This approach results in quick and accurate dovetails.

If you like to use different dovetail angles in different woods, just build two platforms—one for softwood and one for hardwood.

—BRUCE PETERSEN, Canby, Ore., Canada

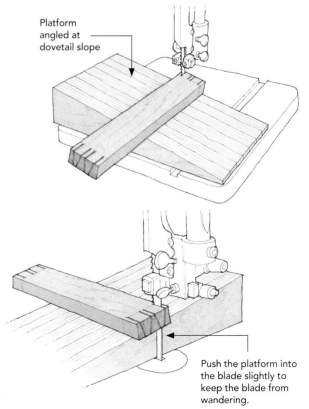

Platform angled at dovetail slope

Push the platform into the blade slightly to keep the blade from wandering.

Dovetail hold-down guides chisel

I've made several aids for hand-cutting dovetails, but the most useful is this hold-down fence. It not only clamps the workpiece but also guides the chisel while chopping out the pins.

The hold-down consists of two sturdy hardwood blocks, 1 in. thick or so, drilled to receive two carriage bolts. The holes in the blocks should match the spacing of the dog holes in your workbench. To use, push the top block down through the bench, and slide the bottom block over the bolts. Clamp the workpiece under the top block, carefully aligning the face of the fence with the scribed line on the workpiece. Tighten the knobs. You're now ready to chop one side of the pins or tails. Don't chop all the way through. Rather, flip the workpiece, re-align it, and complete by chopping from the other side.

—CLARK KELLOGG, Houston, Texas

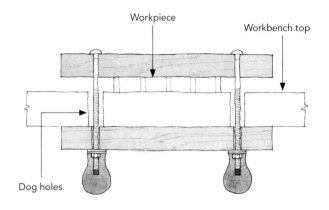

Workpiece

Workbench top

Dog holes

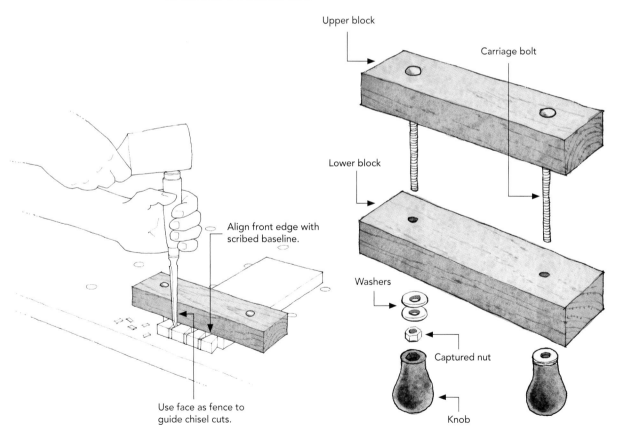

Align front edge with scribed baseline.

Use face as fence to guide chisel cuts.

Upper block

Carriage bolt

Lower block

Washers

Captured nut

Knob

Cutting square pin walls in half-blind dovetails

After I cut the initial kerfs in half-blind dovetails, I use a modified saw to finish the kerf squarely. I took an inexpensive dovetail blade and filed off the teeth from about 2 in. of the forward end of the blade. Some people use an old scraper blade for this technique. While that will work, I prefer a sawblade that has a spine. The spine protects the striking tool, which, in turn, lets me make better contact with the pin corners.

Once the initial diagonal kerfs have been sawn, I set the toothless part of the blade in the kerf, sighting it to line up with my layout lines. Then I pound out the channel with a deadblow hammer or mallet. I don't try to get the blade all the way in with one blow. That's a sure way to split out the sides. Instead, I pound out a little at a time, working the toothless blade out of the kerf, resetting and pounding it in a bit farther, and pulling it out again. I repeat these steps until the saw fits squarely into the corner of the pocket. It usually takes about three repetitions until the chisel has a clear path to follow.

The toothless blade cuts cleanly to the base of the pin wall, reducing the leftover diagonal of wood to a tiny corner nib. This method makes cleanup of the pins more accurate, too.

—KAREN WALES, Chamberlain, Maine

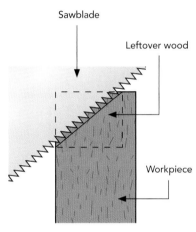

Saw a diagonal kerf. The kerf of a half-blind dovetail leaves a diagonal of wood that can be difficult to chisel out clearly.

Sawblade

Leftover wood

Workpiece

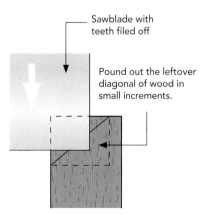

Sawblade with teeth filed off

Pound out the leftover diagonal of wood in small increments.

Define the walls with a modified sawblade. Pound out pin walls in small increments, tapping the blade out of the kerf, realigning it, and driving it in farther, until the pin walls are defined.

Clean out the corners with a skew chisel. Use a bench chisel to clean out the majority of the tail pockets. Then turn to a skew chisel to remove the corner nib, which is hard to reach with a flat-edged chisel.

MITERS

A hidden spline for miter joints in furniture

There are many different ways to strengthen a miter joint: dovetails, mortise and tenons, half laps, and, of course, splines. I recommend using a hidden-spline miter. This joint is used by many furniture makers because it's quick, easy, adds strength, and conceals splined edges in furniture.

Cutting the hidden-spline miter is as simple as setting up your tablesaw. First, cut and fit the miters as you would on any other project, saving the miter waste for later. Make a simple 45° sawing block that is a little thicker than the frame stock, tall enough to give you a good reference, and long enough to clamp to the rip fence. Like your miters, the sawing block should be exactly 45°.

Adjust the dado set on your tablesaw to about one-third the thickness of your stock. Set the distance from the rip fence to the center of the dado set, which should be the exact center of the frame stock. It is helpful to draft a plan view of a corner to determine blade height and cut length. Tracing the dado set with these two dimensions figured out will give you the exact shape of the spline.

Once you've adjusted the rip fence, pass the sawing block through the dado set. Set the block to the appropriate locations determined by the drawing. Mill a couple of sample pieces while you mill the frame stock so you can test-cut all of your settings and adjust, if necessary.

Using the sawing block as your guide, gently plunge the miter into the sawblade, then pull back on the stock to remove it. The piece will not kick back because the block acts as a stop. Repeat this on all of your miters to achieve the slots for the splines.

Mill spline stock to fit the slots snugly but not too tight. Oversize splines could split the stock. Take the time to glue on the miter cutoffs from the first step. This allows you to get great clamping pressure on all four corners, with the flexibility to use the clamps for adjusting the frame. After the glue has set, the clamping blocks may be removed. Bandsaw or handsaw off the blocks close to the frame and flush the excess with a handplane.

—DAN FAIA, East Wakefield, N.H.

Careful setup. Cut a sawing block to 45° and pass it over a dado set, with its kerf adjusted to about one-third the thickness of the stock. The distance from the fence to the center of the blade should equal half the stock thickness.

Clamping down. Set the block into place over the blade, making sure that the blade kerf won't cut through the outside end of the miter. Once the positioning is correct, use a heavy clamp to hold the block in place.

Plunge-cut into the blade. Lower the mitered workpiece onto the blade, using the block as a guide. Once the kerfs have been cut on two mating pieces, spline material is thicknessed, shaped, and set into place.

No-measure mitered boxes

Here's a technique for making mitered boxes that eliminates all of the measuring and fussing to get the mitered parts to fit perfectly. I use the technique on veneered boxes with medium-density-fiberboard cores, but the basic approach will work with any box where the four sides and top join with miters.

Start by applying veneer to a core piece for the top and the sides, including a little extra material for the mitered bevels. Rip all four sides of the box to width (box height) and then square the sides to a little over their final lengths. With the tablesaw blade set at 45°, bevel one long edge and one end of each side piece. Then bevel one edge and one end of the top.

Now set the fence to the desired width of the top. Bevel the other long side of the top and—without changing the fence setting—bevel the two short sides to length. Reset the fence to the desired length of the top and bevel the short side of the top. Again, without changing the fence setting, bevel the two long sides to length.

Run a ¼-in.-wide by ¼-in.-deep groove on the inside of each side piece, ¼ in. up from the bottom edge. This groove will hold the bottom of the box. Cut the bottom from ¼-in. plywood to fit the groove and glue up the box with web clamps or masking tape. Later, after the glue has set, saw the top off the box to produce the lid.

If your fence is square to the blade and your blade is accurately set at 45°, the joints are guaranteed to be perfect. The top will drop into the bevels in the sides with a satisfying precision.

—PAT GRIFFITH, Ottawa, Ont., Canada

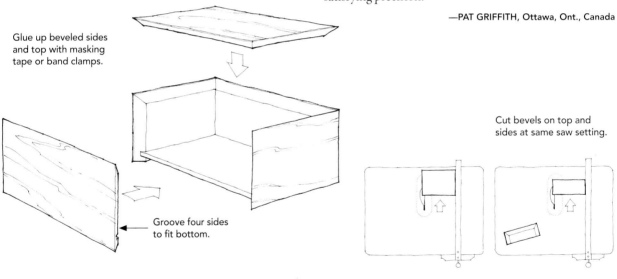

Glue up beveled sides and top with masking tape or band clamps.

Groove four sides to fit bottom.

Cut bevels on top and sides at same saw setting.

Painless miter joints

Making strong, tight miter joints can be a daunting job. Miter joints are inherently weak, hard to clamp and—for me—difficult to cut accurately. Notwithstanding those obstacles, I've discovered a couple of tricks to cut tight, strong miter joints quickly and easily.

First of all, I rough-cut the mitered members on my chopsaw. Then I move each frame member to a shooting board, where I can quickly produce a dead-accurate polished miter with a low-angle jack plane, as shown in the sketch. I seal the end grain with a thin coat of glue, let it absorb into the end grain, then add a little more glue and assemble the joint. If I've done a good job shooting my miter cuts, the whole thing almost holds itself together with just the tack of the glue. I then add one of those nifty little pinch clamps to each corner—the kind that are applied by hand. (The ding that the pinch clamp makes is eliminated in the next step.) Masking tape also works well to pull the miter joints together.

After the glue has thoroughly set, I carefully clamp one corner of the frame in my vise at 45°. Using a stiff

backsaw or dovetail saw I cut a kerf in the joint to accept one or two reinforcing splines. I cut spline material from veneer, apply glue, insert the spline in the kerf, and clamp across the kerf. Once the glue has set, I plane or sand off the protruding portion of the spline.

—ANDREW DIZON, San Diego, Calif.

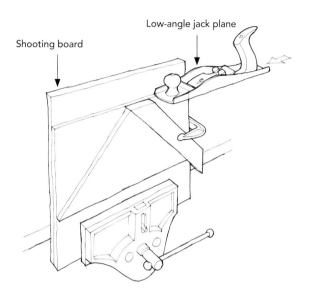

Shooting board

Low-angle jack plane

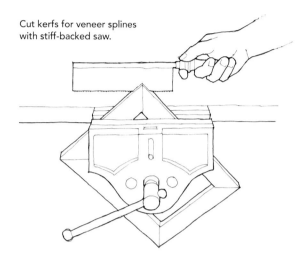

Cut kerfs for veneer splines with stiff-backed saw.

Tablesaw miter jig

This tablesaw jig has helped me to cut accurate miters for 25 years. To make it, cut two table-length rails from well-seasoned oak or hickory and sand to a sliding fit in the slots. With the rails in place in the channels, set the ½-in. plywood base (cut a little smaller than the saw table) on the rails so that the midpoint of the forward edge is aligned with the sawblade. Fasten the base to the rails with ¾-in. flathead screws. Now slide the jig back, raise the sawblade, and saw into the jig 3 in. or so. From the center of the kerf, extend the saw line to the backside of the jig. Mark two lines 45° from the saw line with a draftsman's triangle and fasten the two 1-in.-wide fences on the lines with screws.

Ordinarily, I use the front edges of the fences to hold the pieces to be cut. But to cut, say, the four pieces for a

picture frame, cut the pieces square to length plus twice the thickness of the sawkerf and use the back edges of the jig fences. One fence aligns the work, the other serves as a stop.

—BAYARD M. COLE, Marietta, Ga.

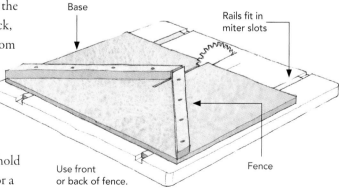

Base

Rails fit in miter slots

Use front or back of fence.

Fence

Cutting spline slots with a biscuit joiner

This technique for cutting spline slots in the corners of small boxes is safer and faster than using a sliding 45° jig on the tablesaw. The splines not only add strength to the corner joint, but they also are quite attractive.

To make this jig, start with a base of ¾-in.-thick plywood and add two sets of fences to the top—one to register the box and another to register the biscuit joiner 45° to the box corner. Adjust the biscuit-joiner fences high enough that you can raise the joiner with spacers to cut splines at different heights off the bottom. I use spacers that are ¼ in., ½ in., and ¾ in. thick to produce several height combinations.

To use the jig, place the box into the corner, against the registration fence, and bring the biscuit joiner into position at the height for cutting the first slot. This may require a spacer. You want the spline slot to be as deep as possible without cutting through to the inside of the box. Set the depth (by varying the biscuit-size setting) and then cut the slot by plunging the joiner into the box. Rotate the box to cut slots in all four corners at that setting, then flip the box and repeat the process. Raise the joiner again with a spacer and repeat the process as many times as needed to cut the desired number of spline slots in all four corners.

Cut the spline material from a contrasting wood and glue it in the slots. After the glue dries, you can trim and sand the splines flush with the box sides.

—WALTER E. ERCK, Mount Prospect, Ill.

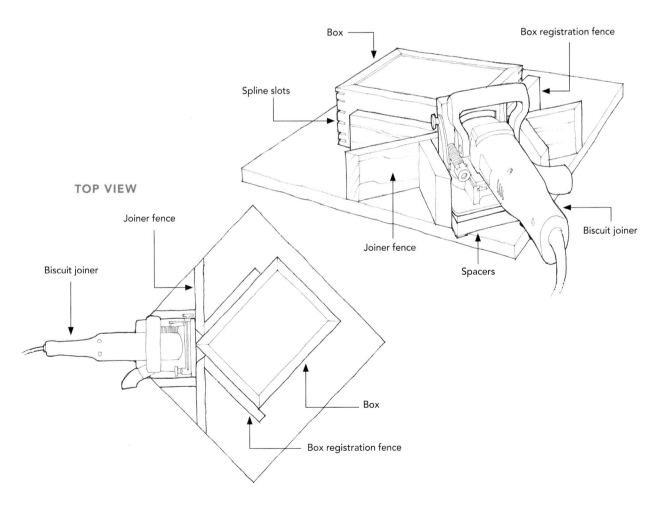

TOP VIEW

Box

Box registration fence

Spline slots

Joiner fence

Joiner fence

Spacers

Biscuit joiner

Biscuit joiner

Box

Box registration fence

Miters for stock of different widths

In several pieces of my furniture, I have a foot molding where I've joined two pieces of wood of unequal widths in a miter. Mitering stock of uneven widths isn't hard to do, but it does mean that the miter will not be 45°. With pieces of unequal width, you have to use the pieces themselves to help you mark your lines to cut.

First scribe the width of the narrower piece onto the wider piece, and then the width of the wider piece onto the narrower piece. Now mark a diagonal cut line from the outside corner of the piece down to the line you've just marked.

You may need to make the cut by hand or on a bandsaw because a chopsaw may not be able to handle this angle. Clean up your mitered edges with a handplane or sander for the best fit. The two pieces will join at 90°.

—CHRISTIAN BECKSVOORT, New Gloucester, Maine

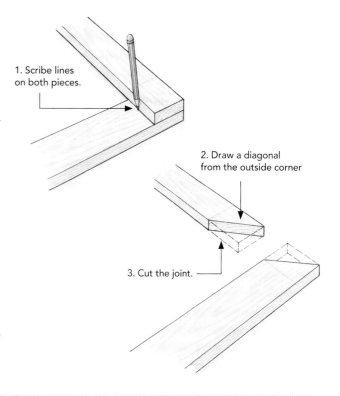

1. Scribe lines on both pieces.

2. Draw a diagonal from the outside corner

3. Cut the joint.

Miter-saw shooting board

I like to add cock-bead trim to the drawers and doors of my furniture. In the past, I have mitered the cock bead using a 45° shooting board and a chisel. To speed things up, I decided to make a shooting board for my miter saw.

Here's how to make it: Laminate a piece of solid-wood scrap to a plywood bottom to make a block about 1½ in. thick by 4 in. wide by 16 in. long. Then, on the tablesaw, cut a groove lengthwise in the solid-wood part of the jig to hold the cock bead. The plywood on the bottom provides stiffness once this groove has been cut. The groove needs to provide a snug fit for the cock bead and be cut deep enough to support the entire width of the stock to prevent splintering when it's cut.

Next, clamp the shooting board to the miter saw and make a 45° cut. Without moving the shooting board, place the cock bead into the groove, adjust its length and make the miter cut. The jig will allow you to set the length perfectly and cut a miter that is as smooth as glass.

—JON C. UITHOL, Madison, Ind.

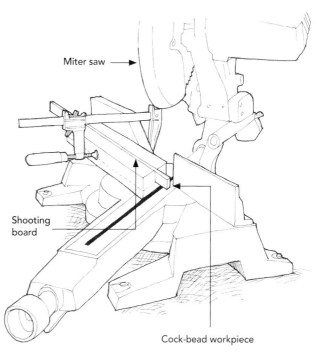

Miter saw

Shooting board

Cock-bead workpiece

Router jig for keyed miter slots

When building a large picture frame for a friend, I needed to add keys to the miters for strength. The problem was that the frame was more than 60 in. long on each side. In the past, I had always used a simple cradle jig on the tablesaw to hold the frame upright while cutting the slot. But this frame was much too large for that. My solution was to use this simple fixture and a bottom-bearing-guided, slot-cutting bit in a router.

To make the jig, cut two plywood pieces at 45° and attach them to a ¼-in.-thick plywood base so they meet at 90°. The fences should be the thickness of or thicker than the frame, and the base should be sized so that it supports the frame sufficiently. To use, clamp the frame into the notch and run the bearing-guided router down the fixture to cut the key slot in the corner of the frame. You'll need to make test cuts to get the slot height just right.

—GARY BRACKETT, Oneonta, N.Y.

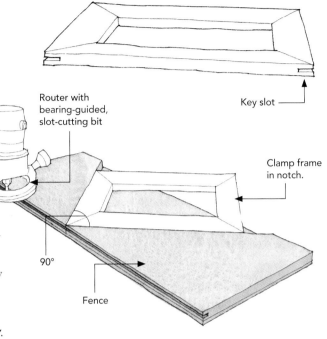

Router with bearing-guided, slot-cutting bit

Key slot

Clamp frame in notch.

90°

Fence

Accurate cuts using a tablesaw's miter gauge

Here's a simple, precise method for cutting 45° miter joints using your tablesaw's miter gauge. All you need is a pair of drafting triangles.

Place the long edge of one triangle against the miter gauge. Adjust the gauge so that its leading edge is pointing toward the blade. Set the other triangle against the body of the blade, not a tooth. Now slide the miter gauge forward until the triangles meet; once the triangles are flush to each other and to the blade and gauge, lock down the miter gauge, and you're ready to go. Check the setup using scraps before you use your good stock.

—STEVE LATTA, Gap, Pa.

Simple method for perfect miters. Use a pair of drafting triangles to set the miter gauge for a precise 45° cut.

MORTISE-AND-TENON JOINTS

Square holes for square pegs

I like to build Craftsman-era furniture and my pieces usually include square pegs. To cut square holes for these pegs, I bought extra ¼-in. and ⅜-in. hollow-chisel mortising bits and I honed them razor sharp.

To cut a square hole, I place the bit where the peg will be inserted and give it a few whacks with a mallet. I then remove the waste with a chisel and glue the square peg in place. Then I bevel the edges of the peg with a chisel.

—JACK HINKEL, Apex, N.C.

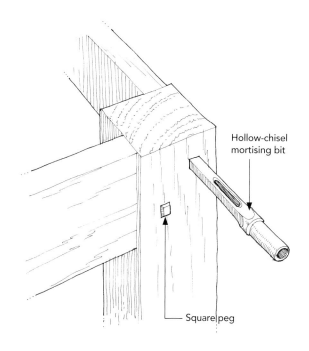

Hollow-chisel mortising bit

Square peg

Chisel handle for paring mortises

Joining furniture with mortise-and-tenon joints can be a problem if you don't have a mortiser to cut square holes. You must either square up the mortises with a chisel or round the tenons with a rasp. I square up, and I've found that the best way to do this is to guide the chisel with my hands while applying pressure to the back of the chisel with my shoulder. But after spending an entire day squaring up more than 100 mortises, I had a sorely bruised shoulder from pushing the chisel.

So I dismantled the chisel and made a new handle with a mushroom-shaped end, similar to an old-fashioned hand drill. (I used a nice piece of boxwood that I had never found a good use for.) It works fine now: Pushing the chisel with my shoulder doesn't give me a pain.

—RUDI WOLF, Les Plantiers, France

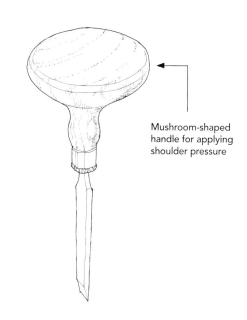

Mushroom-shaped handle for applying shoulder pressure

Jig for making breadboard ends

To keep a tabletop flat, furniture makers often put breadboards on the ends. They're attached to the top with a wide mortise-and-tenon joint. The trick is cutting the tenons so that their top and bottom shoulders align.

This jig slips over the end of the tabletop and provides a router guide to cut the tenon cheeks on the ends of the top. The jig is made of plywood and scraps milled to the thickness of the top. It's held in place by wedges and allows you to rout the tenons quickly and accurately on both sides of the tabletop. Once the cheeks are cut, trim the stub tenons to length with a handsaw or jigsaw.

—SCOTT GIBSON, East Waterboro, Maine

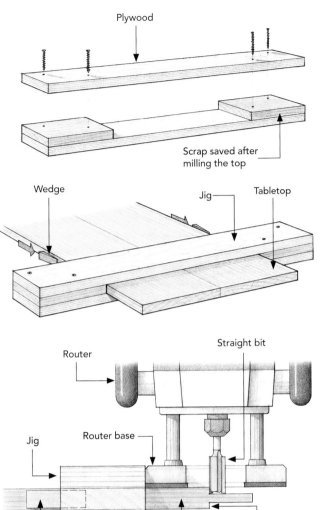

Plywood

Scrap saved after milling the top

Wedge

Jig

Tabletop

Router

Straight bit

Router base

Jig

Wedge

Tabletop

Shoulder

BREADBOARD ENDS KEEP TOP FLAT

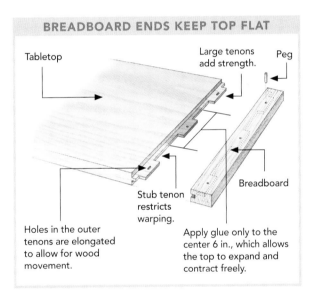

Tabletop

Large tenons add strength.

Peg

Breadboard

Stub tenon restricts warping.

Holes in the outer tenons are elongated to allow for wood movement.

Apply glue only to the center 6 in., which allows the top to expand and contract freely.

USING THE JIG

Hold the jig in place. Tap wedges between the sides of the top and the jig at the back so that it won't move during routing.

Rout the tenon. Butt the router against the edge of the jig. Rout out the tenon waste in two passes.

Flip the tabletop. The best part of this jig is that once one side is done, you simply flip over the board and rout the other side.

Ideal tenon for a wide table apron

For a large table with a wide apron, I recommend a crenellated tenon: two or more large tenons with a shorter stub tenon in between. The joint can also attach breadboard ends to a large panel to keep it flat.

One of the large tenons should be loose in its mortise, allowing it and the width of the apron or panel to move. The stub tenon keeps the parts flush with each other. For example, for a 7-in.-wide apron, make the tenons about 1¾ in. wide each with a ½-in. haunch at the top and a ¼-in. shoulder at the bottom. This leaves 2¾ in. for the central stub portion.

The specific configuration of the joint depends on the application. For instance, the position and fit of the longer tenons on a tabletop should fix the joint at the center and allow movement at both ends. On a drop lid for a desk, the joint should be fixed on the hinge side and only move on the side opposite the hinges. That way the lid will always operate without binding.

Cut the top haunch and top tenon for a snug fit, so when the wood moves, the top edge of the apron will remain flush with the end of the leg. For a 7-in.-wide apron, about ⅟₁₆ in. of room should be left above and below the lower tenon.

—MARIO RODRIGUEZ, Cherry Hill, N.J.

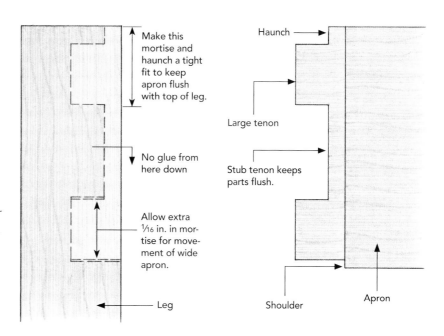

Make this mortise and haunch a tight fit to keep apron flush with top of leg.

No glue from here down

Allow extra ⅟₁₆ in. in mortise for movement of wide apron.

Leg

Haunch

Large tenon

Stub tenon keeps parts flush.

Shoulder

Apron

Tablesaw tenoner

This jig, designed to cut tenons and bridle joints on the tablesaw, performs as well as expensive commercial versions. It consists of a base, which travels in the miter-gauge slot, and a fence assembly. Dadoes in the fence assembly slide on rails in the top of the base to allow the blade-to-fence distance to be varied. The two pieces are locked at the right position by a nut mortised in a block of wood. Make the other jig parts of high-quality ¾-in.-thick plywood.

To use the jig, clamp the work to the fence, or use a hold-down clamp mounted on the fence. Align the jig for the cut and push it through the saw.

—LARRY HUMES, Everson, Wash.

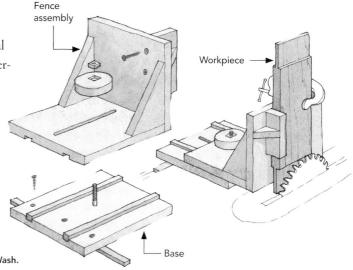

Fence assembly

Workpiece

Base

Large wedge for cutting angled tenons

For right-angle workpieces, cutting tenons on the table-saw is fairly straightforward—just set the miter gauge at 90°, position the rip fence as a stop, and remove the waste with repeated cuts. The process gets trickier, however, for angled tenons.

Setting the miter gauge to the desired angle allows for cutting only one shoulder. And changing the miter-gauge angle for the opposite side is time-consuming. However, this simple wedge-shaped insert makes it easy to cut angled tenons.

Working from plans or a full-scale layout, set the miter gauge to the angle at which the tenoned piece joins its mate. Cut a scrap piece and adjust the miter gauge until it is set just right. Next, you need to cut a wedge insert with an angle twice that of the joint angle. To do

this, first cut an 8-in.- or 10-in.-wide piece of plywood or particleboard at the joint angle. Then flip over the piece and cut off a wedge from the same end. The wedge will have an angle that measures twice the joint angle, and you can use the wedge with the miter gauge to make the tenon cuts on the second side of the angled workpieces. If necessary, secure the wedge to the miter-gauge fence with a brad, a screw, or a dowel to keep it from shifting around during use.

To use the wedge, cut the first tenon cheek using the miter gauge at the angled setting and the rip fence as a stop. Then place the wedge insert against the miter-gauge fence, turn over the workpiece, and cut the second tenon cheek. The shoulders will match exactly.

—LLOYD MARSDEN, Sheridan, Wyo.

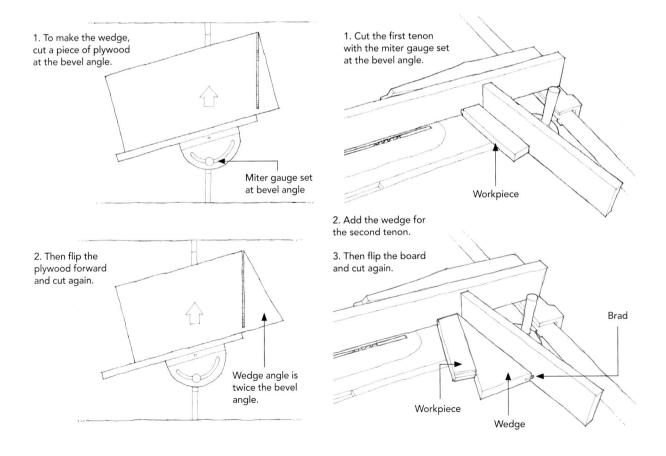

1. To make the wedge, cut a piece of plywood at the bevel angle.

Miter gauge set at bevel angle

2. Then flip the plywood forward and cut again.

Wedge angle is twice the bevel angle.

1. Cut the first tenon with the miter gauge set at the bevel angle.

Workpiece

2. Add the wedge for the second tenon.

3. Then flip the board and cut again.

Brad

Workpiece

Wedge

Router-cut mortises made easy

This simple router-mortising jig has two sections that are clamped to both sides of the workpiece to provide a wide, stable routing platform and to control the length of the mortise cut. The jig, which is used with a fence on the router, can be set to make just about any length of mortise on any thickness of wood. Best of all, you can put it together from scraps in no time.

Each jig section consists of a stop screwed at a right angle to the top edge of a rail. For smaller mortises, ¾-in.-thick by 3-in.-wide stock will work fine for both the rails and the stops. You may want to scale up the jig for larger mortises or use thicker stock to provide a wider platform for mortising thinner workpieces. When sizing the jig, just be sure the rails are long enough so that the stops overlap the rails when the rails are clamped to the workpiece. You also can chamfer the bottom edge of the stops to aid in clearing debris.

Before using the jig, clamp it to a piece of scrap and rout a short mortise by bumping the base of the router against each stop. Use the ends of the mortise to mark a square pencil line across the top of each rail. This line will register the distance from the router baseplate to the outside edge of the bit, and you can use it to align the jig quickly with your mortise layout lines. The registration lines work only for one size of router bit, but the jig is so easy to make that I have a separate one for each bit that I use to cut mortises.

If the mortise is near the end of a workpiece, add a piece of scrap the same thickness as the workpiece to provide a longer clamping base.

—ROB STERLING, Boise, Idaho

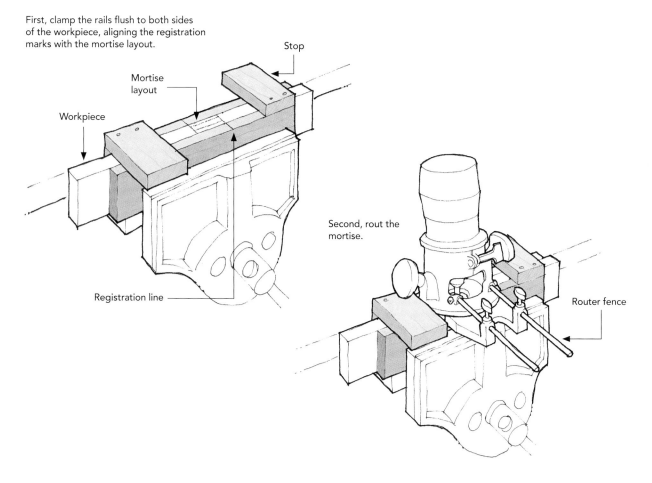

First, clamp the rails flush to both sides of the workpiece, aligning the registration marks with the mortise layout.

Stop

Mortise layout

Workpiece

Registration line

Second, rout the mortise.

Router fence

Router jig cuts many different mortises

This self-contained mortising jig is used with a router template guide to cut mortises of nearly any size.

Made from two pieces of ⅛-in.-thick MDF, a smaller top plate rides on a larger bottom plate and adjusts with paired slots and ¼-in. bolts fastened with wing nuts. Because the paired adjustment slots are at right angles to each other, the rectangular cutouts in the plates can be combined to create an infinite variety of template sizes. Cut the slots and the cutouts with a straight bit in a table-mounted router fitted with a fence. When cutting a mortise, install a ½-in. o.d. template guide in the router and a ¼-in. spiral-cut bit, for an offset of ⅛ in. Square the two plates to each other before locking them down.

—MICHAEL WALKER, Sherwood Park, Alta., Canada

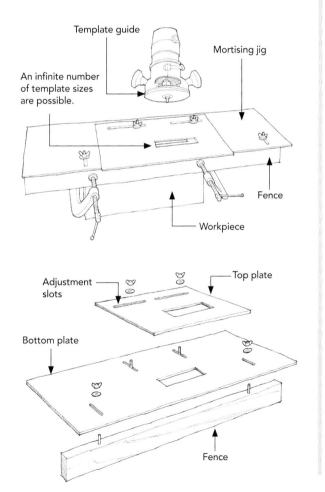

Template guide

An infinite number of template sizes are possible.

Mortising jig

Fence

Workpiece

Adjustment slots

Top plate

Bottom plate

Fence

Two-fence router mortising

By adding an extra fence to your router, you can cut mortises quickly and accurately, and you virtually eliminate the risks of the router wandering or tipping into the cut. Start with a router that has a substantial fence equipped with a threaded micro-adjustment mechanism. Buy a second fence and attach it to the rails, extended through the router base so that it faces the original fence. Sandwich the workpiece snugly between the two fences, and make the necessary micro-adjustments to align the bit with the desired mortise location. Trial cuts on a scrap piece can best confirm the correct alignment. Attach spring clamps to the workpiece to limit the router's travel, and set the length of the mortise.

To cut the mortise, raise the bit from the work, turn on the router, and move it back and forth in the plunge cut until you reach the desired depth. I prefer a spiral up-shear bit for mortising because it clears the chips better than a straight bit does.

This dual-fence arrangement works well when I have to make a series of in-line mortises for Shaker or Mission-style furniture. When mortising close to the end of a workpiece, such as the top of a leg, clamp two legs together in the vise end-to-end to provide more support for the router.

—MANDY KOTZMAN, LaPorte, Colo.

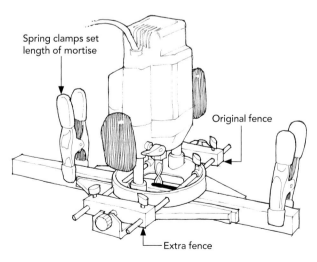

Spring clamps set length of mortise

Original fence

Extra fence

Handsaw guide for tenons

Here is a simple jig that takes only minutes to put together and can make you look like an expert with a handsaw. Use it to cut the waste off the edges of tenons after the two long shoulders and cheeks have been cut on a tablesaw. It allows you to rip perfectly perpendicular to the shoulder of the tenon and to crosscut flush to the shoulder quickly and easily with one setup.

The jig is two 4-in.-square blocks of 1¼-in.-thick hardwood scraps. Align biscuit slots into both squares so that the blocks will overhang each other by an inch or so. Use a ¼-in. piece of plywood as a spacer when biscuiting one of the blocks so that the blocks will be offset ¼ in. when you glue them together. You will have two blocks forming two Ls, offset from each other by ¼ in. and 1 in.

To use the jig, place the lip of the offset onto the shoulder of the tenoned piece and line up the long part of one of the Ls with where you want to cut. Clamp the whole thing into a vise. Use your finger to hold the saw against the jig as if you were going to flush-cut a dowel. Saw down to the bottom of the L, then flip the saw to the short part of the L to finish removing the waste.

—JEFFREY COOK, Plaistow, N.H.

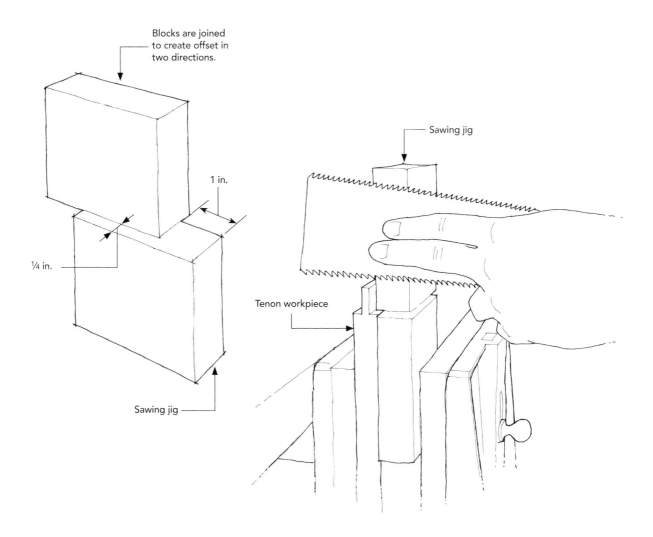

Blocks are joined to create offset in two directions.

1 in.

¼ in.

Sawing jig

Sawing jig

Tenon workpiece

SURFACE PREP

SANDING

Get the most from a random-orbit sander

Random-orbit sanders are wonderful machines. The pad has dual motion: It spins in a circle as well as in an eccentric orbit. These sanders are great for rapidly smoothing large surfaces and leveling raw wood. Five-in.-dia., palm-held models are most common, but you also can buy 6-in.-dia., two-handed versions.

When using a random-orbit sander on the edges of a workpiece, keep the majority of the pad on the wood or you'll risk dishing or rounding over the edge. By the same token, keep these sanders moving; don't concentrate on one spot, or you could create a little bowl.

Orient your project, if you can, so that you're working horizontally. By letting the weight of the sander work for you, you'll gain more control with less fatigue. Also, sand subassemblies before glue-up. It's much easier to sand a frame-and-panel, the aprons of a table, or a drawer's parts before they're assembled.

—DAVID SORG, Denver, Colo.

Random-orbit sanders remove stock quickly. The pad of a random-orbit sander spins in a circle as well as in an eccentric orbit. The motion removes stock rapidly on large surfaces, such as door panels (above) or wide table aprons (right). The sanders use disks backed with either pressure sensitive adhesive (PSA) or hook-and-loop systems.

Use a pad sander for better control in small areas

Pad sanders, also called palm sanders or finish sanders, use a simple orbital pattern, and the pad does not rotate, giving a much slower sanding action but greater control. The square pad allows the tool to get fairly close to the inside corners of a cabinet (but beware getting it too close, where it quickly can chew up the adjacent surface). This type of sander works well on smaller surfaces like the edges of shelves or table legs, as well as on the insides of cabinets and in other confined spaces.

—David Sorg, Denver, Colo.

Pad sanders are great for small parts. Less aggressive than random-orbit sanders, pad sanders are easier to control, which makes them suitable for narrower and more confined areas, such as table legs and frame parts.

How to determine if you're finished power-sanding

By taking this step, you'll avoid the agony of applying a stain only to see scratches jump out.

Wipe mineral spirits on the surface and sight across the wood toward a strong light. Look at the surface for scratches, especially the ugly orbital kind. You should see a uniform appearance with no rough areas or single outstanding scratches. Sometimes it's easiest to see this at the moment of evaporation, when the ruts of the scratches will still be shiny with fluid while the top surface is dry.

—DAVID SORG, Denver, Colo.

Check your progress. With the workpiece lit by a strong light, wipe the wood with some mineral spirits and check the surface for obvious scratches and rough areas.

The right grit for your power sander, from start to finish

With either a random-orbit or a pad sander, I'd rather start with P150-grit than P120-grit paper on most pieces, even though it takes longer to remove some milling marks. For wood that is in good shape, especially with thin-veneered sheet goods, I start with P180-grit paper.

Don't continue using a piece of sandpaper until the sand is all gone and there isn't anything left but the paper. Move to a fresh section of sandpaper as soon as you feel it stop cutting or start to clog, or when it requires you to exert more pressure.

Having experienced this the hard way, let me assure you that it's very important to vacuum and/or blow off the entire piece between grits. I do both, then wipe it with a tack cloth. One piece of P150 grit being swirled around on your P220-grit pad will make you curse when you see the results.

—DAVID SORG, Denver, Colo.

Hand-sanding gives a finishing touch

Using machines for the initial stages of sanding is fast, but you'll want to give each surface some final sanding by hand. Primarily, this is to get rid of the small orbital scratches left by the machines, replacing them with smaller, finer scratches that are all parallel to the grain of the wood and hence less noticeable.

You should back up the sandpaper with a sanding block wherever possible to maintain a flat surface. I find the palm-size rubber blocks most convenient because they also can be used for wet-sanding between coats of finish. Other choices include cork blocks or wood blocks faced with a sheet of cork.

—David Sorg, Denver, Colo.

Breaking the edges. Break the edges on a project not only to reduce future damage but also to prevent finish from forming a mound at the edges.

Sanding the end grain. To lessen end grain's darker appearance when the workpiece is finished, burnish the wood and fill the pores by sanding end grain up to P320-grit paper.

To maintain a flat surface, you should always use a backing block when sanding large areas.

Sanding after glue-up

No matter how thoroughly you sand parts prior to assembly, there still will be small areas to touch up by hand-sanding with P220- or P320-grit paper. Areas where glue was removed with a damp cloth may need smoothing (below left), or there may be two pieces that don't join in a perfect plane (below right). To avoid cross-sanding where grain intersects, mask off one of the pieces.

—David Sorg, Denver, Colo.

How to sand details and molding

Manufacturers advertise detail sanders as the answer to sanding any shape and any confined space. These sanders come with a variety of pads designed to fit different profiles. Although I own a couple of detail sanders, I could live without them, mostly because it's too much trouble to constantly change the paper on them; by their nature, they put their sanding action into a small area of sandpaper that wears very quickly.

Most of the time I think it's quicker to do moldings, interior corners, and other small areas by hand. To keep the moldings crisp, use commercial rubber profiles that cover most convex and concave shapes, or make your own profile blocks from pieces of foam-insulation panel.

The end grain on raised panels requires a special sanding sequence to tone it into the rest of the panel. Start by sanding across the grain with P150- or P180-grit paper to deal with the rough texture. Then sand the entire profile on all four sides of the panel with P180- or P220-grit paper. Last, sand just the end grain with P320-grit paper, going with the grain in short strokes to eliminate any cross-grain scratches and to lessen the end grain's ability to absorb finish.

—David Sorg, Denver, Colo.

Rubber profiles. To keep the edges of the profile sharp while you sand, use a commercial rubber pad that fits the molding.

Tight curves. Contour the paper to fit curves in the wood.

Fun with foam. Insulation foam shaped to match the panel's profile makes a good backing for sandpaper.

Rip sandpaper to any size with precision

My furniture style incorporates lots of curves, and I often make custom sanding blocks in various sizes to smooth those curved areas. To help use expensive sandpaper efficiently, I built this fixture, which allows me to rip sandpaper sheets to any size quickly and easily, with little waste.

The grid surface, which serves as the cutting guide, is a self-healing cutting mat from a dollar store or office-supply store. Following the grid, I can rip perfectly sized sheets not only for my various odd-size sanding blocks but also for my half- and quarter-sheet sanders. Just be sure the lines of the grid are square to the edges of the platform; otherwise, you'll be cutting on an angle.

This is one of the most frequently used fixtures in my workshop. I'm on my second—the first gave out after 30 years.

—MICHAEL FORTUNE,
Lakefield, Ont., Canada

1⅝ in.

1 in.

Fence

½-in.-thick plywood

Fence for half sheet horizontally

Fixture hangs on hook when not in use.

Fence for half sheet vertically

5½ in.

4½ in.

Self-healing cutting mat

13½ in.

Hacksaw blade

6¾ in.

Washer

First line of grid ¼ in. from fence

Softer sanding block

My sanding block is nothing more than a block of wood with felt glued on one side. I cut a block the right size, glue ¼-in.-thick felt on it, and that's it. The sanding blocks are about a third of the size of half a sheet of sandpaper.

—LON SCHLEINING, Capistrano Beach, Calif.

Build better sanding blocks

One day I was thinking about the interminable sanding process—the scratch-scratch-scratching on up through the grits—120, 150, 220—and how I could make it a little more enjoyable. The idea that popped into my head was this supercharged, pimped-out sanding block—what I call a sanding plane—and in less than an hour I had built one.

Since then I've built several more, each adapted to a specific function. You can make a sanding plane with a thick hardwood sole for smoothing flat surfaces; you can use a thinner sole to make a plane that has some flex for smoothing large curved surfaces, like a coopered door; and you can make sanding planes to smooth various molding profiles (a convex version is shown).

To make a flat plane, start with a heavy piece of straight-grained hardwood, milled to about 2¼ in. thick. Cut it to length (the plane shown is about 16 in. long, but you can make them any length) and then joint the bottom and one side. Now rip the block to width, which depends on your selection of sandpaper. This plane uses a length of 3-in.-wide abrasive cloth from a sanding belt, so it's 3 in. wide. I also like to use premium B-weight sandpaper that is 4½ in. wide and comes in 30-ft. rolls (Lee Valley is one supplier: www.leevalley.com). Handles help control the long plane; you can make your own, or salvage them, as I did. To load the sanding plane, slip the paper in the front slot, wrap it around the sole, and then thread it under the cleat and screw it in place.

To make a molding sanding plane, cut a blank to about 9 in. long (the thickness will depend on the profile to be smoothed). Rout the reverse profile on one edge and round over the edges on the opposite side. Cut the slot, add a cleat, and start sanding.

—TOM FIDGEN, Nova Scotia, Canada

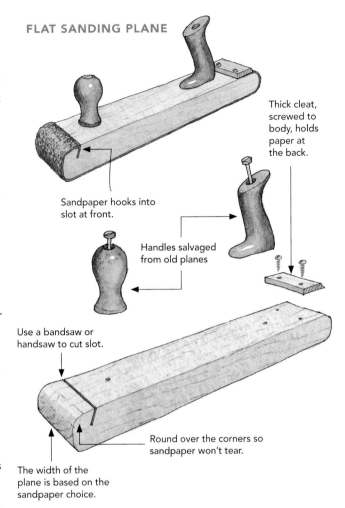

FLAT SANDING PLANE

Thick cleat, screwed to body, holds paper at the back.

Sandpaper hooks into slot at front.

Handles salvaged from old planes

Use a bandsaw or handsaw to cut slot.

Round over the corners so sandpaper won't tear.

The width of the plane is based on the sandpaper choice.

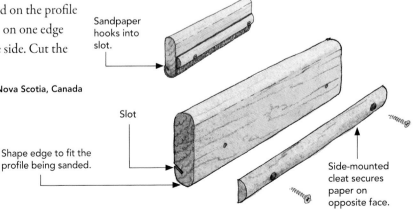

CONVEX SANDING PLANE

Sandpaper hooks into slot.

Slot

Shape edge to fit the profile being sanded.

Side-mounted cleat secures paper on opposite face.

Reverse-profile sanding block for moldings

I use latex patching cement to make reverse-profile blocks for sanding moldings. The material costs much less and is easier to work than two-part epoxy compounds and auto-body fillers. Also, it's strong, and it molds easily to the profile of the molding.

To make a sanding block, cut a short length of molding to use as the form bottom. Coat the surface of the molding with wax so that it will separate easily from the patching cement. Make a sheet-metal or stiff cardboard box to act as a form for the molding and the patching cement. Mix up a batch of the latex patching cement, using as little water as possible. Press the cement into the form around the molding and then cover with plastic wrap to slow evaporation. After the cement hardens, separate it from the molding and cure it in a plastic bag for a few days to maximize its strength and durability. To use the sanding block, simply wrap a piece of sandpaper around the profile side of the block and start sanding—the paper will conform to the shape of the block.

—JAY LI, Chesterfield, Mo.

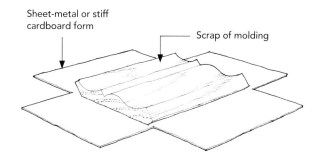

Sheet-metal or stiff cardboard form

Scrap of molding

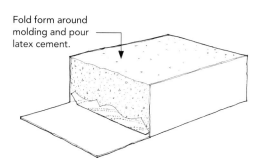

Fold form around molding and pour latex cement.

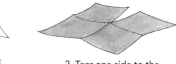

Molded sanding block

How to fold sandpaper to get the most out of a sheet

An old paint salesman showed me how to get the most out of a sheet of sandpaper. Fold the sheet in half in both directions. Then tear the sheet halfway through on the short fold line. Now fold up the sandpaper into a four-layer sanding pad.

The sheet can be refolded different ways to expose a fresh surface. None of the sanding surfaces rub against each other, which results in a longer-lasting sanding pad.

—STEVE CHASTAIN, Bellingham, Wash.

1. Fold sandpaper in half both ways.

2. Tear one side to the centerline.

3. Tuck one side into other side.

4. Completed pack. Sanding surfaces do not rub together.

Two sanding blocks
for inside corners

After gluing up a little shelving unit for my daughter's bathroom, I found that I needed to do a little light sanding in the corners. With a traditional sanding block, I could concentrate only on one surface at a time. So I made a sanding block (top right) that allows me to sand both surfaces of an inside corner at the same time.

Making the block takes only two different settings and four passes on the tablesaw. Starting with square stock, sized to fit your hand comfortably, make two cuts parallel to the outside edges. Then tilt the blade to 45°, reposition the fence, and make two more cuts to define the handle.

—Al Ching, Huntington Beach, Calif.

Block reaches into corners.

Handle

Square corner

I made this special sanding block (below right) to make it easier to clean up inside corners of a box or drawer. The shape was inspired by the profile of a chisel. I started with a scrap of ¾-in.-thick plywood about 1¼ in. wide and 4 in. long. Then I cut a 30° bevel across one end of the plywood to make a pointed end. To use, I cut a strip of sandpaper the same width as the block and wrap it around the block lengthwise. The angle of the block also lets me grip securely on both sides.

—STEVE RESKI, Austin, Texas

Angled tip reaches into corners.

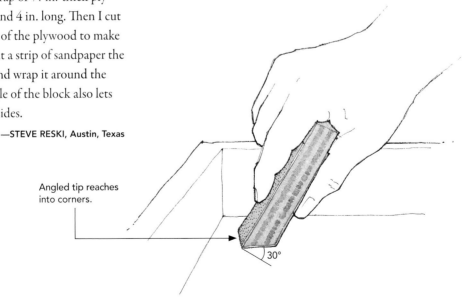

30°

Sand smooth curves
with a belt sander

I make low stools as gifts, each one with a gently shaped concave seat. It was time-consuming to smooth the concave surface, but things got easier when I slipped a rounded piece under the spring-steel shoe of my belt sander.

The rounded piece, or platen, is made by face-gluing three pieces of ⅛-in.-thick hardboard. Use a rasp or file, along with some sandpaper, to shape the platen to the radius of the seat.

To sand the concave side of the seat, simply insert the rounded platen under the flexible shoe from the side. There's no need to use anything special to hold the platen in place; the tension of the sanding belt does that. The thin spring-steel shoe bends to the same radius as the seat, enabling me to sand the entire concave surface. Indeed, by working up through the various grades of abrasive belts, I can finish a seat in no time at all. When the rounded platen is removed, the shoe springs back to its original flat shape.

—NICK ROWE, Greenlane, Auckland, New Zealand

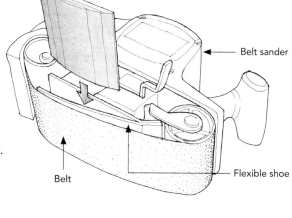

Rounded platen is made from glued-up hardboard.

Belt sander

Belt

Flexible shoe

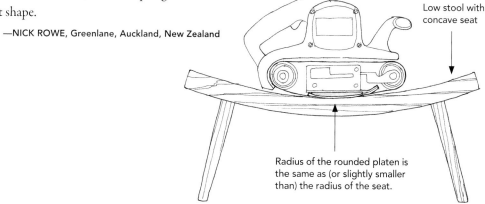

Low stool with concave seat

Radius of the rounded platen is the same as (or slightly smaller than) the radius of the seat.

Reinforce sandpaper with duct tape

There are times when you are sanding a round piece of stock, such as a bedpost, and you need a strip of sandpaper that will fit in a groove. Unfortunately, a narrow strip of sandpaper will not take much strain before it tears. To solve this problem, apply duct tape to the back of the sandpaper before cutting the strip to the width that you need.

—BOB WEEMS, Guthrie, Okla.

How to sand tabletops with breadboard ends

To sand the breadboard ends of a tabletop without marring the panel, you must first make sure that the breadboards and panel are the same thickness before assembling the tabletop. Once the panel has been glued and pinned to the breadboard ends, sand the top with a belt sander, starting with a P150-grit belt, in the direction of the panel grain. At this point you'll leave cross-grain scratches on the breadboards, but don't fret. After repeating the process with a P180-grit belt, those scratches will be barely perceptible.

Next, sand the entire tabletop with a random-orbit sander. Start with a P220-grit disk and give the breadboards a few extra passes to clean up any leftover scratches from the belt sander.

Now hand-sand the panel in the direction of the grain with P220-grit paper. Then carefully hand-sand the breadboards in the direction of the grain. Repeat with P320 and P400 grits. Finally, burnish the tabletop with 0000 steel wool. This should leave a flawless surface, with no scratches visible on either the panel or the breadboards.

—CHRISTIAN BECKSVOORT, New Gloucester, Maine

Start with a belt sander. Use a P150-grit belt first, working in the direction of the panel grain. Repeat with a P180-grit belt.

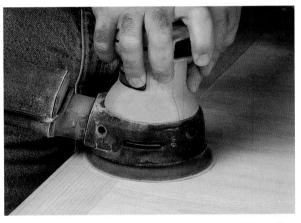

Move on to a random-orbit sander. With a P220-grit disk, work the entire tabletop. Give the breadboards extra attention to remove the belt-sander marks that you just made.

Hand-sand with a block. Using a sanding block, hand-sand the tabletop. Work in the direction of the grain first on the panel, and then on the breadboard ends. Start with P220-grit paper, and work your way up through P320 and P400 grits.

HANDPLANING

Hand screws hold parts for planing—three variations

The workbench I am building doesn't have a vise yet. As an interim solution, I use two large hand screws. I lay the first clamp horizontally on the bench to hold the work. Then I clamp the first clamp to the bench lip with the second clamp (top drawing). This arrangement has the advantages of being cheap, movable, strong, and versatile.

—THOMAS GRACE, Binghamton, N.Y.

Here's a make-do vise I set up until I have the time to build a proper woodworker's bench with a built-in vise. Simply clamp one hand screw to the corner of a sturdy table with another hand screw (center drawing). The bigger the hand screws, the better. This temporary arrangement produces a more-than-satisfactory substitute bench vise. For a more permanent solution, you could secure the hand screw directly to the tabletop with a lag screw. Recently I used this setup to support doors while I planed them to final dimensions.

—JONATHAN PERCY, Newport, R.I.

To hold boards on edge on your workbench for hand-planing, clamp a small hand screw in the end vise, and tighten the hand screw to the workpiece (bottom drawing). This arrangement works well because the benchtop takes all of the downward pressure of planing.

—ANTHONY GUIDICE, St. Louis, Mo.

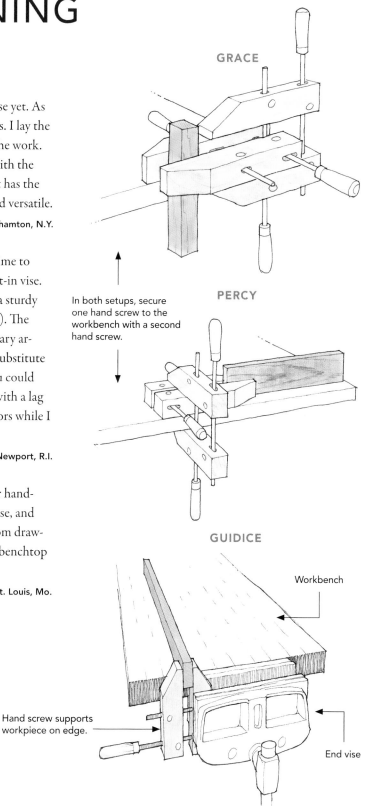

GRACE

In both setups, secure one hand screw to the workbench with a second hand screw.

PERCY

GUIDICE

Workbench

Hand screw supports workpiece on edge.

End vise

Bench stop for planing

My bench has no dogs or other accessories for securing a workpiece to the top for planing or scraping. So I came up with a modified bench stop that performs this function quite well. To make one, screw a generously sized piece of ⅜-in.-thick plywood (mine is 14 in. wide by 18 in. long) to a 2×4 scrap. The ⅜-in. plywood is thin enough that it won't interfere with a plane coming off the end of a ¾-in.-thick workpiece. The jig is wide and long enough to keep the board from moving sideways when planing at an angle to the board's grain. Pressure from the plane usually will keep the workpiece firmly against the jig.

—JUSTIN SMITH, Gustavus, Alaska

Plywood, ⅜ in. thick, screwed to 2x4

Bench stop

2x4

How to determine grain direction for handplaning

When handplaning boards, it is sometimes hard to know which direction to choose to avoid tearing out the wood. Checking the grain on the side of the board is a help, but that does not always tell the whole story. Here is an additional method that works very well.

Look at the end grain of the board. With flatsawn lumber, you get one of two patterns: hills or valleys. Then look at the surface of the wood to see where the grain forms rounded points (called cathedrals). If the end grain is a hill, plane into the points. If the end grain is a valley, plane away from the points.

To help me remember the somewhat complicated directions, I think of an imaginary battle where a band of warriors charges up the hill and into the points of their enemy. The warriors retreat and run back into the valley with the enemy's points at their backs.

—BILLY KING, Oldhams, Va.

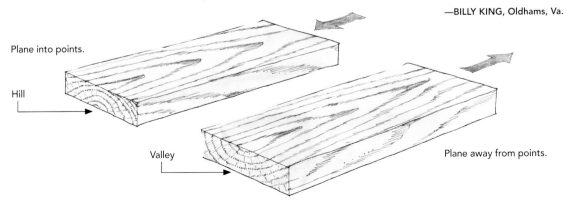

Plane into points.

Hill

Valley

Plane away from points.

Jig makes it easier to plane sides of drawers

It usually is necessary to plane the sides of an assembled drawer in order to get a perfect fit. But it can be a chore to hold the drawer in place for planing.

The typical routine requires that you clamp the drawer to the side of a bench, take a pass with the plane, unclamp the drawer, check the fit, reclamp, take another pass with the plane, and so on.

This simple jig saves time and effort. It consists of two main parts: a yoke that mounts in the end vise and a support board that clamps to the workbench.

Once the jig is set up, you simply slide the drawer in place and plane. Slide the drawer out to check the fit. The jig provides support so that the sides stay flat. It also holds the drawer in such a way that I don't feel like I'm stressing the corner joinery.

The yoke is a rectangular piece of ¾-in.-thick plywood. A 1-in.-wide slot cut in the yoke accepts either the drawer front or back. Attaching a hardwood cleat to the underside of the yoke allows it to be clamped in the vise.

The support board has slots on each side to accommodate drawers of different depths. I hold it in place by sliding a clamp through one of the benchdog holes, which keeps the clamp clear of the planing area. A bench hook also would work. By flipping the piece end for end and moving the clamp to different benchdog holes, I can fit drawers of almost any width or length. If I can't, I just cut a new slot in the plywood.

—MARK EDMUNDSON, Sandpoint, Idaho

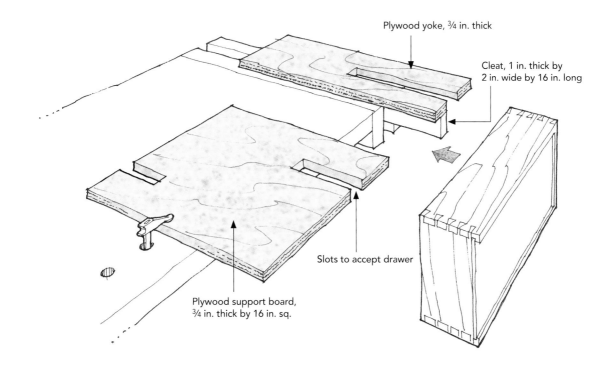

Plywood yoke, ¾ in. thick

Cleat, 1 in. thick by 2 in. wide by 16 in. long

Slots to accept drawer

Plywood support board, ¾ in. thick by 16 in. sq.

GLUING AND CLAMPING

STRATEGY

Two ways to square up a case during glue-up

Ensuring that a case or frame comes together squarely involves more than simply putting the glue-up in clamps and tightening. It requires careful clamp alignment.

Compare diagonal measurements. Any difference signals an out-of-square case. Correct it by realigning clamps, shifting them toward the longer diagonal.

—**STEVE LATTA,** Lancaster, Pa.

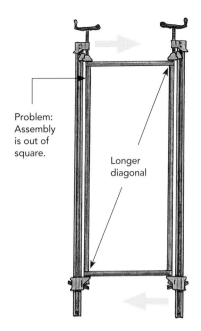

Problem: Assembly is out of square.

Longer diagonal

Solution: Shift the clamps in the direction of the longer diagonal.

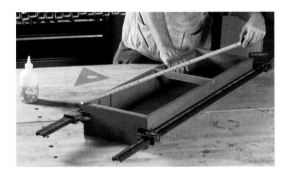

When clamps won't bring a case into square, a simple clamping form made from a square piece of ¾-in.-thick MDF can help bring one corner into square. This typically will bring the entire case into alignment.

Drill a series of holes large enough to accommodate a clamp head, so the form can be held firmly to an interior corner of the glue-up.

—**STEVE LATTA,** Lancaster, Pa.

Clamping form

Cut holes large enough to fit the clamp heads.

90°

Inexpensive shopmade clamps

In the display business where I work, we never seem to have enough clamps. One day, after I ran out of clamps one too many times, I made a large number of the simple, wedge-activated clamps shown above.

I chose to make several sets of clamps in 3-in. increments, but you could make them in any sizes that you find handy. I wouldn't recommend using solid lumber because the grain will be weak at the inside corners, regardless of how you cut the clamp pattern from a board. Either medium-density fiberboard or a good grade of plywood will be less likely to break.

Cut the wedges and the spacer blocks from hardwood. The wedge profiles should be sized for no more than 1 in. of thickness for every 6 in. of length. The spacer blocks (wider than they are thick) serve two purposes: They spread out the clamping force over a larger area, and they also act as space adjusters because they can be used either on edge or flat.

To use one of these clamps, simply find a combination of clamp, spacer, and other material to make a tight fit for the wedge. Then pound the wedge into place. A simple tap on the downhill side of the clamp body will release it immediately.

I used scrap pieces of MDF to make the clamp bodies. But even if I cut the bodies out of a new sheet of MDF, the cost would be only about 10 cents each.

—ROBERT B. CHAMBERS, Richardson, Texas

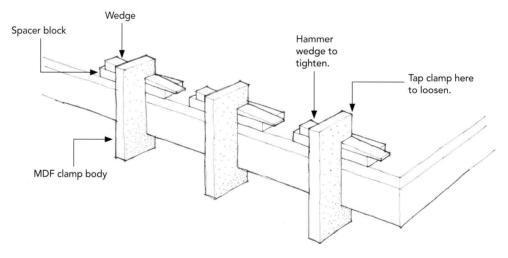

Spacer block · Wedge · Hammer wedge to tighten. · Tap clamp here to loosen. · MDF clamp body

Gripping small clamp handles

If you have trouble gripping those small handles on wood clamps, just wrap the handle with non-slip drawer liner—that soft foam waffle-weave material that is sold at discount chain stores. I hot-glue one end of the material to the handle, wrap it around two or three times, and then hot-glue the other end. This provides a soft, easy-to-grip handle.

—DON PETERSON, Fergus Falls, Minn.

Preventing squeeze-out problems in drawers

To prevent glue squeeze-out problems when assembling drawers, simply finish the insides of the drawers before assembly. Sand all of the inside drawer parts and apply two or three coats of shellac, carefully avoiding the surfaces that will be glued. Later, when you assemble the drawers, any bead of glue will pop right off after it has dried.

—JOE BARRY, Lumberton, N.C.

Shopmade wrench for tightening hand clamps

To multiply the clamping pressure of your hand clamps, use a drawknife to cut opposing flats on the handles. Then rout a slot in a piece of hardwood to make a wood wrench like the one in the sketch. With this combination you can apply tremendous clamping pressure and then easily loosen the clamps later.

—ANDY OLERUD, Driggs, Idaho

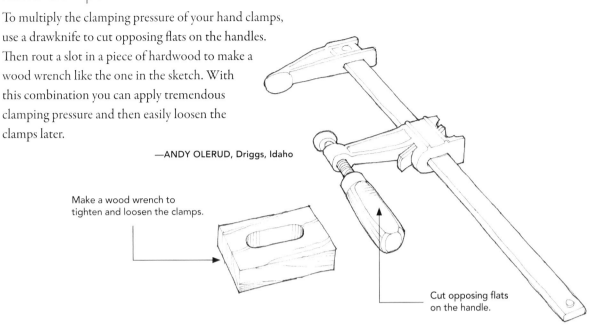

Make a wood wrench to tighten and loosen the clamps.

Cut opposing flats on the handle.

Handy jig for clamping large curved work

Gluing the rear rail into this demilune table would be a challenge with standard clamps alone. The curved aprons offer no secure clamping surface. For work like this, glue a pair of blocks, on which standard clamps can be applied, to a length of veneer that rests on top of the curve.

—STEVE LATTA, Lancaster, Pa.

Using band clamps for squaring during glue-up

Here is a simple technique to pull a case square after you've applied glue and clamped it together. Pass a band clamp behind the clamps diagonally across the case in whatever direction you need to pull the case to square it up. If a lot of force is needed to square up a case, then use the ratchet mechanism of the band clamp. More likely, however, a small amount of force is all you'll need. So you simply can pull on the two ends of the band clamp until the case is square, and then snap on a spring clamp to hold the band clamp in position.

—MARSHALL W. FLETCHER, Dover, Del.

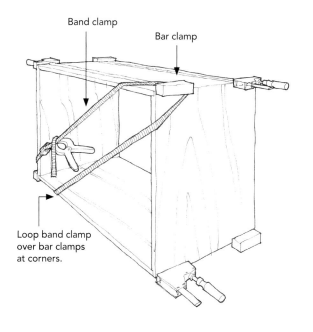

Band clamp

Bar clamp

Loop band clamp over bar clamps at corners.

Curved cauls reach across long shelves

For deep cases, clamp using convex curved cauls, which will extend pressure to the center of interior panels. Curved cauls also can distribute pressure along a long edge, bailing you out if you don't have enough bar clamps. You can curve a caul with a few passes of your handplane or belt sander.

—GARY ROGOWSKI, Portland, Ore.

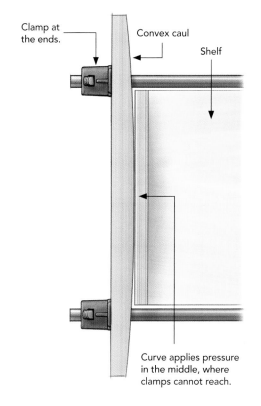

Clamp at the ends.

Convex caul

Shelf

Curve applies pressure in the middle, where clamps cannot reach.

Non-marring clamp pads

I dip the working ends of my clamps in Plasti Dip® (www.plastidip.com), a rubber coating that generally is used for tool handles. With three coats on the pad area of my clamps, I can clamp up lumber without worrying about marring or denting the work. I've had the coating on my clamps for about 10 months, and it's still working fine.

—ELIZABETH A. FRIEDRICH, San Diego, Calif.

Focus pressure with clamp pads

Clamp pads and cauls should be part of every glue-up, but they do more than just protect the work. Properly sized and located, these tools will direct the clamp pressure and help achieve a tight, square assembly.

The pads built into most clamps are too large for many jobs and will distort an assembly like this door frame (see top photo in Step 1). Shop-made cauls or pads, properly sized, will keep the pressure in line (see bottom photo in Step 1). Cut the pads about ⅜ in. shorter than full length; the space at each end lets you

hook on a measuring tape to check corner-to-corner dimensions.

Tape the shop-made pads into place on the workpiece (see left photo in Step 2). This simplifies the task of getting the clamp and pads where you need them. These pads are cut long to distribute even pressure to both rails. Then use a support block to keep the clamp parallel to the work while you tighten it (see Step 3). The block should be dimensioned to locate the clamp pads precisely.

—STEVE LATTA, Lancaster, Pa.

1. CUT PADS TO FIT WORK

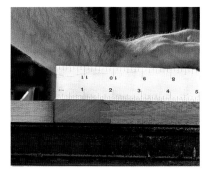

2. TAPE PADS IN PLACE

3. A SUPPORT BLOCK KEEPS CLAMP PARALLEL TO WORK

Extralong clamps

I recently needed some long clamps to span an 8-ft.-long dining table, but my Jorgensen® parallel-jaw clamps were too short. So I made a clamp twice as long as the original by removing the sliding head from one clamp, then removing and reversing the head on a second clamp. Using the hole in the bar where the sliding jaw goes, I fastened the two bars together with a short bolt. I had to enlarge the sliding jaw's hole slightly to accept a ⅜-in.-dia. bolt. (Keep in mind, though, that the jaws no longer will stay parallel in all situations.) You can use this technique on Bessey® clamps if you file off the stamped keeper dimples and drill a hole for the bolt at the end of the bar.

—GEORGE BURMAN, Madera, Calif.

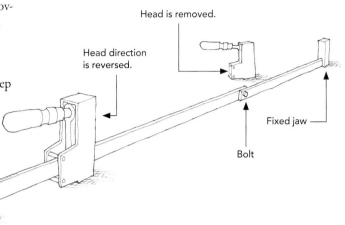

Head is removed.

Head direction is reversed.

Fixed jaw

Bolt

Bridge increases the reach of the clamps on a wide workpiece

Sometimes the width of a workpiece makes it hard for clamps to deliver pressure where it's needed. With two pads and a length of ¾-in. stock, it's possible to use a standard clamp to apply pressure in the middle of a wide panel, to glue in an inlay, for example.

—STEVE LATTA, Lancaster, Pa.

Felt pads work as clamp pads

The felt pads made to cover furniture feet, protecting the floor, also make great clamp pads. Sold at most hardware stores, the pads have an adhesive backing that permanently adheres to a clean surface. For pipe clamps, I buy the felt pads in sheets and cut them to fit the clamp heads. For smaller clamps, I buy the felt disks.

—JIM DION, Lawrenceville, Ga.

Working glue into a crack

Unwaxed dental floss often comes in handy when I want to work glue into a crack. First, I coat the floss with glue. Then I use the floss to work the glue deep into the crack.

—ANNETTE DUBE, Ipswich, Mass.

Small lid makes great glue dish

I use the plastic lid from a yogurt container as a glue dish. When the leftover glue dries, it peels right off, and I can use the lid again.

—MATT NAGEL, Lehi, Utah

Gluing laminated curves
with screw blocks

Here is a method for gluing up laminated curved components that eliminates the need for large numbers of expensive clamps. By using simple hardwood clamping blocks and drywall screws, you can get all of the clamping pressure you need.

First, you'll need to make a curved form for the laminated workpiece. The form should be just a bit wider than the workpiece. Then make screw-attachment blocks for both sides of the form, using construction-grade 2× lumber cut roughly to the shape of the curve. Screw the attachment blocks to the outsides of the form, recessing the curved edges slightly.

Next, cut a few dozen ¾-in.-thick hardwood clamping blocks long enough to span the full width of the form,

including the attachment blocks. Drill pilot holes for screws about 1 in. from each end of the clamping blocks.

After a dry run, spread glue on each of the lamination plies and stack them together on the form. Place an extra (unglued) ply on top to help spread the clamping pressure and to prevent marring the workpiece. Starting at the center of the form, screw the clamping blocks in place, perpendicular to the curved plies. Space the blocks about every 2 in., more or less, depending on the radius of the curve. You can adapt this same basic concept to laminate inside curves or to add edge-banding to irregular contours.

—DAVID GILMORE, Maple Ridge, B.C., Canada

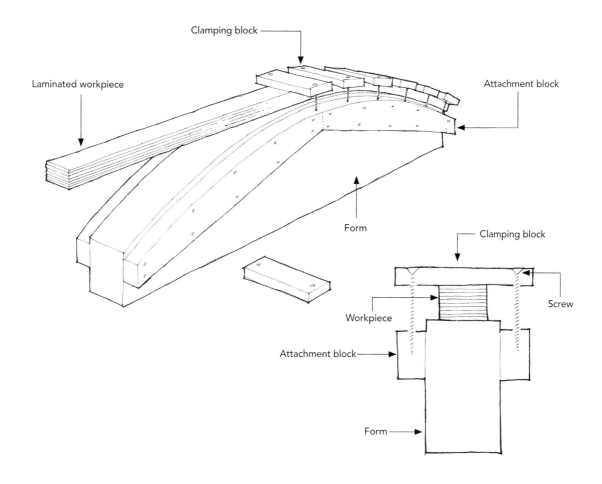

How to remove glue squeeze-out cleanly

Poor stain absorption on areas affected by yellow-glue squeeze-out is a common problem among woodworkers. There are several ways to remedy this. The first is to use less glue. Most woodworkers feel as though they must have bountiful squeeze-out to have a good glue bond. Not so! Apply just enough to have tiny beads barely squeezing out.

Then, there's option two: Don't touch the excess glue. Don't wipe it. And absolutely do not use a wet rag to remove it. The rag is full of dissolved glue, which, when wiped on the wood, ultimately seals the pores. This causes uneven stain absorption. Allow those tiny pearls of squeezed-out glue to harden a little. When they're skinned over, a sharp chisel pops them off perfectly. A little sanding, and then—voilà!—no glue spots. If the joint is a tabletop or some type of flat surface, sanding is in order anyway. If it is a table apron mortised into the leg, there is no need to put glue on the shoulder of the tenon area—it is edge grain and won't add strength anyway. Skip the glue on the outside shoulder entirely.

—TERI MASASCHI, Tigeras, N.M.

Don't wipe wet glue. Wiping causes blotches. Wiping along the glueline seals the pores of the wood, making it impossible for stain to penetrate evenly.

Let it dry and pare away. Chisel slightly hardened glue. Allow beads of glue to skin over but not completely harden. Then, use a sharp chisel to slice them off. The stain absorbs evenly for an imperceptible glueline.

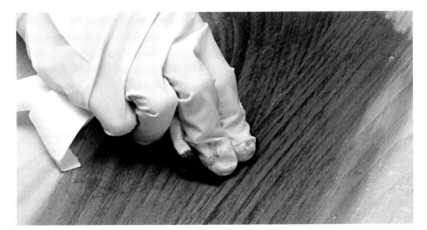

Clamping without clamps

When using a regular clamp won't work, sometimes common items like packing tape or rubber bands can hold odd shapes securely.

—STEVE LATTA, Lancaster, Pa.

Wrap it up. Inexpensive, lightweight packing tape has a little stretch, letting you pull together a joint like the miters on this cabinet base (top photo). The taped-together joint is secured with a clamp between cauls to keep the assembly flat (photo above).

Close a miter with packing tape. A straightedge keeps this mitered bracket foot aligned as a packing tape hinge is applied to the outside of the joint (top photo). The tape keeps the corner together as the miter is closed. After gluing and folding the miter together, wind more tape around the assembly several times to clamp the joint securely (photo above).

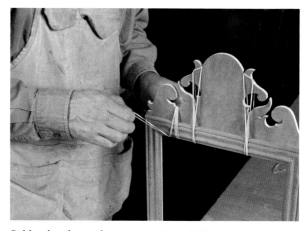

Rubber bands go where tape can't. For light clamping of irregular parts, like the scrollwork on this Chippendale mirror, rubber bands apply pressure where other methods can't reach.

Use offcuts as pads for clamping irregular shapes

Standard clamps can't get a solid grip on shapes that aren't rectilinear. Offcuts from workpieces can serve as perfect-fitting clamp pads.

—STEVE LATTA, Lancaster, Pa.

Complex profiles. The scrollsawn offcut for a bracket foot is ideal for applying pressure evenly. A piece of plywood gives the clamp a flat surface underneath instead of a profiled edge.

Invert the pattern. An inverted offcut helps secure the crown molding on a Pennsylvania spice box. The reversed molding hits its mate at the critical upper and lower edges for even pressure.

Simple curves. The band-sawn cutoff for a curved table apron makes an ideal clamp pad for gluing a bead along the apron's bottom edge. A narrow strip of foam padding helps even out the pressure.

Get a better, stronger grip on your bar clamps

As a woodworker who occasionally suffers from carpal-tunnel syndrome, I have found a measure of relief by retrofitting my bar clamps with ¼-in. dowels. I first drill a ¼-in.-dia. hole in the wood handle with a brad-point bit and follow that with a ⁹⁄₃₂-in. twist bit to enlarge the hole enough to let the dowel slide freely. In that hole I insert a section of dowel just long enough that it doesn't interfere with the bar, and I tape the ends of the dowel so that it doesn't slide out of the handle.

The increased leverage enables me to tighten the clamps with much less effort and strain on my wrists, and I have yet to break a dowel or a clamp handle.

—DAN DEKOVEN, Evergreen, Colo.

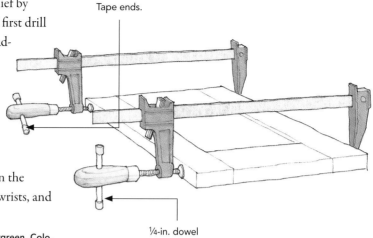

Tape ends.

¼-in. dowel

Nesting frames help with glue-ups and more

These nesting square frames, which I call multi-task shop helpers, take up very little space but pack several functions into a small package.

The frames are great for both panel and carcase glue-ups. They are notched to hold bar clamps on one side and pipe clamps on the other, which makes them handy for panel assemblies. And the frames can be used to help keep a carcase, a box, or a drawer square during assembly.

The frames are handy for cutting stock, too. I use two of them to elevate a board above my bench for crosscutting. In addition, each frame is the same height as my miter-saw bed, so they can be used as outfeed support there.

—SERGE DUCLOS, Delson, Que., Canada

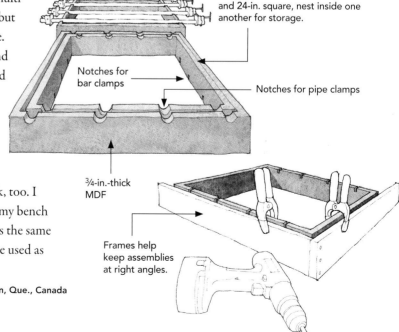

The three frames, 20-in., 22-in., and 24-in. square, nest inside one another for storage.

Notches for bar clamps

Notches for pipe clamps

¾-in.-thick MDF

Frames help keep assemblies at right angles.

MORTISE-AND-TENON JOINTS

Give the glue a place to go

Like other woodworkers, I'd had problems with glue squeezing out of mortise-and-tenon joints as they're clamped up. So I came up with the idea of chamfering or rounding over the top edge of the mortise. As the tenon is inserted, excess glue collects in the channel created by the chamfer, instead of oozing out. The tiny chamfer will not weaken the joint. You can make the chamfer with a carving knife or a roundover router bit with a small pilot bearing. I use a ¼-in. roundover bit with a ³⁄₁₆-in. pilot and adjust the height to give a roundover between ¹⁄₁₆ in. and ⅛ in. Miniature brass-pilot roundover bits as small as ¹⁄₁₆ in. are available from Eagle America (www.eagleamerica.com) and other suppliers.

—CURTIS WHITTINGTON, Boerne, Texas

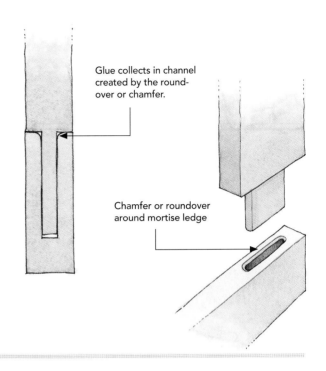

Glue collects in channel created by the round-over or chamfer.

Chamfer or roundover around mortise ledge

Seal through-tenons before glue-up

Through-tenons squeeze their way through a glued mortise like a car through a car wash. They come out completely wet with glue. That glue absorbs quickly into the end grain, where it can prevent the finish from soaking in, leading to blotches.

To prevent the glue from getting into the end grain, I seal it with thinned-down dewaxed shellac (2-lb. cut or lighter). Be careful to keep the finish off the gluing surfaces, and wipe away the squeeze-out as soon as possible.

—GARY ROGOWSKI, Portland, Ore.

PANELS

Grooved clamping blocks don't stick to the work

A common procedure while edge-gluing several boards into a panel is to use clamps at the joints to align the boards. But this often traps glue under the clamp heads. To avoid this problem, I use grooved blocks under the alignment clamps. I start with a 4-in.-wide piece of ¾-in.-thick scrap. I rout a ¼-in.-wide by ¼-in.-deep groove down the center, then cut 3-in.-long blocks from that workpiece. During glue-up, I place one block above and one block below the glueline, with the grooves straddling the joint so that no glue touches the blocks.

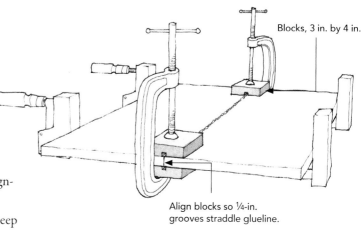

Blocks, 3 in. by 4 in.

Align blocks so ¼-in. grooves straddle glueline.

When the glue starts to set, after 30 minutes or so, I remove the blocks and peel the soft glue off the joint with a chisel.

—ROBERT HONEYCOMBE, Kitchener, Ont., Canada

Prevent glue squeeze-out with tape

Here's a technique that keeps squeeze-out off the wood when you're gluing up panels. When the boards have been jointed, just before gluing, apply a strip of box-sealing tape on the face of each board along the jointed edge. Let the tape overhang the jointed edges by ¼ in. or so. Press the tape tightly along the corners. Then trim the overhang with a new safety razor, taking care not to nick the jointed edges. Glue as usual. Any glue squeeze-out will go onto the face of the tape and not your panel.

After the glue cures, remove the clamps and pull the two pieces of tape off the joint. There may be a hairline bead of glue at the seam, but this is easily removed. Don't let the tape stay on the work too long because the adhesive may become hard to remove.

Exhaustive tests (not really, I just like the sound of that phrase) have determined that the best tape for this job is 3M's® Scotch premium commercial box-sealing tape. Avoid using duct tape, masking tape, cheap packing tape, or regular Scotch tape.

I much prefer spending the time applying tape than scraping off glue residue, which can cause finishing problems. Taping also has the advantage of isolating clamp bars from the stock, thus eliminating iron stains.

—JIM WRIGHT, Berkley, Mass.

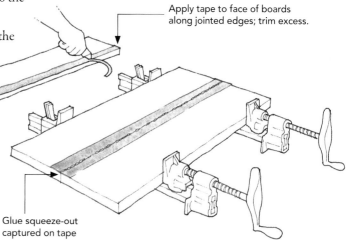

Apply tape to face of boards along jointed edges; trim excess.

Glue squeeze-out captured on tape

Make pipe-clamp saddles from PVC pipe

I always wanted several sets of pipe-clamp saddles but never wanted to pay for them. When I discovered that 1-in.-dia. (schedule 40) gray PVC pipe snaps perfectly onto ¾-in.-dia. iron pipe, I was able to make all of the pipe-clamp saddles I needed for pennies each.

To make the saddles, cut a 1¼-in.-long section of the 1-in. PVC pipe, then mark the centerline on the end of that section. With the centerline as a guide, use a bandsaw to slice out a less-than-half section (about 150°) of the PVC pipe. This gives you a little more than a semicircle of conduit. The inside diameter of the PVC pipe is just a little smaller than the outside diameter of the ¾-in. iron pipe, so it will snap onto the pipe firmly and won't slide around. Drill and countersink a couple of short drywall screws through the PVC section into a block of wood to make a saddle.

Because the saddles are made of PVC, it is easy to glue them to each other or to other PVC materials to make an infinite variety of jigs. You could make a clamping jig by screwing several sections of the PVC saddles to a longer piece of wood to space out your pipe clamps evenly. Or you could use the saddles to fasten your clamps into a storage rack.

—JIM FOLEY, Mickleton, N.J.

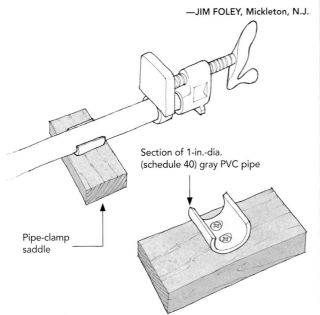

Pipe-clamp saddle

Section of 1-in.-dia. (schedule 40) gray PVC pipe

Pipe-clamp spacers ease panel glue-ups

These simple pipe-clamp spacers, made from ¾-in. plywood scraps, elevate a glued-up panel away from the pipes, leaving enough room to wipe glue squeeze-out from the pipes and preventing unsightly pipe stains on the workpiece. The spacers also allow the pipe clamps to sit upright on a table, making panel glue-ups a breeze.

Place the blocks between the clamp head and tail, making sure you use enough spacers to support all of the boards being glued.

—RALPH PASQUINELLI, Batavia, Ill.

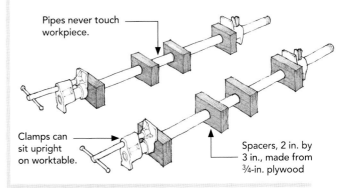

Pipes never touch workpiece.

Clamps can sit upright on worktable.

Spacers, 2 in. by 3 in., made from ¾-in. plywood

Prevent panels from buckling under pressure

When clamping up boards to make a panel, pipe clamps can ride up on the fixed jaw, causing the pressure to be uneven and the panel to buckle. This is caused by the angle of the jaw changing as the pressure comes on. If this bothers you, take a dowel with the same diameter as the thickness of the panel and lay it between the jaws and the work. Now the pressure will be applied on the center of the panel edge just where it should be. The dowel will likely dent the edge, so you may want to add a piece of scrap as a buffer.

—HENRY T. KRAMER, Somerville, N.J.

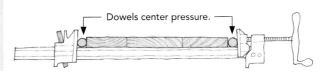

Dowels center pressure.

DOVETAILS

Softwood clamp pads for dovetails

I once taught at a place where another instructor told students that they should make corner clamping cauls, or pads, with cutouts similar to finger joints that would fit around the ends of the pins that protrude slightly. He said you needed those spaces in the clamp pads to pull the dovetail joints together properly. I humbly disagree. I don't waste a lot of time on something that is not part of the finished piece—especially something that will be discarded when the clamping is done. Instead, for clamp pads I use a scrap of white pine the length of the joint, by whatever thickness and width is handy. I find that the end grain of hardwood pins always digs into the softer pine, even the end grain of pine—it's no contest. So, unless you want to kill a lot of time, forget the tedium of making elaborate clamping cauls and just use a strip of pine to clamp the dovetail joints together.

—CHRISTIAN BECKSVOORT, New Gloucester, Maine

Use pine for clamp pads. Use scraps of pine to protect drawer cases from being damaged when clamping pressure is applied during glue-up.

Apply pressure evenly from all sides. Use spring clamps to hold the clamp pads in place, then use bar clamps to pull the joints together (left). Indentations left in the pine clamp pads indicate that they did the job to bring the drawer pieces together tightly (right).

Apply glue sparingly

To avoid squeeze-out inside a case, apply glue to all of the long-grain surfaces of the cheeks of dovetail pins and tails. Put only a dab on the outside edges of the end grain (right) where squeeze-out is more likely to occur. Drive the joint home with a deadblow mallet (far right), which won't mar the workpieces. Wipe away the squeeze-out before clamping.

—GARY ROGOWSKI, Portland, Ore.

MITERS

Clamp blocks for cases

Use these angled clamp blocks to ensure that miters close completely and accurately. The blocks can be glued, taped, or clamped to workpieces.

—GARY ROGOWSKI, Portland, Ore.

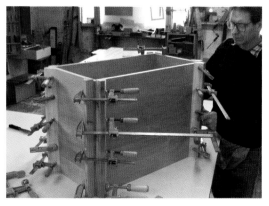

Attach blocks to large mitered cases. Angled blocks direct clamping pressure through the joints. If you glue on the blocks, make them out of a softer wood so they are easy to remove.

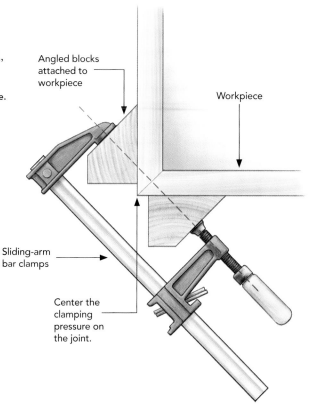

Angled blocks attached to workpiece

Workpiece

Sliding-arm bar clamps

Center the clamping pressure on the joint.

Seal end grain for a stronger joint

Miters are an end-grain-only joint, and they soak up a lot of glue. To add some strength, apply a preliminary coat of glue—called size—to close up all of the porous end grain. Scrape away any excess and wait a few minutes before applying glue again.

—GARY ROGOWSKI, Portland, Ore.

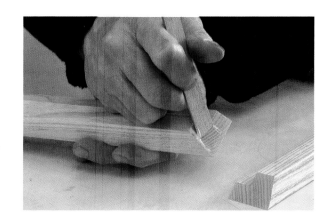

Jig simplifies glue-up of large mitered frames

I bid on, and won, a job that included a dozen 4-ft.-high cabinet doors. The frames of the doors had mitered corners. It wasn't until somewhat later, when I had to build the doors, that it occurred to me I didn't know how to clamp miters on such a big door. Thankfully, this fixture I made solved the problem.

It uses a large, flat base made from ¾-in.-thick medium-density fiberboard, four corner pieces also made from MDF, four hardwood blocks, and eight hardwood wedges to create the necessary clamping force.

Dry-fit the frame parts inside the layout lines, then lay in the corners. Next, slip the wedges in place (with the thin ends opposing each other) and screw the four blocks to the base. Use a pencil to scribe a reference line around the perimeter of the frame parts.

To assemble the frame, dry-fit it first to check the miters, using the reference line to position the parts. Then apply glue and position the workpieces on the jig. (A few pieces of waxed paper will keep the frame from sticking to the base.) Add the corner pieces and wedges, then lightly tap the wedges with a hammer to provide the clamping force.

—DICK JOHNSON, Grand Junction, Colo.

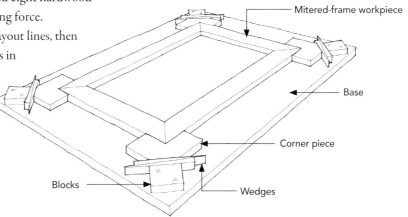

Mitered-frame workpiece

Base

Corner piece

Blocks

Wedges

EDGES AND FACE FRAMES

Clamping face frames with wedges

Recently I had to fabricate a large face frame that required more and longer clamps than I own. I solved the problem with a shop-built wedge-clamping assembly at each glue joint. The wedge-clamp is made entirely with drywall screws and scrap face-frame cutoffs.

First, I screwed a scrap piece to the back of the stile so that it extends 6 in. or so past the rail. Then I screwed a pivot block onto this extension with a single screw. This allows the block to pivot to fit the wedge's angle. When the face frame has been assembled, I drive a wedge home with a mallet to apply sufficient pressure to get a tight joint.

—JAMES BASCOM, Bel Air, Md.

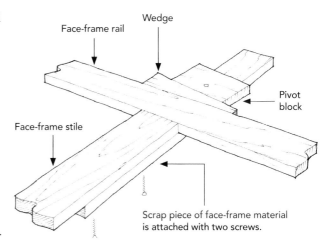

Face-frame rail

Wedge

Pivot block

Face-frame stile

Scrap piece of face-frame material is attached with two screws.

Racking clamps

I often glue edging or strips to the edges of dozens of same-size boards. I may need 50 clamps at a time. Metal clamps are too heavy, expensive, and slow to set up. So I use what I call racking clamps, which I make from wood I'd otherwise discard. The clamp is really a very broad, very shallow C-shape with the opening about ⅛-in. wider than the board plus the edging to be glued.

When making the clamps, I notch the corners to prevent glue squeeze-out sticking to the clamps, and I take care to cut the faces at a perfect 90°. To use, I install a clamp every 6 in. or so by racking, which is bumping one end until the clamp wedges into place. The clamps apply plenty of pressure, and they set up easily. They also disengage instantly to realign the joint if necessary.

—TOM SCHRUNK, Minneapolis, Minn.

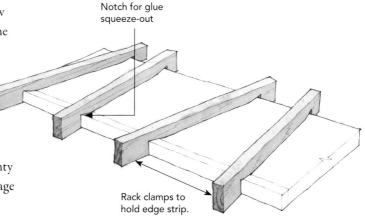

Notch for glue squeeze-out

Rack clamps to hold edge strip.

Shopmade face-frame clamp

When I had to assemble a large face frame, I realized my bar clamps were not long enough and were so heavy that they would probably distort such a light framework. So I made several of the clamps shown below based on a commercial clamp designed for face-frame assembly. The clamp uses a common pipe-clamp head to apply pressure and a tailpiece that grips the stock between two offset, cantilevered hardwood blocks faced with 100-grit sandpaper. A square U-bolt provides the pivot that joins the blocks.

Because I own a pipe tap, I was able to attach the tailpiece by

drilling and tapping the end of the bottom block. Alternatively, you could drill a slightly oversized hole in the block and pin the pipe in the hole with a small bolt. A little flex in the joint is good because it allows the assembly to be somewhat self-aligning.

Wing nuts on the ends of the U-bolt allow it to be reversed to the other side to accommodate left- or right-hand application on a frame. The maximum opening between the blocks (determined by the location of the pivot holes) should be a little more than the thickness of the stock to be joined. A ⅞-in. opening is about right for ¾-in.-thick stock.

—JEFFREY P. GYVING, Point Arena, Calif.

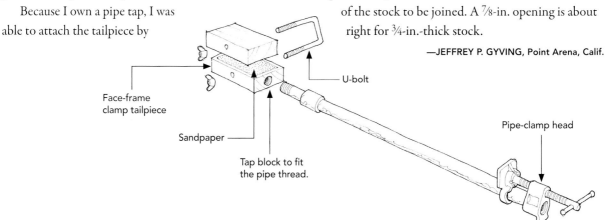

Face-frame clamp tailpiece

Sandpaper

Tap block to fit the pipe thread.

U-bolt

Pipe-clamp head

Using wedges for edge-glueing— two methods

A few wedges are all you need to clamp solid edging to plywood while the glue cures. After applying the edging with glue, simply place a few adjustable clamps along the front edge of the workpiece. It's a good idea to use scraps as clamping blocks to avoid marring the surface. Then tap a pair of wedges under each clamp bar to apply pressure to the edging.

—TED ASOUSA, Broomall, Pa.

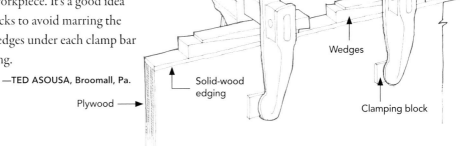

Wedges

Solid-wood edging

Plywood

Clamping block

Glue-ups are among the most frustrating procedures in woodworking. When you expect it to be a bear, it's a lamb, and when you expect it be Little Bo Peep, it turns out to be a grizzly bear. This tip was born out of desperation during what was perceived to be a Little Bo Peep procedure— gluing a wood edging strip to a curved top.

I know there are several kinds of dedicated clamps designed for gluing edges. In my opinion these clamps are too pricey, take up too much precious real estate when they're not being used, and they're too limited in the thickness they can accommodate. Not so with this simple technique, which requires only the quick-action clamps you probably already own and a package of door-installation shims.

Simply tighten your quick-action clamp close to the edge of the top to be glued, accounting for the thickness of your edging and the shim. Apply some decent pressure to the clamp. Add some sandpaper blocks and really cinch down the clamps if you need a lot of pressure. Apply glue and set the edging in place. Then smack a softwood shim between the edging and the bar of the clamp to hold the edging tightly in place until the glue sets.

—DAVID GUARINO, South Plainfield, N.J.

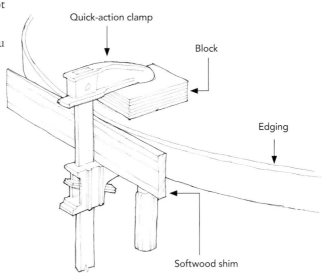

Quick-action clamp

Block

Edging

Softwood shim

FINISHING

REPAIRS

Repairing scratches and tearout

Sometimes you don't see surface defects until you apply stain or dye. Maybe a random-orbit sander left its signature pigtail marks, or you didn't use the right paper to eliminate scratches left by coarser grits. If the first swipe of stain shows vivid swirls or scratches all over the work, stop.

Sand the piece again, this time changing paper frequently and working your way systematically through the grits. If you've oiled or stained the piece and find that swirls show up in only one or two spots, sand those areas by hand with P220-grit wet-or-dry paper, wetting it with some of the same finish you used. This method works well with most oil finishes or oil-based pigment stains. If you used stain, reapply it carefully to match the surrounding stained areas.

If you used a dye, resand a stand-alone area, such as an entire stile. If it is a large surface, sand the damaged area, feathering the edge between sanded and unsanded parts. Then apply more dye.

To eliminate tearout, sand, plane, or scrape the surface. Wipe the surface with mineral spirits to check the smoothness. If the imperfections are small enough (generally no larger than a pinhead), you can fill them after you've stained and sealed the piece, using fill sticks, which are wax crayons sold for touching up scratches.

—TERI MASASCHI, Tijeras, N.M.

Smoothing slurry. Wet-sanding with the oil or stain you used helps eliminate swirls more rapidly without ruining the color.

Removing glue residue and squeeze-out

You can get rid of some gluey fingerprint residue by wet-sanding with the stain you used, or by lightly sanding and reapplying the stain.

Use a sharp chisel to eliminate dried glue from around a joint. Use sandpaper to clear up areas where you didn't completely wipe away squeeze-out. Wrap P220-grit paper around a hard block and sand with the grain, using firm pressure. To avoid scratching adjacent surfaces, use a 6-in. flexible drywall knife as a shield.

—TERI MASASCHI, Tijeras, N.M.

Uneven oiling. Glue residue on this mortise-and-tenon joint prevents the wood from absorbing oil evenly.

Touch-up. When removing glue squeeze-out, sand with the grain using P220-grit paper. Keep the block flat against the work to avoid rounding over an edge. Shield adjacent surfaces with a wide drywall knife.

Repairing burn-through of finish or color

If you've burned through the underlying color while sanding the topcoat, (removing both the topcoats and the stain), carefully apply more stain, protect it with a light coat of shellac, and then replace the topcoats. If you've burned through the finish only (a frequent occurrence on edges, moldings, and carvings), delicately reapply it. When the repairs are thoroughly dry, rub out those areas to blend them in with the rest of the surface.

—TERI MASASCHI, Tijeras, N.M.

Burned up. If you sand the topcoat too aggressively or don't keep the sanding block level, you risk removing some of the finish.

Restore the color. Use a small artist's brush to reapply stain to the sanded-through area.

Seal the color. Brush a light coat of shellac over the stain touch-up.

Clear pitch-pocket filler

To fill pitch pockets, use a five-minute epoxy, which is clear and sets up quickly. Let it harden for at least two hours, then sand it smooth with silicon-carbide paper. Scratches leave a cloudy appearance, so sand with progressively finer grits until you get down to P600-grit or P1,200-grit. Epoxy does have drawbacks; it is not resistant to ultraviolet light, and it eventually will turn opaque and crumble from exposure to bright sunlight. Finally, check for compatibility with the varnish you'll be using.

—CHRISTIAN BECKSVOORT, New Gloucester, Maine

Epoxy is an invisible filler for pitch pockets. To fill pitch pockets without discoloring them, mix a small amount of five-minute epoxy in the base of a paper cup.

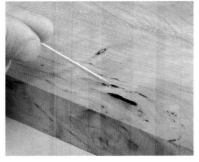

Use care in filling pockets. Flat toothpicks are a handy tool for dripping small amounts of epoxy into holes without spillage.

Sand after the epoxy has cured. Use a hard sanding block to avoid causing a hollow in the wood surrounding the pocket.

Repairing witness lines

When rubbing out a film finish like varnish, you cut through the layers of finish. Witness lines are shadowy craters of this cut-through (see the far right photo). They seldom occur with shellac or lacquer because new coats of those finishes dissolve into the old ones.

To repair witness lines, use fine sandpaper and a light touch to sand the surface to level it as much as possible. Then apply at least two more fresh coats of finish.

—TERI MASASCHI, Tijeras, N.M.

Witnesses. Sanding too much can produce witness lines, whitish areas exposing earlier coats of finish.

Add another topcoat. Apply more of the topcoat to the entire surface, not just where the witness lines had been.

Correcting the wrong stain color

The stain you applied threw the wood color way off. Generally, a stain will appear either too red or not red enough. Either way, it spoils the appearance of the piece.

Correct the color with a glaze. I've had good results with Behlen and Mohawk® glazing stains. Apply a washcoat (a thin coat) of shellac over the stain, then gently scuff-sand with P320-grit paper when it's dry. Use a glaze that contrasts with the stain to bring the color back into line.

For example, if the stain looks too red, tone it down with a raw umber glaze, which is greenish in tone. Alter-natively, you can use a black glaze to change the color's tone. If the stain doesn't have enough red, warm up the color with burnt umber or burnt sienna, which is predominantly reddish.

Brush on the glaze liberally, let it sit for a minute or so, then lightly remove most of it with a clean rag, leaving a thin film of color. Once you've corrected the color to your liking, protect the glaze with another washcoat of shellac before you apply the topcoat.

—TERI MASASCHI, Tigeras, N.M.

Tone it down. A contrasting glaze usually will correct a color that's wrong. Here, black glaze will tame a too-red stain on this oak door (left). Wipe off the excess glaze almost immediately, revealing a better color (above).

Identifying finishes for repair

Before you repair a finish topcoat, you have to know what you're working with. First, remove any wax on the surface by rubbing it with a cotton cloth dampened with mineral spirits.

Next, in an inconspicuous spot, place a drop of denatured alcohol on the surface, wait a few minutes, and then rub the area with a paper tissue. If the finish is shellac, you'll rub some off.

If the surface stays hard, repeat the test with a drop of lacquer thinner. If the surface becomes sticky, the finish is lacquer or a water-based finish. The latter was rarely used before the 1990s, so lacquer is the only candidate on older pieces.

If the surface remains undamaged by the lacquer thinner, you have a reactive finish such as varnish.

In the case of a shellac or solvent-based lacquer finish, a fresh coat of the same finish will melt into the existing finish, making repairs relatively simple if the existing finish is in good shape.

A fresh coat of a reactive finish, however, won't chemically bond to an old coat, so you'll either need to sand the existing surface to create a mechanical bond or, if the existing finish is too badly damaged, strip it entirely and start again from bare wood.

—MARK SCHOFIELD, Newtown, Conn.

Solvent identifies finish. To know which finish you're dealing with, try to dissolve it. Test a hidden spot. You'll know the finish by which solvent removes it.

What to do if red oak turns blue

The blue color in red oak is caused by iron contamination which can occur during milling or by rubbing with steel wool. When sufficient moisture is present, the trace iron particles left on the surface of the wood react with the tannic acid in the wood. That blue-black stain actually is iron tannate.

A diluted solution of oxalic acid will remove the stain. Most hardware stores carry oxalic acid as deck cleaners or in the form of crystals. Follow the manufacturer's directions for proper protection. Dissolve about one tablespoon of crystals in one pint of water to make the oxalic-acid solution. Be sure to use a plastic or glass container to make the solution; the acid will react with metal. Apply the solution with a brush or rag. There's no need to neutralize the acid, but be sure to rinse off the excess thoroughly with water and let the wood dry. Neutralizing sometimes will reverse the reaction of the acid solution, and the blue stain may reappear.

—CHRIS A. MINICK, Stillwater, Minn.

Oxalic acid will remove a blue stain from red oak. This piece of oak, which was wetted to raise the grain and then rubbed down with steel wool, has turned blue. To get rid of the stain, apply a solution of oxalic acid.

Invisible patch for lumber defects

The best repair for small knots and blemishes in wood is an invisible one. This means that any patch should match both the color and the grain of the surrounding board. The best source is a cutoff or scrap from the same board.

Select a flatsawn scrap that has a 2-in. to 3-in. section clear of any growth rings. Plane it down so it's ⅛ in. to 3/16 in. thick. If you don't have a suitable piece, make it at the bandsaw by cutting a flatsawn board to minimize the number of growth rings visible. Cut a diamond-shaped or triangular patch, but not a rectangle. Cuts that run diagonally across the grain are far less visible than those running perpendicular to it.

Plane or sand the edges of the patch smooth and bevel them slightly for a tighter fit. Then place the patch over the damaged area and lightly trace around it with a marking knife. Rout away the waste and clean up the edges and corners with a sharp chisel. Glue and clamp the patch in place. After sanding the patch flush to the surrounding wood, use a brown pencil to lightly draw in grain lines that connect to the surrounding wood.

—CHRISTIAN BECKSVOORT, New Gloucester, Maine

Not all defects are natural. Buckshot and bullets can lie hidden beneath the surface of even the most beautiful board.

No grain allowed. The best patches are made from flatsawn stock with no visible grain. Resaw between grain lines if possible to minimize them.

Shape of patch is key. Diamond-shaped and triangular patches disappear better than square ones, because cuts that run diagonally across the grain are far less visible.

Scribe around the patch. Use a marking knife to trace the patch's outline (left). The precise mark allows you to cut an accurate mortise, which helps hide the patch. After routing away the waste and cleaning the edges with a chisel, glue the patch onto the mortise (above).

Artistic license. Grain lines, drawn with a brown pencil, make the patch disappear.

Finish-based filler hides defects

Shopmade sawdust putty does a great job filling in mistakes, natural defects, and gaps in dovetails and other joinery. Instead of using glue for the binder, however, I make the putty by mixing sawdust with a solvent-based finish—whichever one I am going to use for my first sealer coat. When both the sealer and the putty are made from the same resin, the light reflection, absorption, and refraction of the patched surface and the sealed wood are identical. The patch virtually disappears.

I use dewaxed shellac as the binder in my sawdust putty, but you can use any common solvent-based wood finish (such as lacquer and varnish). Note that putty made from oil-based varnish takes a very long time to dry (several days if the patch is deep).

This method works great for projects that are not stained. If the wood is to be stained, liquid hide glue is the best binder to use. Hide glue will take stain much like wood.

—CHRIS MINICK, Stillwater, Minn.

Disappearing act. Sawdust putty makes a great filler for small cracks and defects like this hole left by a pin knot. After the repair has been sanded and the sealer coat applied, the small hole becomes much less obvious.

Shellac protects wood from contaminated finish

If small craters appear as you are applying a topcoat to a flat surface the surface has some sort of contaminant. Often from the first brushful, the coating literally "crawls" into an odd formation that resembles a crater or fisheye. You can't do anything ahead of time to prevent this contamination. It may come from lubricants used on a tablesaw or jointer bed. It can also occur if you put a water-based finish over an oil-based stain.

Don't even begin to think you can keep brushing to eliminate the problem. Wipe off all the coating, then brush or spray on a light coat of shellac. The shellac forms a barrier to keep the contaminant from coming up through subsequent layers of finish. When the shellac dries, continue applying the topcoat you want.

—TERI MASASCHI, Tijeras, N.M.

Attack immediately. Wipe off all the contaminated topcoat as soon as you see it crawl. A light spray of shellac will isolate the contamination, so you can reapply the topcoat.

Repairing sand-through on face veneer

If you've sanded through the finish and face veneer, don't panic. Here's a simple fix. Use a scrap of the same plywood to duplicate the mistake and serve as a sample board for the remedy. Apply the same finish you plan to use on the piece, then sand through a portion of the face veneer to give yourself a place to experiment with a repair.

Mix thin shellac with a touch-up powder such as Behlen Master Furniture Powder (www.woodworker .com) or Mohawk Blendal Powder Stain (www.mohawk finishing.com). Put a piece of glass next to the sand-through on the practice board and begin developing your color. Quickly dip the brush into the shellac, then into one of the touch-up powders. Swirl the brush around on the glass to incorporate the powder and shellac. Dab on more shellac and a different powder to blend the color you need. Work in thin layers, sneaking up on the color rather than painting it in. If you aren't happy with the results, wipe away the color and start over.

When you've done a reasonable job of covering the sand-through on the scrap, take a deep breath and do the same thing on the real project. A glaze—a type of stain used on a semisealed surface—brushed on and then lightly wiped off will help blend in the patch.

—TERI MASASCHI, Tijeras, N.M.

Practice patch. Make a similar burn-through on a scrap of the same plywood. Mix touch-up powders with thinned shellac to match the color of the face veneer and hide the sanded-through spot.

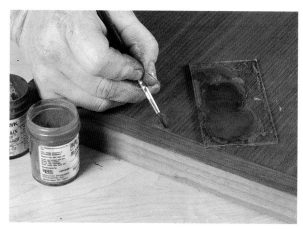

Faux finish. Carefully paint the tinted shellac over the sand-through. Apply a glaze to help blend the patch into the surrounding wood.

Evening out dye stain

If a dye-based stain looks stronger or more intense in some areas than in others as you're applying it, you'll end up with an unevenly colored surface or lap marks where you wanted uniformity.

Pull a damp rag over the surface. That will lift the dye, so you can "move" or remove it to make the color even. Work the rag around to blend the color evenly. Then apply a washcoat of shellac and the stain you want to use.

—TERI MASASCHI, Tijeras, N.M.

Easy fix. This maple door didn't take dye well, leaving lap marks on the frame. A wet rag rubbed over the dye will even out the color, minimizing blotchiness.

Fixing drips and sags in topcoat

If you used too heavy a hand in applying the topcoat and the coating drools down the side of your beautiful project, there is a solution.

Wait until the sag is totally dried. It should feel hard, not resilient, when you push on it. Wrap a cork or hardwood sanding block with P320-grit paper and lightly sand to level the mess. If you start sanding while the sag is still gummy, you'll just make the mess worse. Check your work frequently and change the paper often. You want to flatten the lumps without going through the stain color or down to the bare wood.

Or, if you only have one or two drips, you can scrape them off using a fresh single-edge razor blade. Be sure to scrape carefully to avoid cutting through the finish.

—TERI MASASCHI, Tijeras, N.M.

Scrape or sand. Once a drip has dried completely, scrape it off with a razor blade (left) or sand it flush (right).

Shellac is a cure for blotchy stain

With some woods, a pigmented stain won't take evenly, a problem called blotching. Pine, cherry, maple, birch, and alder are the most likely to blotch.

If the surface is very blotchy, you'll have to remove the stain by stripping, sanding, or both, and start over. This time, apply a washcoat of shellac and then the stain.

If the blotching isn't severe, try using a glaze to soften the contrast between the deeply colored and lighter areas. Once the initial stain is dry, apply a washcoat of shellac. Let it dry, then gently scuff-sand with P320-grit paper. Brush on a burnt umber or other brownish glaze; wipe gently to remove most of the excess.

—TERI MASASCHI, Tijeras, N.M.

Sand lightly. Pine is one of several woods that blotch easily. To even things out, begin by scuff-sanding.

Apply a glaze and wipe it off. Brush on a glaze to help cover up the blotches (left). Once the excess glaze has been wiped away, the door's color is much more uniform (right).

Invisible fix for nick in plywood

If you've nicked your nice piece of hardwood plywood, don't panic. Here's an easy fix. Start by planing thin shavings (0.003 in. to 0.004 in.) from a piece of scrapwood of the same species, color, and grain pattern as the plywood. Trim a dozen or so shavings somewhat longer than the bare spot. Dab a thin layer of yellow glue onto the bare spot and place one shaving on it.

Repeat this procedure until you've filled the void and then some—seven to 10 layers. Work quickly in order to finish before the glue dries. Place a business card or a piece of waxed paper on top of the mound and immediately clamp a hardwood block over the repair. A second block underneath the workpiece will prevent denting.

Let the repair dry overnight before removing the clamp and blocks. Now, carefully handplane the mound with a sharp, standard-angle block plane. As you get close to the surrounding surface, switch to a scraper and/or sandpaper for better control. (For an open-grained species like oak, I also put in fake grain lines with an awl to match the surrounding wood.)

Because of the high wood content and the thin glue bond between layers, the repair holds up and takes stain beautifully.

—HENDRIK VARJU, Acton, Ont., Canada

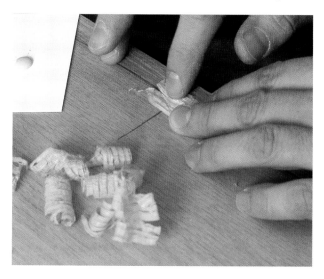

Fill and conceal. Glue thin shavings from matching wood to fill the nick (left). Once the glue dries, plane, scrape, and sand the patch. With a finish applied, neither the nick nor the patch is visible (above).

Solvents reveal planer marks

Planer marks can be tough to remove by sanding and can be hard to see, often showing up after the finish has been applied. But here's a secret to highlighting them before it's too late. Before you apply a finish to a surface, wipe on a solvent such as naphtha, mineral spirits, or denatured alcohol, which, unlike water, will highlight planer marks without raising the grain. The solvent will evaporate quickly and won't interfere with subsequent stains or finishes that you may apply.

—MATT BERGER, Newtown, Conn.

TECHNIQUE

How to hide sapwood

The contrast between pale sapwood and darker heartwood is an issue with both walnut and cherry. Such an extreme difference in appearance can ruin a design. Here's a quick, simple, and effective way to blend sapwood with the heartwood.

First, get a sample board that's the same species as the workpiece. Of course, be sure it has both sapwood and heartwood. Next, wipe the board with denatured alcohol to highlight the sapwood.

Now mix up a dye that is close to the color of the alcohol-wetted heartwood. Be sure to keep the heartwood wet so you can see the true color you are trying to match. Use dye powders that dissolve in water (www.wdlockwood.com and www.woodworker.com), not pigment stains, as these will muddy the appearance of the wood. Test the color on the sapwood of the sample board and, if necessary, tweak it. In this case, I used Lockwood's® walnut crystals for the dark brown color, but added a very small amount of rose pink to match the underlying tone in the heartwood.

If anything, err on the side of sapwood that's slightly darker than the heartwood. When the dye dries, it will appear much darker than the heartwood, but as soon as a clear finish is applied, the two areas will blend into one and no one will know your secret.

—PETER GEDRYS, East Haddam, Conn.

The sapwood revealed. Wiping the surface with denatured alcohol reveals what the walnut's dark heartwood and pale sapwood will look like under a clear finish.

Find the color that matches. Test dyes on a piece of wet scrapwood until you find the perfect match. Then apply the dye, or combination of dyes, to the actual workpiece.

The sapwood concealed. When the dye dries, it will appear darker than the heartwood, but the two will blend together when clear finish is applied.

Simple, two-step, food-safe finish for the inside of a bowl

The finish you apply to your bowl depends somewhat on the bowl's intended use and the surface you prefer. Personally, I don't like high-gloss finishes, partly because they eventually break down and are difficult to refurbish, but also because I like my bowls to be used.

I employ a very quick and easy oil and beeswax finish. The finish also provides a good base for regular refurbishing with just about any furniture polish. With constant use and little or no oiling, wood will develop a wonderfully soft patina. With regular polishing, any wood will soon gain a deep antique glow. The secret to tactile surfaces is frequent use and attention.

I finish the bowl while it's spinning on the lathe, first slopping on a generous dose of mineral oil. Then I hold a lump of pure beeswax firmly against the wood to build up a thin layer of wax inside the bowl. Then I press the oil-soaked cloth firmly against the spinning bowl to burnish it. Any surplus remains in the cloth. (The cloth can become so impregnated with oil and wax that on dense woods you can dispense with the oil and wax and just apply the cloth.)

The finishing technique should work on bark if you have cut and sanded it. If the bark is rough, just oil it with boiled linseed oil, wipe off the surplus, then buff the surface by hand when it's dry, which is usually after 24 hours.

—RICHARD RAFFAN, Holder, ACT, Australia

1. WIPE ON MINERAL OIL

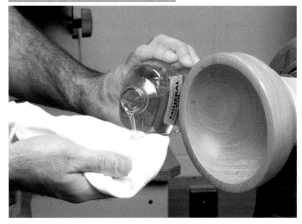

Use a generous amount of mineral oil. With the bowl spinning, burnish the oil into the bowl using a cloth. Use moderate pressure and caution so as not to get the rag wrapped into the lathe. The bowl will take on a satin finish.

2. APPLY BEESWAX AND THEN BURNISH

Hold the block of beeswax firmly against the wood and apply a thin, even layer inside the bowl. With the same rag you used for the mineral oil, press firmly into the bowl until you see a shine. Save this rag for the next time you need to burnish a bowl.

How to brush with no brush marks

Here's a method of brushing on a finish without leaving telltale brush marks in the dried finish film.

First, be sure the viscosity of the finish is right for brushing. With most finishes, a viscosity of roughly that of half-and-half cream flows well. If necessary, thin the finish with the manufacturer's recommended solvent to get the consistency you want. Before dipping the brush into the varnish, wet the bristles in the solvent, which prevents dried finish from building up at the base of the brush.

The first stroke covers just a small area, starting about 3 in. from the edge. The second stroke starts just behind the wet edge and goes to the opposite side. Increase the angle of the brush from about 45° at the start to about 90° near the end. This allows varnish from the reservoir to flow onto the surface and makes it easier to decrease pressure on the bristles so they don't run over the edge on the opposite side.

After coating the whole panel, level out any uneven areas by lightly dragging the bristle tips of the unloaded brush through the wet finish. After each coat dries, scuff-sand with P220-grit paper to remove nibs or dust specks.

—CHRIS A. MINICK, Stillwater, Minn.

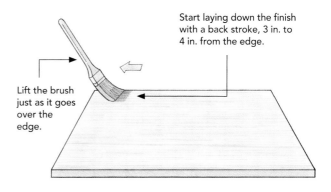

FIRST STROKE

Start laying down the finish with a back stroke, 3 in. to 4 in. from the edge.

Lift the brush just as it goes over the edge.

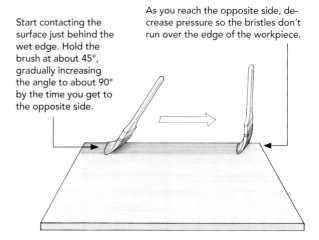

SECOND STROKE

Start contacting the surface just behind the wet edge. Hold the brush at about 45°, gradually increasing the angle to about 90° by the time you get to the opposite side.

As you reach the opposite side, decrease pressure so the bristles don't run over the edge of the workpiece.

How to stain mahogany to match an antique finish

When matching an antique finish, the process you follow is more important than the exact colors and products you use. First, use a dye stain that matches the color between the dark grain lines of the antique. Test the dye on a scrap piece, and strengthen or weaken it until it's just right. After it has dried, seal the dye with a 2-lb. cut of dewaxed shellac. Let it dry for two hours, sand with P400-grit sandpaper, and remove the dust. Next, apply an oil-based grain filler that matches the grain lines on the antique. Let it dry for two days and then apply another coat of dewaxed shellac (2-lb. cut). After the shellac has dried, you can use a gel stain to alter the color. Finally, apply a clear finish. Shellac is a good choice.

—JEFF JEWITT, Strongsville, Ohio

Three-step finish.
Start by dyeing the field, then fill the grain in a darker color. Tweak the color with a gel stain.

Wipe on varnish in three steps

Here's a no-fuss, no-muss method of wiping on varnish. First, strain it through a cone-shaped painter's strainer or a piece of lint-free cheesecloth stretched across the top of an empty can. Dilute the varnish to a 50/50 mixture with the appropriate solvent. Then pour the mixture into an aluminum pie pan.

Dip an applicator (see p. 212) into the mixture, and then tap the sides of the pan lightly until nothing is dripping from it. I always start with the smaller, more intricate parts of a piece of furniture (see the photo at right).

For the larger surfaces, apply the finish in a circular motion, and don't worry about neatness at first. Work quickly because the thinly applied coats dry rapidly. Next, use long, gliding strokes in the direction of the wood grain. At the far end of a flat surface, lift the ball from the surface just as you come to the edge. Repeat until you have deposited a smooth, continuous layer of varnish. Refresh the applicator when it becomes dry or begins to drag. Do the edges of tops last.

Let the varnish dry before applying the next coat.

—**THOMAS E. WISSHACK**, Galesburg, Ill.

Start with the intricate details. Work quickly and use a gentle touch to avoid drips and runs.

Large, flat surfaces. Work in a circular motion first, then work across the surface going with the grain. Finish the edges last.

TOOLS

When varnish is past its prime

Refinishing old furniture with vintage varnish has a certain romantic appeal, but I fear that doing so is asking for hair-pulling frustration. Varnish dries, or more appropriately cures, when the oil-based finish molecules combine with oxygen (from the air) to form a polymerized finish film. Metallic driers or catalysts that speed up the polymerization process are added by the manufacturer to ensure that the finish dries in a reasonable length of time. Unfortunately, these catalysts deactivate with time, even in the factory-sealed container. It is just a fact of chemistry—the older the varnish, the longer it will take to cure. Reasonable dry times can be expected from varnish that is less than one to one-and-a-half years old, but varnish older than three or four years will remain tacky for what seems like eons.

Adding a small amount of Japan drier, a commercially available mixture of metallic driers, can sometimes revive aging varnish. The exact proportion needed varies between manufacturers, so follow the directions printed on the label. Be aware, though, that more drier is not necessarily better. Too much can result in a brittle finish film, form a white haze called drier bloom, or inhibit drying altogether. Experiment on scrap to ensure the proper drier concentration before committing the doctored varnish to your project. Money spent on Japan drier is probably better spent purchasing fresh varnish instead. Besides, it is a lot less frustrating.

—CHRIS A. MINICK, Stillwater, Minn.

Applicator for wipe-on finishes

The ideal applicator for wiping on varnish is a wood finisher's ball made from a soft cotton cloth—about 8 in. by 8 in.—and cheesecloth. Wrap the cloth around the cheesecloth to form a small pillow. A rubber band holds the ball together and makes a convenient handle.

—THOMAS E. WISSHACK, Galesburg, Ill.

Make custom pads for wipe-on finishes

To apply wipe-on finishes, I make small custom pads out of the replacement pads sold for paint edgers. I cut them to a workable size, about 1 in. by 1½ in., and then mount them to a block of wood with double-sided tape to make a handle. I pour a small amount of finish in a saucer, load the pad, and apply it to the workpiece with long, low strokes that just kiss the surface.

—JOHN BUCKHAM, Wauchope, NSW, Australia

Tea makes great stain for raw wood

Paint tea onto raw wood for an inexpensive and natural-looking stain. The stronger the tea, the darker the stain. After it dries, seal with shellac or varnish.

—SAM BRUIN, Brooksville, Fla.

Three light finishes for maple

The ideal finish for maple is colorless, avoids the darkening effect you get with most finishes on light woods, will not yellow over time, and will keep the maple itself from yellowing, which occurs when the wood is exposed to air and oxygen. I recommend an acrylic finish, and you can go two routes:

The first is to use a water-based acrylic or acrylic/urethane blend. This has both the advantage of being colorless when dry and, due to the coalescing nature of the way it forms a film, of keeping the finish resin on the surface of the wood.

This route leads to the slightest deepening effect from the wetting-out of the cellulose. Applied by spraying, brushing, or wiping, this finish looks like plain sanded maple. To pop the grain a bit, first wipe the maple with an ultrapale shellac sealer.

The second route is to use a solvent-based acrylic or butyrate lacquer or blend, such as a CAB-acrylic. CAB stands for cellulose acetate butyrate. This will give you more wetting-out of the cellulose and hence more figure. The finish will be just a touch darker than the aforementioned choice. Also, you must apply this type of finish by spraying.

You also could try an amino-alkyd or vinyl conversion varnish. This finish requires careful preparation and application because it's sprayed. But it's tough as nails once it cures. Avoid conversion lacquer, which is the amino-alkyd resin with nitrocellulose added. Nitrocellulose will yellow significantly over time.

A final option is a dewaxed colorless shellac. Ultrapale and super blonde will have just a hint of color, while bleached shellac has virtually no color. All will deepen the color of the wood but won't provide any UV protection.

Of all of these, I prefer to use an acrylic finish on maple. An acrylic is not only colorless, but it also has a natural screening effect for blocking UV light, which yellows maple.

—JEFF JEWITT, Strongsville, Ohio

More figure. A solvent-based acrylic pops the figure but needs to be sprayed.

Deeper wood figure now, yellow later. While a shellac will give a good finish now, it offers no UV protection, so the wood and finish may yellow.

Clear finish with no yellowing. A water-based acrylic is easy to apply and remains clear over time, but it brings little depth to the grain.

Cleaning brushes extends their life

You can make brushes last for years if you clean them the right way. My method works for both synthetic and natural bristles.

With oil-based finishes, you don't necessarily have to clean the brush each time you use it. If I'm brushing a traditional, multilayered varnish that is recoated each day or every other day, I don't wash the brush after each coat. I wipe the excess finish out of the brush with a lint-free rag, then store it in its solvent. For most oil-based finishes, the solvent is mineral spirits. For lacquer, it is lacquer thinner. Before reusing the brush, I press out the extra solvent.

After I've applied the final coat, it's time to give the brush a good cleaning. First I remove most of the finish using a solvent. Then I rinse the brush with a citrus cleaner and water and hang it to dry. When it comes to water-based finishes, I clean them after each use, using water and some dishwashing detergent.

—DAVID SORG, Denver, Colo.

Hang it out to dry. Once the brush is clean, shake it out and wring out the bristles with your fingers. Hang it on a nail to dry overnight, then wrap the bristles in paper to keep out dust. This goes for brushes used with both water- and oil-based finishes.

WATER-BASED FINISHES

Detergent helps water do its job. Dishwashing liquid will help remove all of the finish material. Use warm water, and massage the soap into the bristles. Rinse and repeat as many times as necessary.

OIL-BASED FINISHES

Remove most of the sludge with a solvent. Fill a jar halfway with solvent and dip the brush in it. Wipe the brush semi-dry with paper towels. Repeat a time or two, especially if there's a lot of finish up in the ferrule. Then hold the brush a little above the container and dribble on some virgin solvent. Repeat.

Rinse with water. Once the brush is free of sludge, rinse it under clean water.

Rinse with citrus cleaner. When you think the brush is clean enough, follow up by rinsing it in household citrus cleaner. A little sludge is normal on the first rinse. If you find a lot of sludge, you probably didn't rinse the brush enough in solvent and you should repeat that step.

Shopmade disposable foam brushes

Here's a way to make simple disposable foam brushes for glue, paint, stain, or epoxy. Slice strips of foam, then cover one side of the foam with spray adhesive—Elmer's® Craft Bond works well. Press tongue depressors or other sticks onto one side of the foam at appropriate intervals. Now fold the foam over the sticks evenly, press, and cut the segments apart. I make dozens of different sizes at a time. Upholstery shops have foam scraps of all thicknesses, and it doesn't take much to make a bunch of brushes—a few feet of ⅜-in.-thick material goes a long way.

—JOHN KINDSETH, Lodi, Calif.

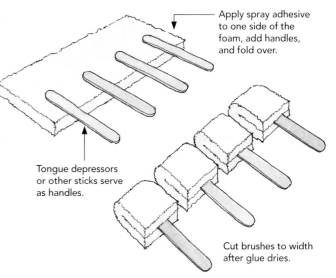

Apply spray adhesive to one side of the foam, add handles, and fold over.

Tongue depressors or other sticks serve as handles.

Cut brushes to width after glue dries.

HOLDING WORK

Magnets and screws make small parts easy to finish

Before applying finish to small wooden parts, like knobs or handles, I drill a small hole in the base of the part and insert a flathead wood screw a few turns. The screw need only be long enough to allow me to grasp it without touching the part.

Once I've applied the finish, I place a rare-earth magnet on the end of the screwhead, then place the magnet, screw, and finished part on a flat metal surface. The magnet sticks firmly to both the metal surface and the screw, so I don't need to worry about the wood part tipping over before the finish dries.

—MIKE WATSON, Sherwood Park, Ala.

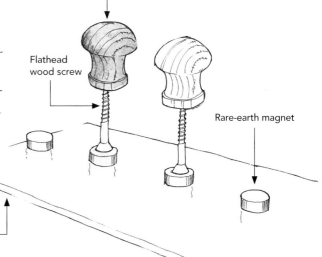

Knob

Flathead wood screw

Rare-earth magnet

Steel plate

Spray-finishing small parts

Holding small parts while you spray-finish them can be a problem. Air pressure from the spray gun blows the parts around. And finish blowing back from the surface the parts sit on can create unexpected runs.

A simple solution is to hold small parts with common hardware cloth or hail screen, as it's sometimes called. Cut a suitable piece of the screen and staple it to scraps of wood to produce a stable base. Then simply place items to be finished on the screen and spray. If you want to make sure the small parts don't move, snip out small sections of the screen to create wire fingers to grip each item. Because of the open nature of the screen, you won't have any problems with finish blowing back.

—R.B. HIMES, Vienna, Ohio

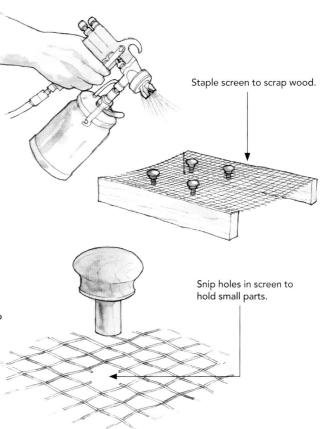

Staple screen to scrap wood.

Snip holes in screen to hold small parts.

Jig rotates legs for finishing

Finishing some table legs recently, I discovered how difficult it can be to get a spotless, dripless finish on such parts. The project became a lot easier after I built this rack from scrap.

The rack is just two lengths of 2×4 stock screwed to a plywood base. Common nails serve as spindles and let me rotate the legs as I finish each side. Allow about ½ in. of clearance on either side of each leg. Drill holes the same diameter as the nails in the 2×4s at appropriate intervals. Make some indentations in the top and bottom of each leg to act as bearing points for the nails.

—BARRY BORTNICK, Calgary, Alta., Canada

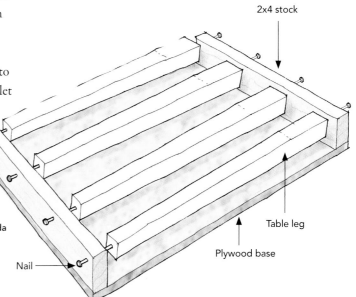

2x4 stock

Table leg

Plywood base

Nail

Oversize lazy Susan helps with finishing

In the past, when brushing or spraying pieces, I often managed to mar the finish by leaving fingerprints on the workpiece as I tried to maneuver it for access, or by inadvertently dragging an air hose across it.

At a flea market, I bought an old telephone operator's chair, the kind that swivels and adjusts up and down. I offered $5 for it, took it home, removed the chair, and bolted a piece of ¾-in.-thick plywood to the chair bracket. Bingo! In just 10 minutes, I had a large lazy Susan that gives me access to an entire workpiece without having to touch areas I've already finished. This simple device allows me to turn the workpiece any way I want and adjust the height to any level. It isn't beautiful, but it sure works great.

—ERNEST M. CUZZOCREO, Sonora, Calif.

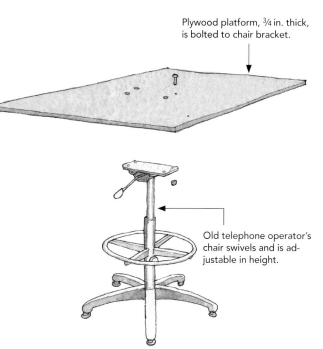

Plywood platform, ¾ in. thick, is bolted to chair bracket.

Old telephone operator's chair swivels and is adjustable in height.

Joining plates suspend items for finishing

I use metal joining plates as supports for finishing. The plates serve the same purpose as driving fine nails or brads into a block of wood, except that the plates are ready-made. You can find them at a lumberyard that stocks metal framing anchors or at a roof-truss builder. A couple of common brands are Gang-Nails and Simpson Strong-Tie®.

The sharp points that project from the plates hold the workpiece being finished above the table and leave little or no marks on the underside of the workpiece. Use one plate to support a small item or several to support a larger item. I've used the plates to support objects as large as a chest of drawers.

—DAVID E. KING, Pendleton, Ore.

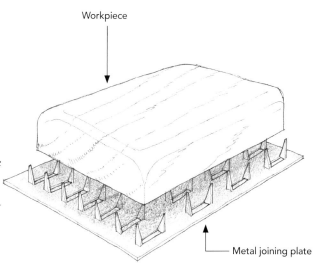

Workpiece

Metal joining plate

MAINTENANCE

Maintaining finely finished furniture

When you touch a piece of fine furniture, you are not touching the wood; you are touching the finish. And the function of any finish is to enhance the beauty of the underlying wood and to protect the piece of furniture from the ravages of everyday life. So the object of furniture care is to maintain the finish. The finish will take care of the furniture.

Furniture finishes can be divided into two broad classes: film-forming finishes and non-film-forming finishes. This distinction is important, because different care procedures are required by each.

Film-forming finishes, as the name implies, form a film much like kitchen plastic wrap over the entire piece of furniture. Most furniture-care products will remove the accumulated dirt and grime, but, more important, leave behind a low-friction coating on the film finish. This slick coating preserves the integrity of the film by deflecting direct blows that would abrade the finish. As long as the finish film is completely intact, with no cracks or deep scratches, it matters little whether you choose an aerosol product containing silicone or a traditional paste wax for furniture. Both work equally well, and neither harms the finish or furniture. However, if the finish surface is scratched, cracked, or chipped, use only paste wax. Aerosol silicone products may seep through the finish cracks and cause future refinishing problems.

By the way, lemon oil is really mineral oil with an added lemon scent. It's okay for cutting boards but probably not the best choice for furniture.

Non-film-forming finishes, such as linseed oil, have no film to protect the wood, so both aerosol silicone products and paste wax should be avoided. Simply remove surface dust and smudges with a dry or slightly water-dampened rag. Periodic oiling, once a year or so, will maintain the appearance of the piece.

—CHRIS A. MINICK, Stillwater, Minn.

Keep walnut from fading

When finished, walnut has a very appealing, deep, rich color. But over time, the color can fade from exposure to ultraviolet light and oxygen. Add a barrier, and you reduce fading. My unstained walnut table, finished with a light coat of oil-based varnish, has sat under the living-room window for more than 20 years. Most finishes won't totally seal out ultraviolet light and oxygen, but they can keep walnut from fading in your lifetime.

Danish oil is a good finish option; three or four coats will impart a hand-rubbed look and provide some protection from fading, too. Plus, Danish oil will not mask the nice purple highlights in air-dried walnut. Best of all, a Danish-oil finish is easily renewable. If your project starts to look dull after a few years of use, wipe on another coat of Danish oil, and it will look like new again.

—CHRIS A. MINICK, Stillwater, Minn.

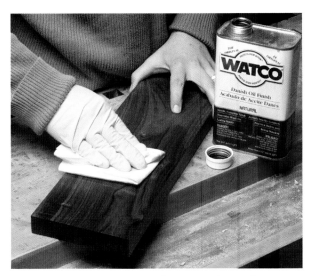

Prevent walnut's rich color from fading. Use three or four coats of Danish oil to preserve the dark, rich color of walnut while giving the piece a hand-rubbed look.

FURNITURE CONSTRUCTION

CABINETS

Fixture for mounting cabinet doors

I work by myself and find it awkward to hold cabinet doors in a perfect position while I mark and mount the hinges. So I made the device shown here that holds the door and allows small adjustments in and out or up and down to put the door into perfect alignment.

To make this fixture, start by fabricating a simple stand with two uprights and a crosspiece. Each upright should have a pair of arms spaced apart by the thickness of the door. Install the crosspiece several inches below the final door height. Then clamp two hand screws to the crosspiece and use the screws on the hand screws to make fine adjustments in the door's position.

—JAMES THOMPSON, Union City, Tenn.

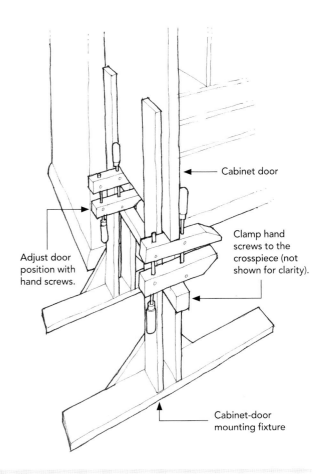

Cabinet door

Adjust door position with hand screws.

Clamp hand screws to the crosspiece (not shown for clarity).

Cabinet-door mounting fixture

Magnetic cabinet catch

A cabinet door that always opens on its own is a big nuisance. However, the problem can be solved easily with a pair of rare-earth magnets. The magnets install in minutes, and they keep the door securely shut. One magnet goes in the door, one in the stile. Drill a ½-in.-dia., 5mm-deep hole in both. Be sure the polarity is right, then glue the magnets flush with a drop of cyanoacrylate glue. You'll be amazed at how well they hold.

—LES ROBERTSON, Carson City, Nev.

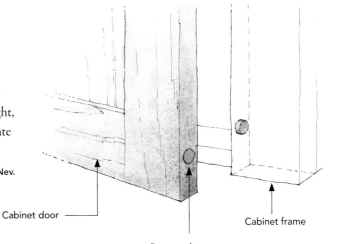

Cabinet door

Rare-earth magnet

Cabinet frame

Simple method for wall-mounting cabinets

This simple method for hanging wall cabinets is fast, easy, and accurate. Rip a ¾-in.-thick board in two at a 45° angle. Screw one cleat to the wall to form a perch and the other cleat to the cabinet back, which should be recessed ¾ in., as shown. Then just slip the cabinet over the wall cleat—a one-man operation. As a bonus, the cabinet can easily be removed whenever needed.

—GEORGE C. MULLER, Union, N.J.

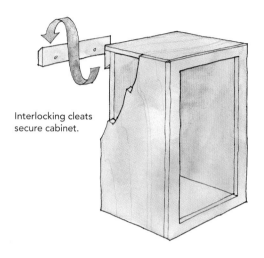

Interlocking cleats secure cabinet.

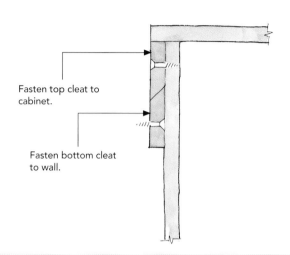

Fasten top cleat to cabinet.

Fasten bottom cleat to wall.

Using foil tape to locate lock mortises

Here's how I use aluminum-foil tape to find the exact bolt location for a drawer, box, or cabinet door lock. Stick a piece of the foil tape close to where the bolt will make contact. Then insert the drawer with lock in place and turn the key in the lock with a little extra pressure so that the bolt presses against the foil. The bolt will leave an imprint in the foil in the exact location where the mortise should be.

Mark through the foil with an awl at the corners of the impression to transfer the mortise location to the wood. Foil tape is used in the heating and air-conditioning trade to seal sheet-metal ducts and can be found at most building-product centers.

—DENNIS KUCHENBECKER, Chippewa Falls, Wis.

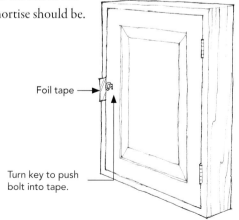

Foil tape

Turn key to push bolt into tape.

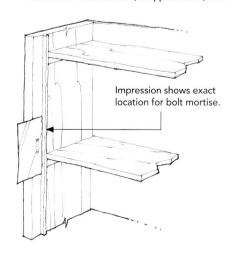

Impression shows exact location for bolt mortise.

DRAWERS

Cut slotted screw holes in a drawer bottom

When installing a bottom in a solid-wood drawer, a slotted screw hole is critical. Without it, the drawer bottom would be trapped between the drawer front and the screw. And with nowhere to go, the bottom's seasonal expansion would eventually damage the drawer's joints, if not tear them apart altogether.

You can make the hole quickly and easily with a countersinking drill bit, a handsaw, and a chisel. First, drill a clearance hole and countersink in the drawer bottom, drilling from the underside. On the top side, mark a line from the outside edges of the pilot hole to the back edge of the drawer bottom. Use a handsaw to cut along both lines and open up a slot. Then, on the underside of the bottom, chamfer the slot with a chisel to match the taper of the screw head.

—MICHAEL PEKOVICH, Newtown, Conn.

Drill a clearance hole in the bottom. For a ½-in.-thick back, the hole should be less than ½ in. from the edge of the bottom. Otherwise, it will be visible from inside the drawer. Countersink the hole.

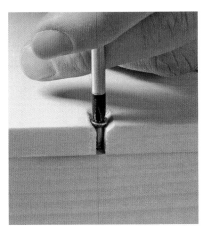

Cut the slot and chamfer it with a chisel. Extend layout lines from the edges of the hole. Then use a backsaw and cut along the inside of the lines (left). For the screw head to move freely in the slot, the walls must be chamfered (right) to match the underside of the head.

Slide in the bottom, and insert the screw. But don't screw it in too tightly. The drawer bottom should be able to expand and contract freely.

No-math layout for drawer pulls

More often than not, drawer handles are located in the middle of the drawer front, both vertically and horizontally. The intuitive method most of us use to locate the holes for the handle takes about five steps and requires measuring the dimensions of the drawer front and the handle. But I have a method that requires no math.

I simply transfer the width of the handle (between hole centers) onto each end of the drawer front and draw diagonals as shown. The points where the diagonals intersect are the locations for the holes. There's much less chance for a mistake with this method, but it's critical that the drawer front be square on the ends. Also, if the height is small compared to the width, it is easy to introduce a small error in the hole location. In that case, checking the hole spacing before drilling is a good idea.

—SCOTT COLLINS, Slidell, La.

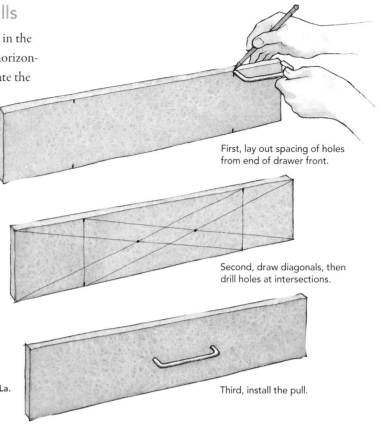

First, lay out spacing of holes from end of drawer front.

Second, draw diagonals, then drill holes at intersections.

Third, install the pull.

Protective finish for drawer sides

When finishing the sides of a drawer and any other secondary areas, such as the back and bottom of the drawers, keep it light. A light finish will seal each drawer without causing it to stick.

Apply two to three thin coats of super-blond shellac. Mix three tablespoons of shellac flakes with one cup of denatured alcohol. After the first coat dries, sand it with fine-grit paper, then apply the second and third coats. Rub out each coat with extra-fine steel wool and then finish with a little paste wax.

The result is a smooth, low-luster satin finish that seals the wood and protects the drawer against dirt and discoloration.

—MARIO RODRIGUEZ, Cherry Hill, N.J.

Use shellac on drawer parts. A light finish on the sides, back, and bottom seals the wood, and a light coat of wax ensures smooth operation.

Installing a muntin in a wide drawer

A muntin, or divider, is placed in the middle of a wide drawer bottom—oriented front to back—to help prevent the drawer from sagging when it's loaded with stuff.

To install a muntin, begin with a drawer bottom, still in two pieces, and place it into grooves cut in the muntin. Next, set in the muntin with a tenon fitting into the drawer's bottom groove. Finally, rabbet the muntin's back end to lay it onto the drawer back, and screw it into place.

—GARY ROGOWSKI, Portland, Ore.

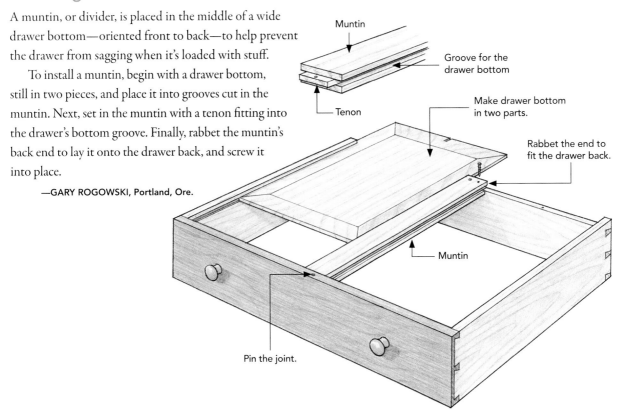

Muntin

Groove for the drawer bottom

Tenon

Make drawer bottom in two parts.

Rabbet the end to fit the drawer back.

Muntin

Pin the joint.

Wood-screw drawer stops

I recently built a display cabinet that included a couple of small drawers without drawer slides. Because this was my first project with such drawers, I wanted them to be as adjustable as possible. This drawer-stop technique is pretty low-tech, but it worked for me.

Rather than use typical wood drawer stops, I simply added two wood screws inside the back of the cabinet. When the drawer is closed, the back of the drawer bumps into the heads of the screws. That way, even if the drawers end up a little out of square, I can adjust each screw to compensate. Now the drawer faces are flush with their supporting web frames, and no one is the wiser.

—MIKE REPEDE, Rochester, Minn.

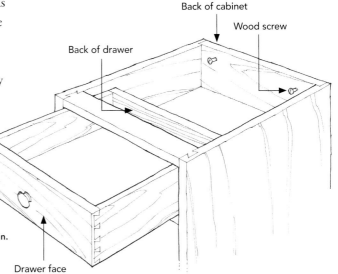

Back of cabinet

Wood screw

Back of drawer

Drawer face

TABLES

Improved tabletop button fits slot every time

An apron slot that's a little too high or low won't make a difference to this tabletop button. A kerf under the working end of the button gives it the flexibility to bend up or down as needed to slip into the slot.

—PETER WALLIN, Malmö, Sweden

Front screw applies pressure to apron slot.

Back screw holds button in place.

Tabletop fastening button

Tabletop

Slot in apron

Button

Kerf

Tabletop attachment slots

While building a small table, I had the idea of using my biscuit joiner to cut the slots in the apron for attaching the top with small, L-shaped buttons. I discovered that the approach held several advantages over routing the slots or chiseling them by hand. First, it is easier to set the proper distance of the slot from the top by setting the joiner's fence. And it is easier to adjust the width of the slot by simply lowering or raising the fence after cutting the first slot. Finally, each slot has rounded ends that enable you to turn the button into position easily.

—IAN WELFORD, North Yorkshire, United Kingdom

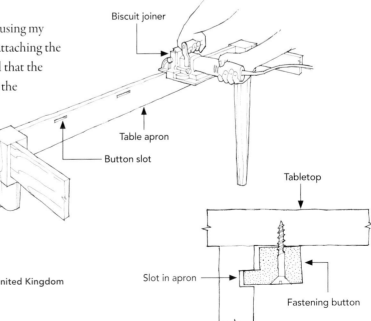

Biscuit joiner

Table apron

Button slot

Tabletop

Slot in apron

Fastening button

Mitered tenons add strength in table construction

When building a large table, say a dining table, you want the joinery to be as strong and stiff as possible. Your first instinct may be to join the table as you would a door—with tenons centered on the aprons, and mortises centered or slightly offset on the legs. But if you follow this logic, your tenons will butt together and one or both of them will be very short and thus weak (the longer the tenon, the stronger the joint). Mitering the tenons where they meet inside the leg increases strength by allowing more glue surface on the outer cheeks of the tenons. Mitering the tenons also provides more room for pegs to reinforce the joint.

Another trick to getting longer tenons is to offset the tenons toward the outside of the aprons—a ⅛-in. shoulder is more than enough to register the outer face of the apron against the leg. Offsetting the tenons will call for an extra setup at the tablesaw when you cut the tenons, but it's worth the trouble. To keep the top of the leg strong, the tenon should stop ½ in. or ¾ in. short of the top end, though you can leave a short haunch there.

Once the tenons have been cut, trim the ends to 45° using a handsaw, which causes less tearout than a tablesaw or miter saw. Don't bother trying to get the miters to meet up exactly inside the leg; it won't add significant strength to the joint.

—MATTHEW TEAGUE, Nashville, Tenn.

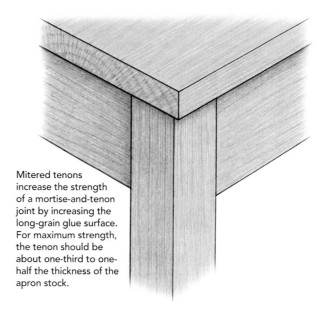

Mitered tenons increase the strength of a mortise-and-tenon joint by increasing the long-grain glue surface. For maximum strength, the tenon should be about one-third to one-half the thickness of the apron stock.

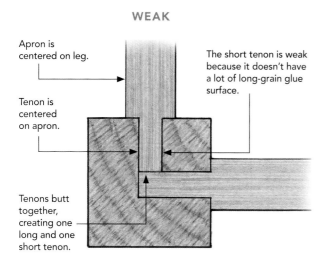

WEAK

Apron is centered on leg.

The short tenon is weak because it doesn't have a lot of long-grain glue surface.

Tenon is centered on apron.

Tenons butt together, creating one long and one short tenon.

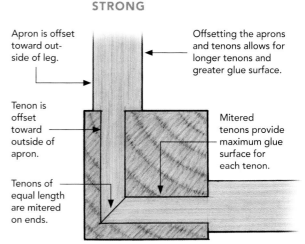

STRONG

Apron is offset toward outside of leg.

Offsetting the aprons and tenons allows for longer tenons and greater glue surface.

Tenon is offset toward outside of apron.

Mitered tenons provide maximum glue surface for each tenon.

Tenons of equal length are mitered on ends.

The best backsaws for cutting tenons

If you prefer cutting tenons by hand, you'll do yourself a favor by getting two types of backsaws. Cutting the cheeks (the face, or glue surface, of the tenon) is an operation that requires a ripsaw because you are cutting with the grain. Cutting the shoulders (the part that butts against the table leg) requires a crosscut saw. Get the best saws you can afford. Look for well-shaped, comfortable handles, stiff brass backs, and well-tempered blades. As for length, 12 in. is a good compromise for both saws.

—CHRISTIAN BECKSVOORT, New Gloucester, Maine

A ripsaw cuts tenon cheeks. Cutting the cheeks (or faces) of a tenon is done most efficiently with a ripsaw because they are cut with the grain.

A crosscut saw is best for shoulders. A 14-teeth per inch (tpi) crosscut saw produces a clean, accurate cut across the grain.

Orienting growth rings in a tabletop

There are two schools of thought regarding growth-ring orientation when gluing up a tabletop. The drawings below show what type of distortion results from each method. The rings-in-the-same-direction school holds that alternating the boards makes the cupping more obvious and that the resulting wavy top is hard to fasten down. Orienting the rings in the same direction forces the board into an arch. This method has merit if the top is tightly held down.

On the other hand, alternating the boards has merits, too. Alternating the cupping helps maintain an appearance of over-all flatness in the finished top and, perhaps even more important, less stress will develop at the gluelines.

More important than growth-ring orientation, make sure that the moisture content is uniform from board to board and that the wood has reached an equilibrium moisture content with its environment before you glue up the top.

—R. BRUCE HOADLEY, Amherst, Mass.

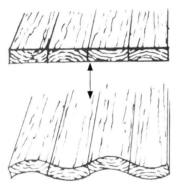

Alternating rings can make a panel wavy when wood moves.

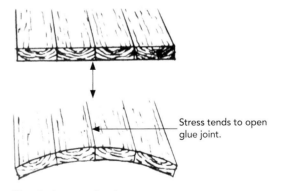

Stress tends to open glue joint.

Rings in the same direction can cause a panel to cup when wood moves.

Matching hardwood tabletop and veneered sides

If you're making a tabletop from hardwood plywood and want to cover the edges with veneer, you'll get the best match by wrapping the edges with veneer cut from the same plywood used to make the top. This veneer will take dyes, stains, and finishes the same as the top.

You can cut veneers that run with the grain or across the grain, so you can match any side of the plywood.

—CECIL BRAEDEN, Anacortes, Wash.

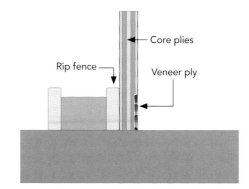

Core plies

Rip fence

Veneer ply

RIP THE VENEER FROM THE PLYWOOD

Accurate setup is the key. To get a clean cut from the plywood, set your fence so the blade slices off just the veneer ply.

Cut the veneer free. Position the fence 1 in. from the blade and make a ripcut with the veneer side up.

GLUE THE VENEER TO THE EDGES

Yellow glue works fine. A caul ensures that the clamping force is applied evenly along the strip. To allow the strip to overhang the underside of the workpiece, place spacers under both the workpiece and the caul.

Trim the veneer. Once the glue has dried, use a sharp knife to cut the veneer flush with the end of the piece. Then use a wide chisel to pare away the veneer overhang. Veneer the panel ends and smooth the joint with a sanding block.

METRIC CONVERSION CHART

INCHES	CENTIMETERS	MILLIMETERS		INCHES	CENTIMETERS	MILLIMETERS
⅛	0.3	3		13	33.0	330
¼	0.6	6		14	35.6	356
⅜	1.0	10		15	38.1	381
½	1.3	13		16	40.6	406
⅝	1.6	16		17	43.2	432
¾	1.9	19		18	45.7	457
⅞	2.2	22		19	48.3	483
1	2.5	25		20	50.8	508
1¼	3.2	32		21	53.3	533
1½	3.8	38		22	55.9	559
1¾	4.4	44		23	58.4	584
2	5.1	51		24	61.0	610
2½	6.4	64		25	63.5	635
3	7.6	76		26	66.0	660
3½	8.9	89		27	68.6	686
4	10.2	102		28	71.1	711
4½	11.4	114		29	73.7	737
5	12.7	127		30	76.2	762
6	15.2	152		31	78.7	787
7	17.8	178		32	81.3	813
8	20.3	203		33	83.8	838
9	22.9	229		34	86.4	864
10	25.4	254		35	88.9	889
11	27.9	279		36	91.4	914
12½	30.5	305				

CREDITS

All photos and illustrations © The Taunton Press, Inc. The following photographers and illustrators have contributed to this book:

p. iii: Bob LaPointe
p. 2: (left) Timothy Sams; (center) Matt Kenney; (right) William Duckworth

Chapter 1
pp. 5–6: Heather Lambert
p. 7: (top left) Michael Pekovich; (top right & bottom) Heather Lambert
pp. 8–14, 16: Jim Richey
p. 15: Vince Babak
pp. 16–19: Jim Richey
p. 20: Mark Schofield
p. 21: (top) Jim Richey; (bottom photos) Mark Schofield
p. 22: (top) Vince Babak; (bottom left) Jim Richey; (bottom right) Karen Wales
p. 23: Jim Richey
p. 24: (top) Jim Richey; (bottom) Vince Babak
pp. 25–38: Jim Richey
p. 39: (top left) Kelly J. Dunton; (top right) David Heim; (bottom) Jim Richey
p. 40: (top) Jim Richey; (bottom left & right) Courtesy Fine Woodworking
p. 41: (top) Marcia Ryan; (bottom) Jim Richey
pp. 42–43: Jim Richey
p. 44: (top) Jim Richey; (bottom) Kelly J. Dunton
pp. 45–46: Jim Richey
p. 47: Matt Kenney
pp. 48–49: Jim Richey
p. 50: (top) Jim Richey; (bottom) Marcia Ryan
p. 51: Jim Richey

p. 52: (left) Michael Pekovich; (right) Vince Babak
p. 53: Jim Richey
pp. 54–59: Jim Richey
p. 60: Kelly J. Dunton
p. 61: (top) Marcia Ryan; (bottom) Kelly J. Dunton
p. 62: (top) Marcia Ryan; (bottom) Vince Babak
pp. 63–65: Jim Richey

Chapter 2
p. 67: (top & bottom left) Jim Richey; (bottom right) Courtesy Fine Woodworking
pp. 68–72: Jim Richey
p. 73: (top) Charles Reina; (bottom) Vince Babak
p. 74: (left) Anatole Burkin; (right) Bob LaPointe
p. 75: Bob LaPointe
p. 76: (top) Jim Richey; (bottom) Vince Babak
pp. 77–78: Jim Richey
p. 79: Timothy Sams
pp. 80–81: Jim Richey
p. 82: (top) Vince Babak; (bottom) Charles Reina
pp. 83–91: Jim Richey

Chapter 3
p. 93: (top) Mark Schofield; (bottom) Jim Richey
p. 94: (top & bottom right) Jim Richey; (bottom left) Mark Schofield
p. 95: Courtesy Fine Woodworking;
p. 96: Marcia Ryan
p. 97: (top) Jim Richey; (bottom) Marcia Ryan
pp. 98–100: Jim Richey
p. 101: (top) Steve Scott; (bottom) Michael Pekovich

pp. 102–103: Steve Scott
p. 104: (top) Steve Scott; (bottom) Tom McKenna
pp. 105–107: Jim Richey
p. 108: Asa Christiana
p. 109: (top) Courtesy Fine Woodworking; (bottom) Karen Wales

Chapter 4
p. 111: (top) Jim Richey; (bottom) Karen Wales
p. 112: (top & bottom left) Steve Scott; (bottom right) John Tetreault
pp. 113–114: Jim Richey
p. 115: (top) Jim Richey; (bottom) Steve Scott
p. 116: Steve Scott
p. 117: Marcia Ryan
p. 118: (top) Steve Scott; (bottom) Jim Richey
pp. 119–120: Vince Babak
p. 121: Steve Scott
p. 122: (top) Steve Scott; (bottom) Jim Richey
p. 123: (top) Vince Babak; (bottom left) Kelly J. Dutton; (bottom right) Marcia Ryan
pp. 124–125: Jim Richey
p. 126: Steve Scott
p. 127: (top) Jim Richey; (bottom) Asa Christiana
pp. 128–133: Jim Richey

Chapter 5
pp. 135–138: Steve Scott
pp. 139–141: Jim Richey
p. 142: (left) Vince Babak; (right) William Duckworth
p. 143: (top) William Duckworth; (bottom) Jim Richey
p. 144: Vince Babak
pp. 145–146: Jim Richey

p. 147: (top) Kelly J. Dunton; (bottom) Asa Christiana

pp. 148–149: Jim Richey

p. 150: (left & right) Kelly J. Dutton; (center) Vince Babak

p. 151: Michael Pekovich

pp. 152–154: Jim Richey

p. 155: (top) Vince Babak; (bottom) Jim Richey

p. 156: (top) Jim Richey; (bottom) Steve Scott

p. 157: Jim Richey

p. 158: (top) Vince Babak; (bottom) Timothy Sams

p. 159: (top) Vince Babak; (bottom) Jim Richey

pp. 160–163: Jim Richey

Chapter 6

p. 165: (top) Matthew Gardner; (bottom) Mark Schofield

p. 166: Mark Schofield

p. 167: (top right & bottom) Mark Schofield; (top right) Matthew Gardner

p. 168: Mark Schofield

p. 169: (top) Jim Richey; (bottom) Matthew Teague

pp. 170–173: Jim Richey

p. 174: Marcia Ryan

pp. 175–177: Jim Richey

Chapter 7

p. 179: (top left & right) Kelly J. Dutton; (bottom) Steve Scott

p. 180: Jim Richey

p. 181: (top) Jim Richey; (bottom) Steve Scott

p. 182: (left) Jim Richey; (top right & bottom) Asa Christiana

p. 183: Steve Scott

p. 184: (top) Jim Richey; (bottom) Steve Scott

p. 185: Jim Richey

p. 186: Kelly J. Dutton

p. 187: All photos by Steve Scott except bottom right photo by Mark Schofield

p. 188: Steve Scott

p. 189: Jim Richey

p. 190: (top) Jim Richey; (bottom) Asa Christiana

pp. 191–192: Jim Richey

p. 193: (top) William Duckworth; (bottom) Asa Christiana

p. 194: (top left & bottom) Asa Christiana; (top right) Chuck Lockhart

pp. 195–197: Jim Richey

Chapter 8

p. 199: David Heim

p. 200: (top) David Heim; (bottom) Karen Wales

p. 201: (top left & bottom) David Heim; (top right) Kelly J. Dunton

p. 202: (left) Courtesy Fine Wood-working; (right) Marcia Ryan

p. 203: Courtesy Fine Woodworking

p. 204: (top) Michael Pekovich; (bottom) David Heim

p. 205: David Heim

p. 206: (top left) Kelly J. Dunton; (top right & bottom) David Heim

p. 207: (top) Courtesy Fine Wood-working; (bottom) Kelly J. Dunton

p. 208: Courtesy Fine Woodworking

p. 209: Timothy Sams

p. 210: (top) Vince Babak; (bottom) Courtesy Fine Woodworking

pp. 211–212: Jefferson Kolle

p. 213: Kelly J. Dunton

p. 214: Andy Engel

pp. 215–217: Jim Richey

p. 218: Kelly J. Dunton

Chapter 9

pp. 220–221: Jim Richey

p. 222: Courtesy Fine Woodworking

p. 223: (top) Jim Richey; (bottom) Marcia Ryan

p. 224: (top) Vince Babak; (bottom) Jim Richey

p. 225: Jim Richey

p. 226: Vince Babak

p. 227: (top) Karen Wales; (bottom) Courtesy Fine Woodworking

p. 228: (top) Kelly J. Dunton; (bottom) Courtesy Fine Woodworking

INDEX